WHERE
ARE THE
CHRIS✝IANS?

WHERE
ARE THE
CHRIS†IANS?

THE UNREALIZED POTENTIAL
OF A DIVIDED RELIGION

ERIC SHUSTER

PLAIN SIGHT PUBLISHING
AN IMPRINT OF CEDAR FORT, INC.
SPRINGVILLE, UTAH

ISBN 13: 978-1-4621-1206-7

Published by Plain Sight Publishing, an imprint of Cedar Fort, Inc.
2373 W. 700 S., Springville, UT 84663
Distributed by Cedar Fort, Inc., www.cedarfort.com

LIBRARY OF CONGRESS CATALOGING-IN-PUBLICATION DATA

Shuster, Eric, 1962- author.
  Where are the Christians? : the unrealized potential of a divided religion / By Eric Shuster.
    pages cm
  Includes bibliographical references.
  ISBN 978-1-4621-1206-7 (alk. paper)
  1. Christian union. 2. Church--Unity. I. Title.

  BX8.3.S53 2013
  262.001'1--dc23

                                2013002992

Cover design by Angela D. Olsen
Cover design © 2013 by Lyle Mortimer
Edited and typeset by Whitney A. Lindsley

Printed in the United States of America

10 9 8 7 6 5 4 3 2 1

To my children and grandchildren—that their testimonies in Jesus Christ might help them achieve their full spiritual potential and keep them on the narrow path.

WHERE ARE THE CHRISTIANS?
Companion Workbook

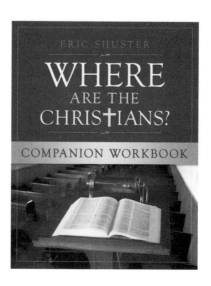

THIS BOOK IS ACCOMPANIED BY THE *WHERE ARE THE CHRISTIANS? COMPANION WORKBOOK*. The workbook acts as a study guide to direct your personal expedition to find your own Christianity.

The workbook includes a more comprehensive review of the materials covered in this book along with exercises to help you ponder more deeply your own beliefs and practices as a Christian and provides a framework for personal improvement. The workbook can be used by individuals or in groups and will bring to life many of the concepts introduced in this book on how each of us can reach our greatest potential as disciples of the Lord Jesus Christ.

CONTENTS

CONTENTS

PREFACE

I HAVE BEEN A CHRISTIAN SINCE BIRTH, ALTHOUGH AN UNCONVEN-
tional one. The first half of my life was spent as a Roman Catholic and
the second half as a Latter-day Saint. These two faith traditions represent
the bookends of Christendom with Catholicism as its oldest and most
celebrated denomination on one end and Mormonism as one of its newest
and most controversial on the other. I'm told my spiritual journey inside
and outside of the Christian mainstream along with my research background allows me to view Christianity more critically and expansively
than most Christians. There are some who take exception to my spiritual
journey leading to passionate exchanges. In these exchanges, I am often
frustrated by the lack of knowledge and understanding of Christianity
from a historical and scriptural standpoint. I've learned emotion and pro-
vincialism are poor substitutes for education and humility.

Living both ends of the Christian spectrum has favored me with a
wide range of experiences prompting me to consider the true potential
of Christianity on a wide scale. This consideration has led me to ponder
four fundamental questions in the classic who, what, where, how style—
questions that I've come to realize many Christians are asking themselves
today . . . or at least should be.

Who are the Christians? Observing the state of Christianity around
me with its seemingly endless numbers of denominations triggered within
me the thought of where it all began and how it all came to be. I marveled
at whom the Christians were historically, the impact of that history on
modern-day Christianity, and how that history has affected me in my
own journey of faith.

What is a Christian? Having been granted and denied the privilege
of being called a Christian simply by virtue of the faith traditions I was

living was baffling. It caused me to wonder how a Christian is defined, who has the right to define it, and how my own beliefs and practices measure up to the Christian moniker.

Where are the Christians? With my understanding the basic tenets of Christianity, it has escaped me for years how a country like America so overwhelmingly populated by Christians could be deteriorating so quickly. I wondered where all of those Christians could be, what they were doing during this tumultuous period of our country's history, and where I stood in the fight for righteousness and liberty.

How will Christianity unite? Knowing the power of Jesus Christ and the teachings of the Bible on the unity of faith produced within me feelings of confusion as to how Christianity was ever going to come together to reach its full potential. I questioned how thousands of faith traditions would eventually live in one accord and what I needed to do in my own life to help move that process along.

Driven by these questions, I set out to research, understand, and reconcile. Resisting the urge to prove my own spiritual convictions, I have instead concentrated on fostering a spirit of religious appreciation, cooperation, and awareness focused on one simple objective: help Christianity reach its full potential by helping you answer the "who, what, where, and how" of Christianity in your own life. This book will help you consider from **whom** you have come from in Christian history (section one); **what** and **where** you are in your Christian faith journey today (sections two and three); and **how** you would like your Christian life to be in the future (section four).

Come take this journey with me to learn about Christianity from the ground up. Let me demonstrate how by applying the who, what, where, and how to yourself personally you will have the knowledge and tools to not only reach our own spiritual potential, but to help your family, church, and community do the same.

–ERIC SHUSTER

ACKNOWLEDGMENTS

LIKE EVERY BOOK I WRITE, IT IS NOT POSSIBLE FOR ME TO NAME ALL those who have had an impact on my life and inspired me to this juncture. Instead of naming them all here, I will strive to show my appreciation in a more personal way to the majority as our paths cross in the future.

There are a few that I will acknowledge here pertaining to this specific work:

To the many involved in interfaith ministries around the world who have long had the vision of a united family in God and have been able to effectively manage theological diversity and focus on the core message of Jesus Christ in serving others.

To all those involved in studying and reporting religious activity including the Barna Group and Pew Research, but especially the team responsible for the National Survey of Youth and Religion including Christian Smith and Melinda Denton. The awareness you generate helps all of us ponder our own beliefs and actions.

To our distinguished interfaith review board comprising ministers and lay people from the faith traditions of the Baptist, Evangelical, Methodist, Mormon (The Church of Jesus Christ of Latter-day Saints), Presbyterian, and Roman Catholic churches, including (in alphabetical order) David Dewey, Brandon Goss, Joe Kirkendall, Reverend Eunice T. McGarrahan, Charlie McIntyre, Reverend Larry Paulson, and Reverend Bill Wolfe. Their generosity of time in reviewing the manuscript and providing feedback are not an endorsement of this work, but rather a demonstration of faith, love, courage, and a vision of what can be realized when people come together in Christ toward a common purpose. Without them, this book would be much less than it is, while I myself am blessed through my association with these incredible people.

To my friend and colleague Dr. Alex Kalamarides for educating me on the original Greek meaning of several key words found in the English translation of the Bible—and what an education it was and continues to be!

To my friend Chuck Sale who taught me how to be a writer and to tell the story in as few words as possible . . . I'm still working on that "few" part.

To Saint Lawrence Academy in Santa Clara, California, for teaching me the importance and worth of Christian values, despite the fact it took me a while to comprehend those teachings and live those values in my own life.

To the many who have challenged me over the years encouraging me to dig deeper into the scriptures, to research more fully the facts, and to more sharply report the findings in hopes of promoting a more productive and worthwhile dialogue.

To my extended family: my mother, brothers Tom and Gordon, sisters Terry and Lisa, and my departed father and brother Robert—you are never far from my mind and have each given me something special that I hold on to and cherish.

To my children, Jason, Dee Dee, and Ryan, for teaching me to be a better father; and to my grandchildren, Austyn, Azriel, Taylor, and Tylor (and future grandchildren) for inspiring me to write the words that I hope will someday strengthen you in your relationship with the Savior.

And finally to my wife and eternal companion, Marilyn: for her patience with my quiet periods, her understanding of my constant tiredness, her support of my mission to change the world, her time in reading and editing the manuscript, and, most important, her unwavering love of me and our family toward the building of an enduring family of Zion.

WHO ARE THE CHRISTIANS?

A History

"One truth stands firm. All that happens in world history rests on something spiritual. If the spiritual is strong, it creates world history. If it is weak, it suffers world history."

—Albert Schweitzer

EVERY CULTURE AND CIVILIZATION IS SHAPED BY ITS HISTORY—CHRIStianity is no different. To fully understand and appreciate the Christianity of today, one must study its evolution and history. That is not to say one cannot gain a testimony of Jesus Christ and be a powerful Christian without doing so; it is simply to say understanding the history of Christianity illuminates many present-day matters and helps one to gain a broader perspective.

To present the history of Christianity from its humble origins to the modern era is challenging. The history of Christianity is exciting, colorful, full of miracles and intrigue, and anything but simple and straightforward. For two thousand years, even more when we incorporate pre-Christian Jewish history, Christianity has endured a continuous parade of characters that have built up, broken down, and expanded the Lord's Church into the massive religious movement it is today.

THE CHALLENGES OF REPORTING
CHRISTIAN HISTORY

Before tackling history, we might consider a bit of expert counsel from those who have made history. Winston Churchill wrote, "History with its flickering lamp stumbles along the trail of the past, trying to reconstruct its scenes, to revive its echoes, and kindle with the pale gleams the passion of former days."[1] The late English statesman warns that history is not easily reconstructed and therefore vulnerable to errors in present day reenactments. Offering a more cynical view, Voltaire wrote, "All the ancient histories, as one of our wits say, are just fables that have been agreed upon."[2] The historian and philosopher Voltaire was leery of the accuracy of historical record keeping and therefore urges the reader to be critical in discernment. Then there is the writer Mark Twain, who exclaimed, "The very ink with which all history is written is merely fluid prejudice."[3] Twain cautions the reader that biases have a way of shaping the way history is reported.

So how is one to reconstruct and summarize over two thousand years of events leading to a useful history of Christianity to educate and edify the reader without bias? The answer is "very carefully." Paul Johnson, author of the book *A History of Christianity*, wrote, "Christianity is essentially a historical religion. It bases its claims on the historical facts it asserts. If these are demolished, it is nothing."[4]

There are volumes written on the history of Christianity, each offering a particular point of view on the events and dynamics that have led to its evolution over the centuries. Catholics will offer their version; Protestants will offer their version; and so on. The challenge in providing a concise and factual history of Christianity is narrowing down significant events into those which truly influenced its present state. Adding to the challenge is creating something of value to the well informed as well as the newly curious while making it interesting and relevant to us all.

The history of Christianity provided in this book will not be exhaustive, but it will be comprehensive in identifying key events. Lest I be singled out as an author biasing the content, the historical point of view I will be offering the reader is one that *Christianity has endured the test of time despite centuries of persecution and corruption that may have otherwise destroyed a lesser religion.*

HISTORICAL SOURCES

Historians who have dedicated themselves to compiling the history of Christianity, especially relating to the early Church, surprisingly have very little to work with. Evidence has been primarily derived from biblical records and ecclesiastical testimony, augmented with historical records and archeological findings in later time periods. Historian Paul Johnson wrote, "When we turn to the earliest Christian sources, we enter a terrifying jungle of scholarly contradictions. All were writing evangelism or theology rather than history."[5] The scriptures are the inspired word of God; however, should one decide to use scriptural records as historical evidence of the early Church a number of issues must be considered according to Johnson:

Writer motivation: the authors of scripture were more interested in dealing with ecclesiastical controversy and evangelization than they were with recording historical facts.

Oral to written conversion: it was common in earlier time periods to rely on oral descriptions of mysterious concepts, which were often passed down. Such concepts are difficult to translate into the written word without avoiding linguistic issues.

Communication linkages: besides oral tradition, scriptural records are often based on transcriptions and the recording of testimonies from observers. For example, the prologue to the book of Luke indicates its content is largely based on earlier written accounts, which in turn are based upon the testimony of firsthand observers—suggesting a multilinkage, multigenerational chain of communications.

Language translations: Johnson writes, "The four gospels declared canonical, for instance, were circulated, but not necessarily first written, in colloquial Greek; but Matthew was almost certainly translated from Hebrew, and all four were either *thought* in Aramaic, or transcriptions from tales which were Aramaic in original circulation, yet which drew on Hebrew quotations and, to a lesser extent, on Hellenic or Hellenized concepts. The possibilities for misunderstanding are infinite."[6]

Handwritten transmissions: the use of scribes to create copies of copies was a common practice and one that created limitless opportunities for error. The books of Luke and Matthew are generally considered to have borrowed content from Mark, although it is unclear if Luke and Matthew borrowed content from one another. Beyond the transmission issues, it would not be out of the question for text to be refined to address theological and social issues, an issue Johnson believes was common in the early manuscripts.

Although these issues relate specifically to scriptural records, one or more can potentially have affected the many available historical records given the volatile and controversial nature of religion throughout history. The later the history the better and more available the sources become. Just to note, the over six hundred unique biblical references in this book have been taken from the traditional King James translation.

SEGMENTING THE PERIODS OF CHRISTIANITY

To help us better understand and manage the staggering amount of historical content available, this book segments historical Christianity into four distinct periods:

- **Evangelization and Formation** (up to AD 299)

- **Legitimacy and Codification** (AD 300 to 999)

- **Corruption and Division** (AD 1000 to 1499)

- **Reform and Denominational Proliferation** (AD 1500 to the present)

Although this segmentation provides clarity and ease of understanding, the fluidity of historical events causes periods to overlap. For example, evangelization continues into the period of legitimacy and codification, while corruption and division continues into the period of reformation and denominational proliferation. Despite such overlaps, this unique segmentation offers the reader a simple way of managing an otherwise complex and overwhelming history.

Chapter 1

THEY WERE
EVANGELIZERS AND BUILDERS
(UP TO AD 299)

THE PROPHETIC HISTORY BEFORE
THE BIRTH OF CHRIST

The origins of Christianity happened long before the birth of Jesus Christ. Direct and indirect references to the Savior (or Messiah) and his ministry are found throughout the Old Testament centuries before the birth of Christ. For example, Genesis 3:15 prophesies of the Savior coming forth from a woman ("her seed") to destroy the adversary ("bruise thy head")—a prophecy that was fulfilled in 1 John 3:8. It was prophesied that Jesus Christ would be born of a virgin and called Immanuel in Isaiah 7:14—a prophecy that was fulfilled in Matthew 1:18–2:1. Or the prophecies of Jesus Christ coming forth from the tribe of Judah and the lineage of David found in Genesis 49:10 and 2 Samuel 7:12–16, respectively, fulfilled in the New Testament passages of Hebrews 7:14–17 and Matthew 1:1–17, respectively.

Therefore, although some might consider Christianity to have begun during the ministry of Jesus Christ, in reality the genesis of Christianity started thousands of years before that time—even at the foundation of the world (John 1:1). Imagine the scholars of Alexandria who translated the Septuagint from Hebrew to Greek around 250 BC—little did they know that less than three centuries later the Messiah would be born, would minister to God's children on earth, and would atone for the sins of all mankind.

THE BIRTH, MINISTRY, CRUCIFIXION, AND RESURRECTION OF CHRIST

Conventional wisdom suggests the birth of Jesus Christ to be in the time period AD (anno Domini) 1 according to the Julian and Gregorian calendars with BC depicting "before Christ." However, the Gospel of Matthew records the birth of Christ in the time period of Herod the Great, around 4 BC.[1] The Gospel of Luke associates the birth of Christ taking place during the first census of the Roman provinces of Syria and Judaea in or around 6 BC.[8] Therefore, the birth of Jesus Christ was likely to be sometime between 4 and 6 BC. I provide this example to demonstrate the difficulty of pinpointing with any degree of accuracy the dates of events relating to this early period of Christian history and thus the terms "in or around" and so forth.

The New Testament provides only a glimpse of Christ before his public ministry including having grown in "wisdom and stature, and in favour with God and man" (Luke 2:52), experiencing baptism (Matthew 3:16, Mark 1:9, Luke 3:21), and being tempted of the devil while fasting in the wilderness (Luke 4:1–2).

Preparing the way for the ministry of Jesus, John the Baptist began his public ministry around the same time as Pontius Pilate's appointment as the prefect of Judea in or around AD 26. The New Testament records John as a naturalist (Mark 1:6), preaching in the wilderness of Judea (Matthew 3:1), reproaching the Pharisees and Sadducees (Matthew 3:7), and eventually being heralded by Jesus as the greatest of the prophets (Luke 7:28). Shortly thereafter the Savior began his public ministry.

The majority of content found in the four Gospels records the public ministry of Christ from his coming forth from the wilderness to his ascension into heaven. Included are the miracles he performed, the doctrines of the gospel he taught, his many interactions with the apostles, disciples, and those who opposed him and, most important, his suffering in Gethsemane, Crucifixion, and Resurrection (referred to in some circles of Christendom as the "Atonement").

As the influence of Jesus Christ grew, so did the opposition to his ministry by the Roman authorities, the Sadducees, the Pharisees, and Herod Antipas—an otherwise divided group brought together in their zeal to have the Savior destroyed. In or around AD 29, John the Baptist was beheaded, followed by the Crucifixion, Resurrection, and Ascension of Jesus Christ approximately one year later.

EVANGELIZATION AND FORMATION AFTER THE ASCENSION OF CHRIST

The evangelization and formation period after the Ascension of Christ was a time for Christianity to establish a footing, despite the enormity of odds against it. The Savior commissioned his apostles to "teach all nations" and to baptize those who believe (Matthew 28:19–20 and Mark 16:15–16), setting into motion the order of Christianity. The new religion, without the earthly presence of Jesus Christ, was up against a well-organized and deeply passionate Jewish tradition in its founding geographies. At this stage it was unthinkable that Christianity could spread outside of Palestine into non-Jewish strongholds where paganism thrived.

This period of Christianity was defined by seven major categories of events: persecution of the Church, martyrdom of its early leaders, the spreading of the gospel outside of Palestine, the conversion of Paul, the formation of the Church, early heresies, and the writing of the New Testament. The dynamics of these events not only broadened the influence of Christianity beyond the geographic ministry of Jesus Christ, but it refined the Church and prepared it for the ongoing challenges it would be faced with in the centuries that followed.

CHURCH PERSECUTION

Jesus Christ told his disciples that persecution would come to those who followed him (John 15:20), teaching persecution for righteousness' sake was a blessing (Matthew 5:10). These teachings were critical and prophetic as persecution came swiftly and with great force. Although Gamaliel, head of the Sanhedrin encouraged tolerance of the Christians

(Acts 5:34–38), Pharisees like Saul (before his conversion and becoming better known as Paul) brought great tribulation to the Church. Persecution could be as subtle as intolerance of religious views, to something more serious as being ejected from public places, torture or even murder. Part of the persecution came as a result of the instability of the early Christian Church in Jerusalem as a hybrid of Judaism and Christianity, giving it the appearance of a "Jewish cult."[3]

Extreme persecution of the Church began under Nero, who blamed the Christians for the burning of Rome around AD 64. This was proceeded by even harsher persecutions under the emperor Domitian following an unsuccessful attempt on his life. The reestablishment of the Sanhedrin under Rabbis Johanan ben Zakkai, Gamaliel II and Simeon around AD 90 led to the expulsion of Christians from the synagogues, further persecution under emperor Domitian, and the eventual exile of John to Patmos sometime between AD 90 and 95. Persecution of the Church became even more widespread under emperors Marcus Aurelius (AD 161 to 180), Septimus Severus (~AD 202), Maximin the Thracian (~AD 235), Decius (AD 249 to 251), and Diocletian (AD 284 to 305).

However, not all Roman emperors were intolerant of Christianity. Antoninus Caracalla, Alexander Severus, Gordian III, and Philip the Arabian during approximately AD 211 to 244 were more tolerant of the new religion. While "tolerance" is somewhat relative, such forbearance under these emperors gave Christianity opportunities to strengthen local leadership, teach the gospel more freely, and grow its numbers.

MARTYRDOM

Persecution of Christianity often took the form of murdering its leaders. During the evangelization and formation period, a number of early Christian Church founders were martyred, including Stephen, James the brother of John, Andrew, Peter, Matthias, Paul, Mark, Simeon (Symeon) bishop of Jerusalem, and Polycarp (the Bishop of Smyrna and disciple of John). In some cases, the martyrdom was executed with great brutality including Mark being dragged through the streets with a rope around his neck[4] or the crucifixion of Simeon.[5]

SPREADING OF THE GOSPEL

Following the Ascension of Christ the spreading of the gospel was accomplished through individuals and events. For example, in or around AD 30–33 Phillip began preaching in Samaria (Acts 8), while in that same time frame Christians were scattered abroad following the expulsion of the Jews from Jerusalem—bringing with them their knowledge and testimonies of Jesus Christ. In approximately AD 35–37, Peter founded the Church in Antioch, helping its expansion outside of Jerusalem.

Christian tradition (and perhaps legend) suggests the evangelization of Christianity continued and reached far outside of the Mediterranean with Joseph of Arimathea traveling to Britain to preach the gospel, Thaddeus establishing the Christian Church in Armenia, and Mark introducing Christianity in Egypt—all around AD 60 to about AD 75. These and other evangelization efforts continued as a primary means of spreading the gospel of Jesus Christ and establishing Christianity as a credible religious sect during this period in history.

CONVERSION AND MINISTRY OF PAUL

Perhaps no single person in history has had such a positive impact on Christianity as Paul. There was a time when just the opposite could be said. Before his conversion, Paul was a Pharisee and inflicted severe persecutions on the believers of Jesus Christ. In Paul's own words, "I persecuted this way unto the death, binding and delivering into prisons both men and women" (Acts 22:4).

Paul became converted to the gospel of Jesus Christ sometime between AD 33 and 35, spawning great anxiety among Jewish leaders who then attempted to assassinate him on several occasions. By about AD 40, Paul was spreading the gospel across the Mediterranean region, boldly declaring Christianity to all who would listen. Between AD 42 and 45, Paul and Barnabas preached in Antioch, where the term "Christian" is believed to have originated. By the end of that decade, Paul and Barnabas would travel to Cypress to preach Christianity in Greece. Between AD 50 and 55, Paul took Silas as a companion and spent well over a year in Corinth preaching and teaching. Paul's third missionary journey commenced shortly thereafter, testifying before Festus, appealing to Caesar, and ending up in prison by the end of that same decade.

Paul's letters eventually became a primary source of content for the New Testament. Of the twenty-seven books of the New Testament, a majority are attributed to Paul. The doctrines of Paul, and even Paul himself, were often at odds with Peter and other "Jewish-Christians," many of whom participated with Jesus in his public ministry (which Paul never did). The historian Johnson writes, "What ensured the survival of Christianity was not the triumph of Paul in the field but the destruction of Jerusalem, and with it the Jewish-Christian faith."[6] The result would be the increased influence of Paul, the alignment of the canonical Gospels (Matthew, Mark, Luke, and John) and the book of Acts to that of the Pauline system of theology and the demise of the Jewish-Christian sect.[7]

The execution of Paul sometime between AD 62 and 68 is infamously connected to his prophetic words to Timothy: "For I am now ready to be offered, and the time of my departure is at hand. I have fought a good fight, I have finished my course, I have kept the faith" (2 Timothy 4:6–7). Paul is considered to be the exemplary figure that symbolizes the evangelization and formation period of Christianity.

FORMATION AND SPIRITUALITY

Evangelization alone was not enough to establish the Church; it took the development of formal organization and a variety of spiritual events to create a foundation on which the Church could stand. Examples of organization include the Council of Jerusalem in AD 48 to 49 (dealing with the Gentiles and circumcision), the appointment of Simeon, son of Cleopas, to succeed James as head of the Church in Jerusalem after his martyrdom, and Mark giving up his position to Annianus as head of the Church in Alexandria around AD 60–63. Examples of spiritual events around this time frame include Pentecost (that is, the birthday of the Christian Church) around AD 30–33, the use of the word "Christian" in Antioch around a decade later, and the death of Mary, the mother of Jesus, in or around AD 50 to 52 (which led to the tradition of Mary being assumed into heaven).

The lack of church structure was troubling to many as Paul freely preached "by the spirit," setting up churches, and establishing Christianity into a set of independent bodies[8] with their own oral traditions.[9] Church organization began to take shape as Linus succeeded Peter as pope of Rome (according to Roman Catholic tradition) in approximately AD 65–67 and as the center of Christianity moved from Jerusalem to Antioch. The clergy of the time integrated both Greek and Judaic concepts with the Jewish-Christian Church, implementing an authoritative structure including bishops and deacons.[10]

It was not until around AD 105–107 the term "Catholic Church" would be used by Ignatius and not until around AD 232 that the title of Pope would be officially used as we know it today (Pope Heracleus, the thirteenth Alexandrine Patriarch).[11] Demonstrating a cultural shift, in AD 135 the first gentile bishop was appointed, Marcus, who unlike his predecessors was not Jewish.

Spiritual events brought tradition and doctrine to the early Christian Church in both good and bad ways. Around AD 125 the first instance of prayer to Mary was recorded (and still takes place today in the Roman Catholic Church) and in or around AD 134–137 the holiday tradition of Christmas was started by the bishop of Rome (Telesphorus) as a means of celebrating the birth of Jesus Christ. Although these spiritual events gave tradition and character to the early Christian Church, they also began a trend of fracture among believers as they gathered themselves into different factions with conflicting doctrines.

EARLY HERESIES

This period of Christianity experienced the beginning of heretical doctrines, or perceived heresies, that sought to indoctrinate Christians into belief systems that were contrary to the prevailing doctrines held by the central Christian Church. Heresies would come and go for centuries, with some having more staying power than others. There were three prominent heresies that marked this period in Christianity: Gnosticism, Montanism, and Monarchianism.

Gnosticism

Drawing from the Greek word *gnosis*, which means knowledge, the Gnostics were loosely established before Christianity, mingling Judaism with Greek philosophy and eastern mythology into a convoluted belief system. At the core of Gnosticism is the belief that salvation of the soul from a materialistic world is found through knowledge. True to its assimilating nature, Gnosticism integrated pieces of Christianity into its belief system, formulating such distorted doctrine as there being "intermediate deific beings who4 exist between the ultimate, True God and ourselves."[12] Gnosticism taught other erroneous doctrines such as all matter being evil and that a divine spirit entered in Christ at baptism and left him at his Crucifixion.[13] Perhaps the most infamous Gnostic of this period was Marcion of Sinope (AD 100–160), the son of a bishop, whose followers are sometimes referred to as Marcionites, or disciples of Marcionism.[14]

Montanism

Frustrated at the perceived lack of passion among Christians, Montanus in Phrygia founded Montanism, a religious sect characterized by fanatical practices and teachings. Established around AD 155–157, Montanists were discouraged from marriage, subjected to regular regiments of fasting, and encouraged to seek out opportunities for martyrdom. A core belief of Montanism was the second coming of Christ and the end of the world were both imminent. Besotted to the end, following intense suppression at the hands of emperor Justinian in the sixth century, the Montanists of Constantinople committed mass suicide by fire.[15]

Monarchianism

Monarchianism, the forerunner to an even more influential heresy in Arianism many years later, taught opposing doctrines that were less obvious to the unsuspecting, attracting even bishops of the time to its ranks. Those aligning to dynamic monarchianism believed Jesus Christ was an ordinary man who gained divine power from God. Those aligning to modalistic monarchianism believed God could manifest himself to be the Father, Son, or Holy Spirit at will according to the need. The followers of modalist monarchianism included Praxeas, bishop of Smyrna, and Sabellius of Pentapolis (followers would later refer to themselves as Sabellians).[16]

SCRIPTURES WRITTEN

Nothing would help solidify doctrinal beliefs and provide guidance to a growing church as the writings of the early apostles—much of which became the canon for the New Testament. The exact dates of their creation are tenuous and mostly based upon oral tradition, but one can get a general idea of the relative timing.

The four Gospels—Matthew, Mark, Luke, and John—were written between approximately AD 50 and 90. The final text of the Gospels was not established until several decades later, perhaps as late as AD 150. The book of Acts, thought to be authored by Luke, was written during the same period.

The writings of Paul are the earliest writings of the New Testament, likely between AD 40 and 50, starting with Galatians, followed by 1 and 2 Thessalonians; and then 1 and 2 Corinthians and Romans between AD 50 and 60. The letters of Paul to the Colossians, Philippians, and Ephesians, along with Philemon, both letters of Timothy, Titus and Hebrews were likely all written between AD 60 and 70. Stirring a bit of controversy, the Christian scholar Origen Adamantius, considered an early Church Father[17] despite his perceived heretical teachings of the premortal existence of souls and subordination of Jesus Christ to God the Father, would later question the authenticity of the letters of Paul.[18]

Other books of the New Testament include the book of James (written between AD 40 and 50), Jude between AD 60 and 70, 1 and 2 Peter written in AD 78–82, the three epistles of John written between AD 80 and 90, and the Book of Revelation written in AD 92–96.

THE STATE OF CHRISTIANITY IN AD 299

While enduring intense persecution, surviving the martyrdom of its early church leaders, navigating a volatile political landscape, and battling heresies, Christianity managed to roll forth and create a lasting framework by the end of the evangelization and formation period. The Church was still in its infancy and subject to competing internal and external forces while it strived to develop one "dominant strain" of Christianity instead of the variety of sects that had formed around a diversity of charismatic leaders.[19] The challenge for Christianity moving into the next period was to achieve large-scale credibility as a legitimate religion with the power not only to save souls through faith in Jesus Christ but also to influence the social and political environment toward the establishment of a global Christian Church.

Chapter 2

THEY WERE LEGITIMIZED AND CODIFIED (AD 300–999)

THE LEGITIMACY AND CODIFICATION PERIOD, FROM AD 300 TO 999, WAS a time for Christianity to continue its global proliferation while codifying its doctrines and legitimizing its place in religion and politics. This was accomplished while enduring ongoing persecution and the battle against divergent sects of Christianity. During this time period the not-so-new religion developed organization and hierarchy to maintain its growth and to defend its doctrines, finding allies and mediators in converted politicians and influential people.

This period of Christianity was defined by seven major categories of events: the continuation of persecution and evangelization, increased heresies, doctrinal codification, hierarchy and politics, validation, and the seeds of corruption. The dynamics of these events firmly established Christianity into the mainstream of society and gave it both spiritual and political power to spread its message of hope and faith in Jesus Christ around the world to become a religious force.

PERSECUTION CONTINUES

Although the persecution against Christianity and its adherents continued, the fervor in which it was executed was less than it was the previous centuries. The emperor Diocletian around AD 303 persecuted the Christians, a persecution which included the burning of Christian books and churches. By this time it was clear that Christianity could not be eliminated and therefore such persecution served to feed the ego of bigoted leaders such as the maltreatment and forcible conversion of the Christians at the hands of King Shapur II of the Sassanid Empire of Persia during his fourth-century reign.[1]

EVANGELIZATION CONTINUES

The spreading of Christianity continued using two primary methods—word of mouth (preaching and proclamation) and the establishment of physical structures for the purposes of Christian worship and teaching. One type of physical structure was monasteries, buildings dedicated to prayer while serving as the living quarters of monks and others who served as evangelists. Between AD 330 and 360 monasteries were built in Egypt, Palestine, Syria, Persia, and Greece. During this time churches were spontaneously emerging around the globe. A church might be as simple as a person's home or as elaborate as a structure built specifically for Christian worship services. An important component of evangelization was the conversion of influential individuals or groups to Christianity such as Constantine in AD 312. These conversions had a ripple effect and led to the spreading of Christianity all over the world in great numbers.

HERESIES INCREASE

As the heresies of the previous period faded away, new—even more prolific—heresies emerged, seeking to indoctrinate Christians into belief systems that were contrary to the prevailing doctrines held by the central Christian Church. Heresies were both spiritually and politically unhealthy for Christianity because each heresy splintered a consolidated Christian movement while challenging the established ecclesiastical leadership. The six major heresies of the Legitimacy and Codification period were Arianism, Dontanism, Apollinarianism, Nestorianism, Eutychianism (Monophysitism), and Pelagianism.

Arianism

Arianism taught Jesus Christ was the literal Son of God, created by God the Father, and thus subordinate to the Father. Arius, born in AD 256, was a priest in Alexandria in AD 318 and based his belief system on such scriptural passages as John 14:28, in which Jesus said, ". . . or my Father is greater than I."[2] Although the Arian belief system was entirely consistent with the available scripture at the time, Arianism was contrary to the prevailing thought of Jesus being one with God—a belief that would later be codified as the doctrine of the Trinity at the Council of Nicaea in AD 325.

Arius was expelled and excommunicated by the patriarch Alexander in AD 320, but he went on to convince bishops and other influential Christian leaders of his belief system. Arius was reinstated by councils of bishops in Bithynia and Palestine, causing further uproar and giving credence to Arianism. Although Constantine convened the Council of Nicaea to refute the Arian doctrine by way of the Trinity, Arians were able to maintain their doctrine by way of interpretation of the Nicene Creed. Despite the anti-Arian conclusion of the Council of Nicaea, in AD 327, Constantine and Eusebius of Nicomedia reinstated Arius out of exile, with Arius said to become one of Constantine's advisors. Constantine's action produced great confusion in Christianity, making it appear Constantine reversed his decision in order to support Arianism over the doctrine of the Trinity.

Donatism

The heresy of Donatism was less about doctrine and more about how the Church should treat those who renounced their faith under Diocletian (the Roman Emperor from AD 284 to 305). During the Diocletian persecutions, Christians were asked to repudiate their faith by way of giving up their scriptures, which many of the wealthier Christians did in order to avoid losing property and riches. Once the persecutions ended, those who renounced their Christian faith were viewed as traitors by the poor who did not renounce their faith.[3] As a result, the Donatists (so called after the bishop Donatus Magnus) viewed any sacraments performed by such traitors to be invalid and refused to submit to the authority of such priests and bishops—many of which returned to their positions of authority under Constantine.

Apollinarianism

Although a minor threat compared to Arianism, Apollinarianism taught that Christ had a human body but that his mind was purely divine.[4] Formulated around AD 360 and named after a bishop in Antioch named Apollinarius, the doctrine of Apollinarianism rendered the physical suffering of Jesus Christ without meaning, making a mockery of the events in Gethsemane, including the pleading of Christ to the Father. Apollinarianism was labeled a heresy and barely survived into the fifth century.

Nestorianism

Taking an opposite approach to that of Apollinarianism, Nestorianism taught Jesus was actually two completely separate persons—both the Son of God and a mortal man.[5] Following this logic, the Nestorianism doctrine concluded that Mary was the mother of Jesus Christ the mortal man, not Jesus Christ the Son of God, refuting doctrines of the day that revered Mary as the Mother of God. Nestorianism is coined after a monk in Antioch named Nestorius, who later became a priest and the Patriarch of Constantinople. When it became apparent that there were no reconciling doctrines concerning Nestorianism, the third Ecumenical Council in AD 431 condemned Nestoriansim, banning Nestorius eventually to Egypt where he later died. Despite the death of Nestorius, in AD 484 the Synod of Beth Papat accepted the Nestorian doctrine of Christ as official doctrine for the East Syrian Church.[6]

Eutychianism (Monophysitism)

Eutychianism, and later Momophysitism, were subtle variations of Apollinariansim, teaching that Jesus Christ was of both human and divine "natures" and merged the two natures into one fully divine nature not equal to the Father but greater than man—thus removing the human element of Christ.[7] Eutyches, the influential head of a monastery near Constantinople, is credited with disseminating the doctrine of Eutychianism and was promptly excommunicated following a synod at Constantinople. Not to be deterred, Eutyches leveraged his influence in having a council of bishops called in AD 449 under Emperor Theodosius II, which not only reinstated Eutyches but also excommunicated Pope Leo.

In AD 451, Pope Leo consolidated his own support in calling a council of nearly 600 bishops at Chalcedon, where a creed was established condemning the three like heresies of Nestorianism, Apollinarianism, and Eutychianism.

Pelagianism

Named after a supposed British monk Pelagius, Pelagianism replaced the doctrine of original sin with the belief that the will of man was capable of making his own choices without the help of God and because of evil choices (sin) there was a need for the Atonement of Jesus Christ.[8] With Pelagianism formulated around AD 400, its author, Pelagius, was found innocent of heresy by a council of bishops in AD 415 but was later found guilty in subsequent councils. To add further confusion, Pope Innocent I declared Pelagius a heretic, but his successor Zozimus reversed that decision to find him innocent only to reverse his own decision shortly thereafter (as did later popes). Some controversy exists today over the theology that children are born with sin and the principle of free will and how that enters into man's relationship with God.

DOCTRINAL CODIFICATION

As Christianity flourished, especially in the face of ongoing heretical battles and persecution, the codification of its doctrines became critical. During this period there was synthesis and establishment of the doctrines themselves, as well as the codification of those doctrines in the form of canonized scriptures.

The First Council of Nicaea

Perhaps no single ecclesiastical event in Christian history had more impact, or was so full of controversy, as the First Council of Nicaea in AD 325. Before understanding what the council accomplished, one must first understand the man who convened the council—the Roman Emperor Constantine I.

Constantine was not a religious or holy man, rather he is said to have been superstitious, a sun-worshipper, murderer, and by all respects having lived a questionable life, not being baptized until days before his death.[9] As a consummate opportunist, Constantine viewed the Church as a means of consolidating political power, unifying and stabilizing his empire, and leaving a personal legacy on par with that of the Apostles. To achieve his design, Constantine contrived an uneasy alliance between himself and the Church.[10] Of this the Christian historian Paul Johnson wrote:

> How could the Christian Church, apparently quite willingly, accommodate this weird megalomaniac in its theocratic system? Was there a conscious bargain? Which side benefited most from this unseemly marriage between Church and State? Or, to put it another way, did the empire surrender to Christianity, or did Christianity prostitute itself to the empire?[11]

From a spiritual standpoint, at least two major stumbling blocks requiring a resolution faced Christianity: 1) the Arian dispute over the nature of Christ; and 2) the need to reconcile the Judaic concern over Christ being the Son of God, creating a polytheistic dilemma. Constantine himself was not concerned over such doctrinal matters and found them to be insignificant, "a point of discussion . . . suggested by the contentious spirit fostered by the misused leisure . . . merely an intellectual exercise."[12] When considering the differences between the Arian belief and what came to be known as the doctrine of the Trinity, Constantine considered the matter to be "too sublime and abstruse" to be settled with certainty.[13]

Seizing the opportunity, explaining he received a vision from heaven, Constantine called a council of bishops, inviting 1,800 bishops from the east and west with an estimated 220 to 318 bishops attending.[14] The workings of the council were much like those of a committee, discussing points of view in hopes of driving to a consensus. Hanging over the attendees was the notion that the Emperor Constantine demanded clear resolutions and would not tolerate dissension—even going as far as to threaten those would not endorse the final resolutions with exile.

Besides establishing a date for the Easter celebration and settling issues relating to early canon law, the council tenuously resolved the issue of the relationship between Jesus Christ and God the Father and in doing so constructed the Nicene Creed.

The Nature of Jesus Christ and the Nicene Creed

Essentially two points of view were debated at the council. Arius argued that Jesus Christ was created by God (Colossians 1:15), that all things were created through the Son, but that the Son was subordinate to the Father (John 14:28). Those opposed to Arius argued God the Father is eternal and therefore his Son is eternal, and as a result they are both one in being (John 14:10).

After months of debate, which by some accounts was reported to be quite heated to the point of physical altercations,[15] the council was able to reach consensus on the following (with three bishops in disagreement):

- The divinity of Jesus Christ, not made but begotten by God the Father

- Jesus Christ is God's Son but is also fully God

- Jesus Christ is "one in being with the Father" or "of the same substance"

To further solidify the consensus a creed was created and agreed upon called the Nicene Creed, which read:

We believe in one God, the Father Almighty, Maker of all things visible and invisible.

And in one Lord Jesus Christ, the Son of God, begotten of the Father [the only-begotten; that is, of the essence of the Father, God of God], Light of Light, very God of very God, begotten, not made, being of one substance with the Father;

By whom all things were made [both in heaven and on earth];

Who for us men, and for our salvation, came down and was incarnate and was made man;

He suffered, and the third day he rose again, ascended into heaven;

From thence he shall come to judge the quick and the dead.

And in the Holy Ghost.

[But those who say: 'There was a time when he was not;' and 'He was not before he was made;' and 'He was made out of nothing,' or 'He is of another substance' or 'essence,' or 'The Son of God is created,' or 'changeable,' or 'alterable'—they are condemned by the holy catholic and apostolic Church.]

The final paragraph, which is somewhat out of step with the rest of the creed, was apparently aimed at Arius and his followers, who disagreed with the doctrine put forth in the Nicene Creed.

Although the Council of Nicaea adjourned having achieved significant progress, the debate over Christian doctrine would not end there.

The phrase "one substance" and its interpretation caused consternation among Church leaders for decades. Adding to the confusion and suggesting his indifference to the importance of Christian doctrine, Constantine reinstated Arius from exile following the Council of Nicaea with two of Constantine's successors being Arian, giving rise to additional theological confusion.

It is important to note that although the efforts of the Council of Nicaea, and the Nicene Creed in particular, were significant support pillars for the doctrine of the Trinity, the concept of the Trinity was discussed long before in the writings of Tertullian and Origen.[16] Tertullian was an early Christian author—at times considered a heretic—while Origen was a scholar and theologian considered to be one of the fathers of the early Christian Church.

Beyond Nicaea and the Modification of the Nicene Creed

Several decades later, loosely attributed to the First Council of Constantinople in AD 381, the Nicene Creed was modified to clarify God the Father's generation of the Son, to provide a reference to the Virgin Mary, and to more fully elucidate the Holy Spirit and his role in the Trinity. The modified Nicene Creed read as follows, with the key modifications from the original version shown in italics:

> We believe in one God, the Father, the Almighty, of all that is, seen and unseen.
>
> We believe in one Lord, Jesus Christ, the only Son of God, eternally begotten of the Father, God from God, Light from Light, true God from true God, begotten, not made, of one Being with the Father.
>
> Through him all things were made.
>
> For us and for our salvation he came down from heaven: *by the power of the Holy Spirit he became incarnate from the Virgin Mary,* and was made man.
>
> For our sake he was *crucified under Pontius Pilate;* he suffered death and was buried.
>
> On the third day he rose again in accordance with the Scriptures; he ascended into heaven *and is seated at the right hand of the Father.*
>
> He will come again in glory to judge the living and the dead, *and his kingdom will have no end.*
>
> *We believe in the Holy Spirit, the Lord, the giver of life, who proceeds from the Father and the Son. With the Father and the Son he is worshipped*

and glorified. He has spoken through the Prophets.
  We believe in one holy catholic and apostolic Church.
  We acknowledge one baptism for the forgiveness of sins.
  We look for the resurrection of the dead, and the life of the world to
come. Amen.

Despite these clarifications to the Nicene Creed the controversy over the nature of Jesus Christ and his relationship to God the Father would continue, mainly due to the stark ambiguities and room for interpretation. There were those who focused on the literal meaning of the available scriptures and those who chose to submit to a more allegorical meaning. Given the power of the universal (Catholic) Church, which crafted and embraced the principles of the Nicene Creed and its interpretation thereof, eventually the Trinitarian belief system (that is, Jesus Christ is begotten and not made, being of one essence with the Father) prevailed and left the opposing belief systems to carve out their niches and exist in some cases until the present day.

Peripheral Doctrines, Practices and Principles

There were other doctrines, practices and principles of Christianity established during this period besides that of the Trinity. The Third Ecumenical Council in AD 431 declared Mary as being the "Mother of God," both reaffirming the Triune doctrine and commencing a tradition in which Mary would be more fully venerated including an intercessory prayer dedicated to her approximately 1,000 years later.[17] During this period came the practices of confession and penance as a means of salvation, use of the Latin language in worship services (~AD 600), and a lengthy controversy over the use of icons and statues in churches (AD 720 to 850).

The Bible

Critical to codification and legitimacy of Christianity was the establishment and publication of holy scripture, allowing the word of God to be taught in a consistent written form. The Bible, as it came to be known as early as AD 223,[18] would include both an Old Testament (before Christ) and a New Testament (from around the birth of Christ until shortly after his Ascension). The compilation of the Bible was a long a laborious process that took many hundreds of years to complete. The process would include the original authoring of the writings, the copying of those writings by scribes, the selection of writings for inclusion, the compilation of those writings and further copying, and the canonization (or approval) of the finished product, which came to be known as the Bible.

Despite the fact that all of the New Testament content was authored before AD 100 during the evangelization and formation period, it would not be until centuries later that the twenty-seven books making up the New Testament would be selected (and other books rejected) for publication in the Bible. Athanasius is credited with identifying the twenty-seven books of the New Testament as part of his festal letter, but it was not until AD 397 at the Synod at Carthage that those twenty-seven books would be ecclesiastically ratified and considered sacred scripture. By AD 400 Jerome translated the Greek Bible into Latin, which came to be known as the Vulgate—both the Old and New Testaments together. The earliest recorded Bible in nearly completed physical form is known as the Codex Vaticanus, a fourth-century document written on vellum (mammal skin).[19]

The compilation of the Bible was not without controversy as the ability to maintain doctrinal consistency and continuity proved difficult. Eusebius of Caesarea desired to demonstrate that from the earliest period of Christianity orthodoxy was part of a continuous tradition and in doing so recognized serious inaccuracies that inhibited that effort.[20] For example the influence of Gnosticism on Christianity in Antioch raised questions regarding apostolic succession, creating inconsistencies in the history used by Eusebius during that time.[21] Furthermore Origen was concerned with textual inconsistencies with the New Testament manuscripts.[22] Despite these and numerous other challenges the anthology of scripture moved forward into the Bibles we have in today's modern era.

The books accepted for inclusion to the Bible are well known, but perhaps less known are the books that were rejected including the Life of Adam and Eve, the Book of Enoch, the Book of Jubilees, the gospel of Mary, the gospel of Nicodemus, and a huge library of fifty-two texts referred to as the Gnostic scriptures of Nag Hammadi.[23] The volumes of writings rejected for inclusion to the Bible are staggering. The reasons for rejection were mainly the fear of forgery and because many of the writings did not support the doctrinal direction of the early Christian Church.

For example, the Gospel of Thomas found among the Nag Hammadi texts (in Codex II) contained 114 sayings recorded by the Apostle Thomas attributed to Jesus Christ. Many of those sayings resembled closely those found in the Canonical Gospels while others were thought to be more of a Gnostic nature.[24]

The Gospel of Thomas was either rejected or simply overlooked by the biblical aggregators. One theory suggests Bishop Athanasius of Alexandria, a fierce opponent of Arianism,[25] ordered the Gospel of Thomas and all other noncanonical scripture to be destroyed (or buried) in his Festal Letter of AD 367 so as to preserve the purity of scripture at the time.[51] If this theory is true, and if instead these texts were given serious consideration, then the Bible of today might have looked quite different in terms of its content. These texts may have brought clarity to doctrines such as the Trinity. Of the compilation of the New Testament, Christian historian Paul Johnson writes:

> An inclusive canon allowed the Church to make a wider appeal to heretical populations or, to put it another way, to include under its umbrella of faith the followers of old and divergent traditions. At the same time, the process of selection and canonization allowed the orthodox leaders to demolish dangerous documents once their adherents had been captured. Thus in the third, fourth and fifth centuries, many written "gospels," particularly those penetrated by gnosticism, were excluded and so disappeared. At the same time, dangerous elements within the canon could be to some extent de-fused by attaching more orthodox documents to their authors.[27]

Although the Bible of this period was well circulated, the process of canonization was not technically complete, meaning the Bible was not fully accepted as being a "closed canon" where no other modifications could be made. This is a matter of some controversy as some like Augustine believed the canon to be closed by the end of the fourth century. However, it was not until the Council of Trent in 1563 that the Roman Catholic canon was officially closed. The version of the Bible recognized at the Council of Trent differs from the Protestant version in circulation today, which removed the Roman Catholic included books of Tobit, Judith, 1 and 2 Maccabees, Wisdom, Sirach, and Baruch along with small enhancements to the books of Esther and Daniel—all in the Old Testament.

HIERARCHY AND POLITICS

As the early Christian Church grew it was inevitable, if not necessary, for an advanced form of organizational hierarch to develop. Christian hierarchy was positive when it provided formal lines of delegation to allocate the work to more effectively spread the gospel and minister to its members. Christian hierarchy was negative when it added layers of formality and politicized the Church by feeding the egos of leaders while removing the influence of its members. Historically speaking, Christianity experienced both.

After the ascension of Christ the Christian Church was loosely organized as witnessed in the letters of Paul. By the early second century, a church hierarchy began to form.[28] Bishops were the first overseers of the local church with priests eventually being added as subordinate to the bishops. Deacons were added and were subordinate to the priests. Paul in his letters writes of apostles, prophets, elders, teachers, preachers, evangelists, and pastors. This formation of a hierarchical clergy was a natural progression and happened slowly and not necessarily in a regionally uniform manner. By the early fourth century, the clergy were the only ones permitted to speak from the pulpit, suggesting a hierarchical structure in which members were subject to the clergy.

Being subject to a Pope had its disadvantages for bishops and priests. In AD 385, Pope Siricius issued a decree that made it forbidden for bishops, priests, and deacons to have sex. Several decades later, in AD 460, Pope Leo made it forbidden for priests to marry, leading to the celibate priesthood of the Roman Catholic Church today.

As the Christian Church grew, it became necessary to introduce additional forms of hierarchy. In AD 343 at the council of Serdicia, the bishop of Rome was appointed to mediate over the Eastern Churches. One hundred years later in the mid fifth century, the Emperor Valentinian III gave a decree that all bishops were subject to the Pope. With the offices of deacons, priests, bishops, eventually cardinals, and the pope in place, the hierarchy of the early Christian Church was in full bloom.

With hierarchy comes politics. Following the decree from Valentinian III, the Council of Chalcedon gave equal authority to the Bishop of Constantinople as that of the Bishop of Rome, signaling the beginning of the East-West schism. The power struggle between Rome and Constantinople continued until the Sixth Ecumenical Council in AD 680 where the Emperor Constantine IV proclaimed the pope as the head of all Christianity. The influence of politics would continue within the Church with such events as the crowning of Charlemagne as emperor of the Holy Roman Empire by Pope Leo III in AD 800 and the election of Pope Sergius III in AD 904 and his successors at the hands of Roman aristocracy. During this period since there were few boundaries between the church and state, each influenced the other.

POLITICAL AND RELIGIOUS VALIDATION

The alliance of Constantine with the Church generated substantial legitimacy and validation for Christianity; however, such a status was well in the works before then. It is estimated by AD 300 there were approximately sixty million people in the Roman Empire with as many as fifteen million (25 percent) professing to be Christians.[29] In AD 301, Armenia adopted Christianity as its state religion—twelve years before Christianity became a legal religion within the Roman Empire, thirty-six years before Christianity became the state religion of Rome, and seventy-nine years before Christianity became the official religion of the Roman Empire. Constantine, although polytheistic in his beliefs and careless in this governance, advanced the legitimacy of Christianity by declaring Sunday as the Christian Sabbath in AD 321, building a church to the Apostle Peter in AD 323 and moving the capital to Constantinople in AD 324. All of these events preceded the political and religious legitimacy of Christianity among the Roman Empire to the point of Theodosius I declaring Christianity to be the sole religion of the Roman Empire in AD 380.

THE SEEDS OF CORRUPTION

Within this period of great advancement for Christianity came the seeds of corruption; seeds that would germinate, grow, and choke the Church in the centuries that followed. The corruption of Christianity would come at the hands of unrighteous men seeking power and riches. Paul Johnson speaks of the rich joining the Church to advance their personal gain and bishops purchasing their way into greater positions—becoming rich as they did so.[30] Such positioning took connections. In AD 904, thanks to the influence of a powerful Roman noblewoman, Sergius

III was elected pope, the beginning of a promulgation that would witness other popes elected by the Roman aristocracy.

A leading indicator of corruption was the abuse of power. Armed with supposed directives from God, the Church and its supporters began a campaign of forced conversion. In AD 612, the Visigothic King Sisebut forced the Jews in Spain to not only release all slaves, but also to convert to Christianity or be exiled. In AD 721, Pope Leo II embarked on a campaign of forced conversion of the Jews. In addition to the abuse of power was the spirit of nepotism that was becoming ripe among Church leaders along with a mentality of entitlement.

THE STATE OF CHRISTIANITY IN AD 999

Despite its ongoing battles with persecution and heresy, by AD 999 Christianity was thriving spiritual and politically. No longer having to worry about the overbearing external forces trying to eliminate its existence as with the previous period, Christianity could now focus on codifying its doctrines, establishing its canon, and building an enduring organization capable of taking the gospel to the four corners of the earth. With all of its strength and vitality moving into the next millennium, the Church began to experience fracture and the beginning of corruption. Richard Daft in his book, *Organization Theory and Design*, explains the four stages of the organizational life cycle as 1) Entrepreneurial stage when there is a need for leadership; 2) Collectivity stage when there is a need for delegation; 3) Formalization stage when red tape becomes excessive; and 4) the Elaboration stage when there is a need for revitalization.[31] Although not a corporate entity, a church operates under a similar dynamic and the Church by the end of AD 999 was evolving between stages two and three.

Chapter 3

THEY WERE CORRUPTED
AND DIVIDED (AD 1000-1499)

As the Christian Church neared the millennial landmark it would begin to be faced with significant issues of leadership that would rupture its unity spiritually and politically. Although Christianity was still spreading throughout the world and doctrinal clarification would continue to evolve, the organization of the Church would be challenged by its integration with the political structure and an increasingly corrupt leadership. These and other trials would lead to the debacle of the crusades, the unwarranted persecution of prominent individuals, the unconscionable inquisitions, and a series of schisms that would divide Christianity into multiple denominations. Accordingly, this period is marked by four major categories of events and activities including doctrinal evolution, church and state integration, corruption, and division.

DOCTRINAL EVOLUTION

The evolution of Christian doctrine would continue during this period, but without the intensity of such developments as the Nicene Creed. Instead the doctrinal developments of this period would bring about refinements such as the defining of the seven sacraments from the Forth Lateran Council in 1215. The seven sacraments would include baptism, the Eucharist, reconciliation, confirmation, marriage, holy orders, and the anointing of the sick. This period of Christianity would bring rise to such spiritual giants as Thomas Aquinas who attempted to reconcile the arguments of religion and science with the publishing of *Summa Contra Gentiles* in 1264.

Because of the growing bureaucracy of the Church—its many layers of leadership and evolving rules of governance—establishing doctrine and dogma was not always a timely process. For example, the theological concept of papal infallibility was reportedly invoked by Popes Bonaface VIII in his Bull Unam Sanctam of 1302, but it would not be until the First Vatican Council of 1870 when papal infallibility would be dogmatically defined.

CHURCH AND STATE INTEGRATION

Christianity's rise to global prominence and legitimization was in part accomplished through strong political alignment. The process of validation and legitimization through politics was a double-edged sword for the Church. On one hand it gave the Church influence and protection, on the other hand the lack of separation of church and state meant the state's influence on the Church could sometimes be exerted in ways that were spiritually counterproductive. After enjoying the fruits of political alliances with the likes of Constantine the Church began to feel the negative side of these uneasy associations.

For instance, it was common for emperors shortly after the reign of Constantine to conduct papal appointments. Such appointments may or may not have coincided with the desires of bishops and other clergy. The last such appointment was made in 1049 when the Emperor Henry III appointed Leo IX as the Pope. Ten years later in 1059 there was an attempt to end the practice of emperor appointments by way of a papal bull by Pope Nicholas II, which established cardinal-bishops as the only electors of the pope with corresponding consents.[1] Despite this action, the state still exerted considerable influence in the elections of Church officials.

While the state exerted its authority on the Church, the reverse also carried weight in the ongoing relationship of the two. Pope Gregory VII believed the Church, and specifically the pope, had the right to remove emperors and attempted to do so in 1076 with Henry IV following the emperor's action to depose Gregory.

The appointments of clergy by politicians were not isolated to the papacy. During this period the practice of "lay investiture" was common.

Lay investiture, the appointment of bishops and other clergy by secular authorities,[2] was a source of income because of the wealth and land commonly amassed by bishops as part of their ecclesiastical assignments. Besides generating revenue, this incestuous bureaucratic process ensured governmental loyalty. In 1111, Pope Paschal II attempted to address the issue of wealth accumulation by declaring church-wide apostolic poverty—something Francis of Assisi would commit himself to nearly 100 years later. In a much broader initiative, the French theologian John of Salisbury in 1159 published the book *Policraticus* outlining the doctrine of separation of church and state where the state was to become subordinate to the Church.[3]

The lay investiture issue continued for several decades until 1122, when Pope Calixtus II and Henry V reached an agreement that would be known as the Concordat of Worms, confirmed at the First Lateran Council in 1123, to abandon the practice with a more amicable process in its place (including veto power of the emperor). Although the process was more acceptable to the Church one might question its efficiency in selecting popes as witnessed in 1268 when it took church cardinals three years to elect Pope Gregorio X in 1271. The newly elected pope later instituted the conclave to streamline the process of electing new popes.

CORRUPTION

The Lord is incorruptible (1 Peter 1:4, 23), but unfortunately the same cannot be said of man. During this five-hundred-year period of Christianity, with the Church becoming a powerful spiritual and political entity, it was common by necessity for leaders of the Church to be spiritual shepherds, politicians, corporate officers, and military strategists—all at the same time. The evolving global dynamics demanded such versatility in Church leadership to navigate and address complex social and cultural issues. Combine this with man's natural desire for power, wealth, and family security, and the unfortunate outcome was often corruption. The corruption of this period included nepotism, immorality, indulgences, and piety.

Nepotism

The most obvious form of corruption facing the Church at this time was that of widespread nepotism. Nepotism is "patronage bestowed or favoritism shown on the basis of family relationship."[4] Such practices were culturally common for the day, but in some cases the abuses were rampant. For example, Pope Nicholas III (1277–80) appointed his nephew, Latino, to the cardinalate and later "took possession of the [Romagna] province" in Italy through Latino. Another one of Nicholas's nephews, Berthold, was later made Count of the Romagna through the influence of Nicholas. Nicholas bestowed important positions of power on close relatives ensuring a legacy of wealth and prominent standing.[5]

Pope Innocent VII (1404–06) appointed his nephew Ludovico Migliorati to the cardinalate. Migliorati was an unstable individual who kidnapped and murdered a group of Roman partisans for rebelling against Innocent.[6] The appointment of relatives not only generated wealth but also made for fiercely loyal subjects.

Pope Callixtus III (1455–58) appointed two of his nephews cardinals, one of which (Rodrigo) later became Pope Alexander VI. In turn, Alexander promoted his alleged mistress's brother, Alessandro Farnese, to cardinal with Farnese later becoming Pope Paul III.[7] Continuing the cycle of nepotism Paul appointed two of his grandsons to the cardinalate, Alessandro Farnese, age fourteen, and Guido Ascanio Sforza, age sixteen.[8]

Pope Sixtus IV (1471–84) may have been the greatest practitioner of nepotism among all popes, appointing six of his nephews to be cardinals[9] while ensuring financial riches to his family through the granting of influential posts with generous salaries. One of Sixtus's nephews, Giuliano della Rovere, who would later become Pope Julius II, was appointed Bishop of Carpentras and later Cardinal Priest of San Pietro in Vincula by the time he was eighteen years old. Another nephew, Raffaele Sansoni Galeoti Riario, was appointed Cardinal of San Giorgio in Velabro at the age of twenty-six. As a wedding gift at age thirty, Sixtus made his nephew Girolamo Riario Lord of Imola and Foli. As a matter of intrigue and politics two of Sixtus's nephews, Pietro Riario and Guiliano della Rovere, aligned themselves with the Pazzi family of Florence and the Archbishop of Pisa to depose the Medici family from power in Florence, murdering Giuliano Medici in the Cathedral of Santa Maria del Fiore.[10] Pietro Riario eventually became one of the richest men in Rome and the chief foreign policy advisor to Sixtus.

Pope Alexander VI (1492–1503) not only fathered children with a mistress,[11] but he also appointed one of his sons (Cesare Borgia) to be a bishop at fifteen years old and shortly thereafter a cardinal.[12]

Pope Innocent XII, disgusted by the historical practice of papal nepotism, issued the bull Romanum decet pontificem in 1692.[13] The papal bull banned popes from granting positions, estates, or income to any relative and allowed a pope to appoint only one qualified relative to the cardinalate.

Immorality

Nepotism often led to the appointment of highly unqualified and questionable individuals. For example, In 1032 a young boy between the ages of eleven and twenty, son of the Count of Tusculum and nephew of Pope Benedict VIII and Pope John XIX, was appointed pope—Pope Benedict IX.[14] Besides lacking ecclesiastical qualifications, Pope Benedict IX engaged in "unsophisticated pleasures" and "riotous living."[15] Making matters worse, the young man eventually sold the papacy to his godfather Gregory VI.

Pope Alexander VI (1492–1503) was said to have several mistresses and fathered illegitimate children while "repleting his treasury in ways that were more than dubious."[16] Pope Paul II (1464–1471) was accused of grave immorality during his papal reign.[17] Pope Sixtus IV (1471–1484) allegedly appointed Giovanni Sclafenato a cardinal for "ingenuousness, loyalty, . . . and his other gifts of soul and body."[18]

Such widespread immorality among the papacy prompted the emperor Henry III to convoke the synod of Sutri in 1046 to address corruption in the office of the pope. Approximately five years later, a monk by the name of Pietro Damiani published *Liber Gomorrhianus*, a work condemning widespread moral corruption within the Church. While these public admonitions were stinging to the Church, they had little effect in curtailing the inappropriate activity among the papacy.

Indulgences

In Christianity, when an individual commits sin, forgiveness is available through repentance made possible by grace in the Lord Jesus Christ through his atoning sacrifice. Sin always carries with it temporal and spiritual consequences, paid for in mortality or in the next life. Imagine if that consequence could be shortened or removed altogether by doing good deeds, offering money, or displaying some form of piety. In the early Christian Church, it was possible to forego the consequences of sin by obtaining an indulgence through payment, an act of devotion, service, worship, attending a pilgrimage, or several other various acts large and small. It was possible to obtain an indulgence by making monetary contributions to Church-sponsored projects for buildings, infrastructure, schools, and other worthy causes.[19]

Over time the practice of selling indulgences for money reached outrageous proportions. Commissaries (Church representatives), often unknown to Church leadership, would inflate the price of indulgences so as to greedily maximize their own profits.[20] There were professional "pardoners"[21] commissioned to make collections for specific projects, often exceeding Church guidelines for the amount to be collected and the extent of the forgiveness offered.[22] All of this was reminiscent of the merchants in the temple who were chased out by the Savior (Luke 19:45–46).

Despite the efforts of the Fourth Lateran Council in 1215 to curb abuses relating to indulgences, the practice continued. In 1392, Pope Boniface IX confronted the Bishop of Ferrara on the unauthorized use of the pope's authority to extract money from individuals in return for indulgences.[23] Johann Tetzel, a German Dominican preacher and commissioner of indulgences for all of Germany under Pope Leo X, reportedly traveled with a supposed official document of Pope Leo X on velvet cushion, preaching to the masses the following as fact:

> Indulgences . . . are the most precious and sublime of God's gifts; this [red] cross . . . has as much efficacy as the cross of Jesus Christ. Draw near, and I will give you letters, duly sealed, by which even the sins you shall hereafter desire to commit, shall be all forgiven you. . . . There is no sin so great that indulgence cannot remit it . . . let him pay,—let him only pay largely, and it shall be forgiven him. Even repentance is not indispensible. But more than all this: indulgences save not the living alone, they also save the dead. . . . The very moment . . . that the money clinks against the bottom of the chest, the soul escapes from purgatory and flies free to heaven.[24]

The concept of indulgences is not itself blasphemous (making sacrifices as a means of penance), but the idea of allowing individuals to buy forgiveness for not only past sins but future sins makes a mockery of the infinite sacrifice made by Jesus Christ. For that reason the selling of indulgences was a true indicator of corruption within the Church.

Piety

Piety is defined as a form of devout religious fulfillment and reverence for God; however, piety can evolve negatively toward piousness, including hypocrisy and pretended religious motives.[25] Because of its political and spiritual influence during this period in history, the Church felt the need to fight wars on three fronts. First, there was the war on real and perceived heretical doctrines and those who promulgated such doctrine. Second, there were wars to advance the cause of Christ through forced conversion to Christianity. And finally, there were wars to fight the invasions of non-Christians into Christian territories. While some may justify one or more of these battles as necessary in preserving Christianity and to free enslaved societies, one can certainly argue that such battles were often unnecessary and manifested a vanity that was unbecoming of the Lord's Church.

Inquisitions: The battles against heresy, or offenses against canon law, were sorely manifest in the many inquisitions facilitated by the Church and political institutions of the day. Although fighting heresy was nothing new, the origins of the inquisitions can be ecclesiastically traced to a papal bull issued against heretics in 1184 by Pope Lucius III, which outlined secular punishments for heretics and those who supported them. In 1252, Pope Innocent IV issued a papal bull that approved the use of torture against heretics,[26] laying the groundwork for future atrocities.

History records two key inquisitions during this period, the Medieval Inquisition (started in 1231) and the Spanish Inquisition (started in 1478). It was not uncommon for inquisitions to include torture and burnings at the stake as a means to extract information and punish the accused.[27] A few of those persecuted for heresy include the following:

- In 1141, Pierre Abelard, a philosopher, was condemned as a heretic for his views on the Trinity and illicit relationship with a French nun.[28]

- In 1215, the Fourth Lateran council prescribed that Jews must wear clothing to distinguish them from Christians.[29]

- In 1244, a group of over 200 individuals practicing Catharism, a sect considered heretical to the Catholic Church, were burned at Montsegur for not renouncing their faith.[30]

- In 1321, Franciscan monk Marsilio da Padova was declared a heretic for preaching separation of church and state,[31] while the Franciscan monk William of Occam was excommunicated for preaching the same, adding the Church should forego property ownership.[32]

- In 1323, the Church declared Pope Paschal II's doctrine on apostolic poverty as heresy.[33]

- In 1415, at the Council of Constance John Wycliffe was declared a heretic for his translation of the Bible into English. His books were burned and his remains exhumed and burned in 1428 at the request of Pope Martin V.[34]

- In 1415, Jan Hus was burned at the stake for heresy pertaining to his opposition in opposing the sale of indulgences and his opposition to selected Church doctrines.[35]

- In 1484, the persecution of magicians and witches in Germany was ordered by Pope Innocent VIII.[36]

- In 1497 Girolamo Savonarola, a Dominican monk, was excommunicated, tortured, and burned for his heretical teachings against the Church.[37]

The lessons of the inquisitions were clear—oppose the Church publicly or spread false doctrines and risk torture or possibly death. Such punishments were often levied against believers only, leaving nonbelievers such as Jews and Muslims free to act on their own and not be held accountable to the same standards.[38]

Crusades: The battles to force conversion and defend Christian territories were evident in the several Crusades that took place during this five-hundred-year period. The Crusades were holy wars sanctioned by the pope against groups of people who were seen as enemies to Christianity. While this definition may sound definitive, the Crusades were more complex than that. Blessed Urban II (1088–99) commissioned the First Crusade in response to the Byzantine emperor's plea for military help against the advancing Turks. At the Council of Clermont, the pope called all Christians to engage in a holy war against the Turks in return for a remission of sins (that is, indulgence) for those who died in the conflict.[39]

The Second Crusade during the time of Pope Eugene III (1145–53) failed in its quest after the fall of Edessa to the Muslims.[40] The Third Crusade commissioned by Pope Gregory VIII (1187) to reclaim the fallen holy land was somewhat successful, but did not achieve its objective of retaking Jerusalem.[41] The Fourth Crusade issued by Pope Innocent III (1198–1216) also failed in its attempt to retake Jerusalem, included a number of ill-fated battles that were contrary to Innocent's orders, and led to a solidification of the schism between the East and West Churches.

There were another five Crusades (nine in all), each failing to retake Jerusalem and having various political, spiritual and military dynamics associated with each one. Some historians will point to the positive impact of the Crusades, including the facilitation of structural changes in Europe, the stimulation of the economy, increased trade, uniting Christianity, and the channeling of military energy. However, alternative views will focus on religious arrogance and the wasted ecclesiastical and spiritual energies on wars that were highly questionable in terms of exemplifying Christian gospel principles including the forced conversion of non-Christians to the Christian faith.

Perspective

During the five centuries that make up the corruption and division period of Christianity there were seventy-five popes and twenty-two antipopes (those challenging the legitimacy of an elected pope). The dynamics of the papacy were complex, and it would be easy to consider the aforementioned acts of papal corruption and conclude Christianity entirely, or at least the Catholic Church as it became to be known at the time was corrupt and beyond repair. However, one must consider that of the seventy-five legitimate popes only a handful during this period committed acts of corruption. Furthermore, at least seven popes during the period could be considered "reformers" (or perhaps a better term might be "refiners"), including Sylvester II (999–1003), Clement II (1046–47), Victor II (1055–57), St. Gregory VII (1073–85), Benedict XII (1334–42), Innocent VI (1352–62), and Blessed Urban V (1362–70)—popes who vigorously opposed the status quo of the papal office and attempted to institute needed changes.

DIVISION

The origins of division among Christianity might be traced back to minor strife among the Apostles as to who was the greatest (Luke 22:24), or the desire of James and John to sit on the right and left hand of Christ in his glory at the displeasure of others (Mark 10:35–37, 41). The ambitions and pride of man often lead to division in family, society and even nations and so was the case for Christianity during this period—approximately one thousand years after the Ascension of Christ.

During this 500-year era, two major schisms divided Christianity. First was the "Great Schism" of 1054, separating the Church into what would eventually be known as the Eastern Orthodox Church (Greek) and the Roman Catholic Church (Latin). The division resulted from intense differences in politics, ecclesiastical matters, and theology. Issues such as the use of leavened bread in the Eucharist, the power of the pope, and the prominence given to Constantinople as the geographic center of Christianity were issues that sharply divided the two factions. So bitter were the differences that in 1054 the Patriarch of Constantinople (Michael Cerularius) and the reigning pope (Leo IX) excommunicated one another.[42] Despite the efforts of the Council of Florence and its treaty of 1439, the reunification of churches was not fully realized, leaving division that remains to the present day.

The second schism came in 1378, often referred to as the Great Western Schism, whereby the Catholic Church experienced a split within itself. Following the death of Pope Gregory XI, who moved the papacy to Rome from France, Pope Urban VI was hastily elected and proved to be a less-than-optimal choice. A group of cardinals who regrettably elected Urban VI removed themselves from Rome to Anagni and elected a different pope (the antipope Clement VII) who promptly moved the papacy back to France—creating two simultaneous legitimate papacies. The impact of the dual elections created not only an ecclesiastical conflict and division, but it also created political turmoil with the effect of dividing Europe and forcing secular leaders to choose which pope they would recognize.

The schism continued under the Roman popes Boniface IX (1389–1404), Innocent VII (1404–06), and Gregory XII (1406–15), and the antipopes Benedict XIII (1394–1417), John XXIII (1400–1415), and Alexander V (1409–1410). It was not until the Council of Constance in 1414 that the matter was resolved with the resignations of John XXIII and Gregory XII, the excommunication of Benedict XIII, and the election of Pope Martin V. Although these actions effectively ended the schism, the damage done to the Church by internal fighting and politicking was extensive. The division of Christianity went well beyond the schisms and into ecclesiastical matters, politics, territorial claims, and calls for reform.

THE STATE OF CHRISTIANITY IN 1499

By the end of this period in Christianity, more than one faction of the Christian Church existed (likely many were unknown or not recognized). The Church was plagued with disagreements on theology, continued power struggles, large-scale corruption, and political and societal unrest. Recalling Daft's organizational life cycle mentioned in the last chapter, the Church by 1499 was evolving from the formalization stage, when red tape was rampant, to the elaboration stage, when there became a tremendous need for revitalization. Another word for "revitalization" is "reform," and the time was right for church reform.

Chapter 4

THEY WERE REFORMED AND SCATTERED (1500 TO PRESENT)

THE FINAL PERIOD OF CHRISTIANITY IS THE LAST 500 YEARS TO THE present, a period this book refers to as reform and denominational proliferation. It is in this last period that individuals came forward to challenge the Catholic Church (commonly referred to as the "Roman Catholic Church" during this period) to reform itself from corruption. When reform did not go far enough, complicated by a host of political and social issues of the day, schisms took place, leading to the formation of multiple denominations of Christianity in our modern era—33,820 Christian denominations as of 2010 according to the *World Christian Encyclopedia*.[1] Accordingly, this period in the history of Christianity is marked by five major activities, including the carryover of corruption; the emergence of refiners, reformers, and restorers; the bringing about of movements and influencers, the propagation of published scripture; and the proliferation of denominations.

THE CARRYOVER OF CORRUPTION

The corruption of the former period continued in the form of ongoing nepotism, immorality, greed, and arrogance. Alexander VI, perhaps the most corrupt pope in history, prolonged his crooked reign with more appointments of cardinals for money, arrangements of marriages of his children for financial gain, and the famous Banquet of Chestnuts in 1501 where the pontiff hosted prostitutes for sex on display among his guests.[2]

Another point of corruption was the papal election in 1513 of Pope Leo X who was not even a priest at the time of his election, and Pope Paul IV's Index Librorum Prohibitorum, when books written by Protestants along with Italian and German translations of the Latin Bible were banned. The persecution of individuals persisted with the Philosopher Giordano Bruno being executed in 1600 for his claims of the universe being infinite[3] and Galileo being compelled to renounce his scientific findings in 1633.[4]

This continuation of corruption in the Roman Catholic Church became fodder for what would become the Protestant Reformation and efforts by refiners, reformers, and restorers to address the issues plaguing the Church—an effort that would last for centuries.

REFINERS, REFORMERS, AND RESTORERS

This five-hundred-year period witnessed three types of individuals who would seek to change the direction of the Roman Catholic Church—the prevailing Christian Church at the time. There were the **refiners**, those who sought to change the Roman Catholic Church from within. Refiners felt the Church could change itself by eradicating corruption and putting into place doctrines, practices, and principles that reflected the discipleship expounded by Jesus Christ during his ministry. There were the **reformers**, those who sought to change the Roman Catholic Church, or eventually influence the Protestant Movement itself, through public debate and open accusation. Reformers felt the Church must make radical changes or face the proliferation of new churches to take its place. Then there were the **restorers**, those who thought the corruption of the Church (the Roman Catholic Church and those that proceeded forth from the Roman Catholic Church), and its doctrinal base had become so corrupt that a complete restoration of the Church was necessary.

All three, the refiners, reformers, and restorers, demonstrated immense courage in the face of overwhelming circumstances in going up against Church establishment. It was the efforts of these brave souls that sparked a revolution in challenging corruption to the Lord's Church and encouraging a return to the discipleship of Jesus Christ in a more simple and undefiled way.

The following are examples of refiners, reformers, and restorers—a list that is by no means exhaustive:

Refiners

Desiderius Erasmus

Desiderius Erasmus was a Dutch Catholic priest, teacher, and theologian, and a man who could be characterized as a "subtle reformer." However, Erasmus chose a strategy of reforming the Church from within as opposed to a more public approach and thus he can be categorized as a refiner. A prolific writer, Erasmus wrote *The Praise of Folly* in 1509, which in a satirical style addressed the corrupt practices of the Roman Catholic Church while expounding the virtues of Christian principles.[5] This brilliant treatise of Erasmus, along with his persistent yet nonconfrontational efforts to address abuses within the Roman Catholic Church (to which he was entirely faithful), would become a catalyst for the Protestant Reformation.

Roman Catholic Popes

The Roman Catholic Church had its refiners of the previous period, including popes Sylvester II (999–1003), Clement II (1046–47), Victor II (1055–57), St. Gregory VII (1073–85), Benedict XII (1334–42), Innocent VI (1352–62), and Blessed Urban V (1362–70). Although not a pope, one might include Saint Francis of Assisi as a refiner in the early 1200s. As the pope from 1534 to 1549, despite accusations of nepotism, Paul III convened the Council of Trent in 1545 to address the issues fueling the Protestant Reformation including the selling of indulgences.

In 1559, Pope Pius IV (1559–1565) was elected to the papacy and reconvened the Council of Trent, which decreed among other things a ban on the sale of indulgences and eventually the cancellation of those indulgences that were granted by way of financial transactions. Although these were welcome developments in refining the Roman Catholic Church, the Council of Trent also strongly sounded its opposition to the Protestant Reformation ushering in centuries of denominational proliferation that would follow.

Reformers

Martin Luther

Born in 1483, Martin Luther became a monk in 1505 and describes being given a revelation in 1508 that man can obtain salvation through his faith in Jesus Christ alone without the need for additional works (a belief contrary to the teachings of the time). Disgusted by the corruption in the Roman Catholic Church, especially with the selling of indulgences and its blatant violation against the principles of confession and penance, Luther compiled a list of ninety-five theses and nailed it to the Castle Church door in Wittenberg, Germany, in 1517. Despite being excommunicated for his actions in 1521, Luther's efforts are widely viewed as being the driving force of the Protestant Reformation and the formation of the Lutheran Church in 1597.[6]

Philipp Melanchthon

A contemporary of Martin Luther, Melanchthon was a highly educated theologian best known for being one of the primary authors of the *Augsburg Confession* in 1530, a defender of the reformation movement, and one who brought into form the teachings of Martin Luther for use in religious education.[7] Although less known than Luther and Calvin as a Protestant reformer, Melanchthon's ability to convey theological ideas into inspirational educational practice made him a powerful component of the reformation movement.

William Tyndale

Inspired by Wycliffe's translation of the Bible in 1382, the Greek translation of the New Testament by Erasmus in 1516, and the tireless efforts of Martin Luther in driving religious reform,[8] William Tyndale translated the Bible into common English in 1525, making available an understandable version of the scriptures (although few could afford to purchase such a work).[9] Tyndale's translation of the Bible was viewed as a challenge to the dominion of the Roman Catholic Church and the English church and state in general. Tyndale's perceived heresy, along with his opposition to Henry VIII's divorce, resulted in his martyrdom of being choked, impaled, and burned at the stake in 1536.

John Calvin

An attorney and French theologian, John Calvin was an outspoken critic of the Roman Catholic Church (which he broke from around 1530), denying its claim to papal primacy, rejecting five of the seven sacraments,[10] and supporting the separation of church and state.[11] Known as one to fiercely debate his views and provide written defenses of Christian theology, the controversial Calvin was a minister in Strasbourg before moving to Geneva where amid local resistance he implemented unfamiliar concepts of the liturgy and church government. In 1536, Calvin published the *Institutes of the Christian Religion* (Institutio Christianae Religionis is the original Latin title) a decisive treatise that doctrinally defined the Protestant faith while criticizing the corruption of the Roman Catholic Church.[12] The influence of this work was far reaching and helped formulate what would later become known as Calvinism, the primary belief system practiced among the Reformed and Presbyterian Churches of the present day.

Heinrich Bullinger

As another lesser-known figure of the Protestant Reformation, Heinrich Bullinger was a theologian and Swiss pastor who became head of the Zurich Church following another unseen reformer in Huldrych Zwingli. Bullinger was not one to pursue open controversy as Calvin or Luther and regularly corresponded with Melanchthon and Calvin on matters of the Reformation. Bullinger is best known for his authorship of the widely adopted *Second Helvetic Confession* in 1561, a proclamation of faith similar to that of the *Augsburg Confession* of 1530. The Helvetic Confession is still considered a widely recognized confession among the Reformed Churches of the present day.

John Smyth

Ordained an Anglican priest in 1594, John Smyth left the Church of England to form a small congregation dedicated to studying the Bible. Smyth, a passionate activist of religious liberty, led the congregation during its growth in Amsterdam when in 1609 it came to be known as the Baptist Church.[13] Before his death, the reformer Smyth transitioned from his earlier Baptist views into those of the Mennonite faith.[14]

George Whitefield

Admired by Ben Franklin and a leader of the First Great Awakening (1730s and 1740s) in Britain and the English colonies, George White-field was an Anglican priest who possessed a powerful gift for open-air preaching—a style that would be embraced and copied by future preach-ers of Christianity. Whitefield was a stalwart traveler with a passion for his theology of a merciful God, the joy of salvation, and the dreadfulness of eternal hell and damnation. Whitefield is credited (with John Wesley) as being one of the founders of Methodism as well as helping to inspire the Evangelical Movement.[15]

John Wesley

John Wesley was a theologian and clergyman for the Church of Eng-land before experiencing a conversion toward living a deeper sense of spirituality through reading the works of Thomas à Kempis and Jeremy Taylor and coming in contact with Moravian settlers.[16] Further enthused by the works of Luther and a love of open-air teaching[17], Wesley joined his brother Charles in or around 1738 to invoke a "method" of study and worship that would become the foundation of the Methodist Move-ment[18]—a movement that eventually inspired Pentecostalism, the Holi-ness Movement, and the Charismatic Movement.

Campbell, Scott, and Stone

Thomas Campbell, his son Alexander Campbell, Walter Scott, and Barton Stone came together during the Second Great Awakening in the United States to lead what is now referred to as the Restoration Move-ment. Thomas Campbell was a Presbyterian minister from Ireland who rejected infant baptism and instead embraced baptism by immersion and joined the Redstone Baptist Association with the understanding he could teach from the Bible as moved upon by the Holy Spirit.[19] Campbell's son was a minister, joining his father in 1809 to help lead his ministry. The Campbells eventually broke ties with their congregation to pursue the concept of a systematic restoration of Christianity,[20] which came to be known as the Disciples of Christ. In 1826, the Campbells were joined by Walter Scott, a native Scotsman and minister, who helped lead their movement forward as an evangelist.[21] In 1832, Barton Stone, an expelled

Presbyterian minister,[22] merged his Kentucky-based group that shared similar beliefs to that of the Disciples of Christ,[23] eventually attempting to bring together a number of denominations that focused on the scriptures.

Restorers

Joseph Smith

Unlike the European reformers who were ordained ministers and theologians of existing religions, Joseph Smith was an American youth with no religious affiliations who claimed to receive a vision from God directing him to restore the Church of Jesus Christ on earth. The restoration included a return to the original organization of the Church (for example, twelve Apostles), the existence of living prophets, ongoing revelation, and an open canon. Smith established the Church of Jesus Christ of Latter-day Saints in 1830 (commonly known as the Mormon Church) in what would be the beginning of a tumultuous history of industrious endeavors, curious religious practices, extreme religious persecution, and a modern day exodus (1846–1869) that led to the establishment of the state of Utah, which entered the union in 1896.

Charles Taze Russell

Charles Taze Russell was an American-bred Christian pastor and restorationist minister focused on spreading God's word "in this 'harvest' time."[24] A chief communications vehicle for Russell was a monthly journal started in 1879 titled *Zion's Watch Tower and Herald of Christ's Presence*. Not interested in forming a church or claiming revelations or visions from God,[25] Russell founded the Bible Student movement from which the Jehovah's Witnesses eventually sprang forth.

Ellen Gould White

Ellen Gould White was a visionary and prolific Christian author who led the founding of the Seventh-day Adventist Church in 1863.[26] The author of over forty books and thousands of periodic articles on a variety of subjects, and thought to be one of the more colorful and controversial figures in modern Christian history, White was a health and lifestyle advocate who promoted vegetarianism and the building of schools and hospitals.

MOVEMENTS AND INFLUENCERS

This period in Christianity was marked by a large number of "movements." These movements were not churches, but rather groups or associations that formed, gained momentum, and helped shape belief systems and, in some cases, specific Christian denominations. There was the First Great Awakening (around 1730 to 1740) that spread from Britain to the English colonies helping people "feel" the gospel of Jesus Christ and challenging the traditional Christian denominations of the time—giving rise to such churches as the Baptist and Methodist. There was the Second Great Awakening (around 1800 to 1870) in the United States where revivals became vehicles to salvation and led to the establishment of reform movements and a large number of new Christian churches. There was the Restoration Movement, which attempted to reestablish the tenets of primitive Christianity fueled by the Second Great Awakening. There were many other movements including the Charismatic, Evangelicalism, Free Grace, Holiness, Methodism, and Pentecostalism.

These movements were important in bringing awareness to Christianity by getting people involved, spawning the creation of many new churches in America. This multibranded approach to Christianity of making available "something for everyone" in the way of churches became one of Christianity's greatest strengths in creating mass appeal. However, this decentralized approach would also become one of Christianity's greatest weaknesses as churches polarized against one another, diluting Christianity's societal influence and splintering its adherents.

Beyond the reformers, refiners, and restorers into the modern era, other individuals and organizations influenced the direction of Christianity. Ignatius of Loyola founded the Society of Jesus[27] that became the Jesuits of today. Billy Graham, a twentieth-century evangelical evangelist, brought Christianity to the masses using radio and television with the largest audience of any evangelist in history as of 2012.[28] There were other TV Evangelists (Televangelists) including Robert Schuller (the *Hour of Power*), Pat Robertson, Jerry Falwell, Jimmy Swaggart, John Hagee, and Jim and Tammy Faye Bakker. With what became a staggering number of Christian denominations, the twentieth-century formation of organizations such as the American Council of Christian Churches, the World Council of Churches, and the National Council of Churches helped to fuel ecumenicalism among Christian Churches.

PROPAGATION OF PUBLISHED SCRIPTURE

The Protestant Reformation and success of the various Christian movements that followed could not have succeeded without the ongoing establishment and availability of the scriptures. Although the Bible was compiled centuries before, it was not until the work of Tyndale to translate the Bible into English that the layperson was able to read and understand the scriptures. Despite the availability of these more functional biblical translations, the lack of economic means and literacy still put the Bible out of reach for the common person.

Since Tyndale's translation of the Bible scholars have brought forth dozens of translations of the Bible into English, including the King James Version, the English Standard Version, the Good News Bible, the Holman Christian Standard Bible, the J B Phillips New Testament, The Living Bible, The Message, the New American Bible, the New American Standard Bible, the New International Version, the (New) Jerusalem Bible, the New King James Bible, the New Living Translation, the (New) Revised Standard Version, Today's English Version, and Today's New International Version. As of 2012 there were ninety-two known translations of the Bible into English. In many cases, the translations are significantly different from one another, allowing readers to choose the translation they feel most comfortable with. The Bible has been translated into dozens of other languages around the globe, making it one of the most widely available books in the world.

Although traditional Christianity operated on the premise of a closed canon (the Bible being the only form of scripture), in 1830 the Book of Mormon was published by Joseph Smith as another testament of Jesus Christ as a companion to the Bible. Over a century later came the discovery of the Nag Hammadi Library in Egypt and the Dead Sea Scrolls in Israel in 1945 and 1947, respectively. The Dead Sea Scrolls are ancient manuscripts, including those from Isaiah, as well as noncanonical texts. The Nag Hammadi Library includes a number of Gnostic scriptures and Christian manuscripts, including the Gospel of Thomas (referenced earlier), the Gospel of Philip, and the Apocryphon of James.[29]

DENOMINATIONAL PROLIFERATION

Since 1500, Christianity has exploded into nearly 34,000 different denominations.[30] The tangled web of Christian denominations forming, merging, splitting, and disintegrating is historically known but not always easily explained. A few examples of how denominational proliferation took place during this time period of Christianity are the following:

- **The Presbyterian Church** came forth in the British Isles from the sixteenth-century reformation in Europe organized around the teachings of John Calvin.

- **Evangelical Churches** can trace their roots back to the protestant William Tyndale, who first used the term in 1531.[31]

- **The Lutheran Church** came forth during the Protestant Reformation in the sixteenth century—its father, Martin Luther, being a former Roman Catholic priest. The Lutheran Church today is composed of dozens of denominations around the world, including the synods of the ELCA (Evangelical Lutheran Church in America), the LC-MS (Lutheran Church-Missouri Synod), and the WELS (Wisconsin Evangelical Lutheran Synod) in the United States.

- **The Baptist Church** is believed to have started in or around 1609 under John Smyth[32] and splintered into dozens of conventions, leading to the formation of the Baptist World Alliance (BWA) in 1905. As of 2012 the BWA accounts for 221 Baptist Conventions throughout the world,[33] with the largest convention (Southern Baptist) severing is membership with the BWA in 2004.[34]

- **Pentecostalism** came forth from a nineteenth century evangelical movement[35] and today comprises hundreds of denominations across a wide range of theologies and cultures.[36]

- **The Episcopal Church** was organized after the American Revolution and is found mainly in the United States.[37] The Episcopal Church came forth from the Anglican Church, which comes forth from the Church of England, which came forth from the Roman Catholic Church.

- **Assemblies of God** was formed in 1914 and is the largest Pentecostal denomination comprising separate, loosely linked churches that share common beliefs with worldwide adherents numbering fifty-seven million as of 2012.[38]

- **The Methodist Church** started as a movement under John and Charles Wesley of the Church of England, fueled by George Whitefield, eventually splitting into three separate denominations, including the Methodist Protestant Church, the Methodist Episcopal Church, and the Methodist Episcopal Church, South. All three then united with the Evangelical United Brethren Church to form The United Methodist Church.[39]

- **The Church of Jesus Christ of Latter-day Saints** was organized as the restored Church of Jesus Christ in 1830 during the Second Great Awakening by Joseph Smith. Following the death of Joseph Smith, a group of members left to form the Reorganized Church of Jesus Christ of Latter-day Saints, which eventually spawned other denominations—some, but not all, claiming the Mormonism label.

- **The United Church of Christ** is the formation of the Evangelical and Reformed Church (ERC) and the Congregational Christian Churches (CCC) in 1957.[40] The ERC came as the result of a merger between the Reformed Church in the United States and the Evangelical Synod of North America in 1934.[41] The CCC came as the result of a merger in 1931 between the General Council of Congregational Churches and the General Convention of the Christian Church.[42]

- **The Seventh-day Adventist Church** was founded in 1863 with Millerite origins,[43] a movement during the Second Great Awakening, which spawned a number of Christian denominations.

- **Jehovah's Witnesses** was established in 1931[44] by Joseph Franklin Rutherford but can trace its origins to the Bible Student Movement started by Charles Taze Russell in the late 1870s.

- **The Churches of Christ** are a group of Christian congregations (recognized by the U.S. Religious Census in 1906) that, although autonomous of one another in governance and some practices, are linked through common beliefs and focus on strict biblical interpretation. Within and from the Churches of Christ are a number of denominations.

The list could go on, especially if the focus were to be expanded across the globe into local regions where language, culture, and an integration of beliefs created new Christian denominations—many of which may not be known or recorded.

COMMENTARY ON DENOMINATIONAL PROLIFERATION

The *World Christian Encyclopedia* (WCE) categorizes the nearly 34,000 sects of Christianity today into seven segments: 1) Orthodox, 2) Roman Catholic, 3) Catholics (Reformed Catholics, New Apostolic, and so on), 4) Anglicans, 5) Protestants (Lutherans, Methodists, and so on), 6) Marginal Protestants (Unitarians, LDS/Mormons, Jehovah's Witnesses, and so on), and 7) Non-White Indigenous Christians.[45] For North America, the WCE further refines this categorization by segmenting Christians affiliated with a particular denomination into Independents, Roman Catholics, Protestants, Marginal Christians, Orthodox, and Anglicans.[46]

This staggering number of denominations gives rise to the question of how there could be one Christian Church in Catholicism around AD 1000 and then approximately one thousand years later that number could explode to over 160 times the number of countries in the world. The answer to this question is not simple and includes several viable answers, including pride, doctrinal differences, cultural nuances, logistical challenges, money, and revelation.

Pride

Isaiah wrote of a land "utterly emptied and utterly spoiled . . . because they have transgressed the laws, changed the ordinance, broken the everlasting covenant" (Isaiah 24:1–6). The Prophet Amos prophesied a similar vision, writing of a "famine in the land . . . of hearing the words of the Lord" (Amos 8:11). These Old Testament prophesies reveal a world that would spiritually suffer and leave people searching, likely because of the pride of man leading to transgression and wickedness.

Pride is of the world (1 John 2:16) and is an evil that comes from within a man so as to defile him (Mark 7:21–23). This same pride can lead to religious corruption followed by separation—a separation that includes forming a new church or a new belief system that satisfies an intellect or particular set of objectives. While one cannot blame pride on the formation of all separate Christian churches, it is not difficult to imagine how pride could have played a role in the formation of many.

Doctrinal Differences

The reformers of Christianity often disagreed with one another on matters of doctrine. For example, Calvin and Luther disagreed on the interpretation of the Eucharist. There was dissensus among sects on the requirements of baptism (infant or adult) and the method of baptism (sprinkling or immersion). There also was disparity in the requirements for salvation (faith, works, or both) and the existence of the afterlife (heaven or otherwise). The vast differences in biblical interpretation, church organization, leadership structure, the nature of Jesus Christ, and countless other matters of doctrine were powerful enough to divide and separate leaders and their congregations.

Cultural Nuances

Churches that started in one country or among a certain group of people were not often sensitive to the cultural needs of another country or group of people. As a result, new denominations that integrated elements from the old with elements of the new were formed. The churches in early America that appealed to middle-class white people did not inspire those who were of color and lesser means. Where in many black cultures singing and vibrant praise are important components of worship, a more reverent tone that focused on sacred hymns and meditation was often preferred among more predominantly white cultures. These clashes of culture resulted in further denominational proliferation.

Logistical Challenges

In the modern era, it may not be unusual to travel many miles to attend a particular church. Earlier in history, however, travel was more difficult; therefore, church proximity was important. If a community did not have a church close by that would meet its needs, then few barriers existed to keep that community from forming a church that did. A church might be formed as a branch of an existing church, or an entirely separate church might be established as a new denomination of Christianity. This was especially the case in remote parts of the world where communication was difficult and people were left to fend for themselves and did so in whatever manner they could.

Money

Perhaps a more cynical view of denominational proliferation is the motivation for money. Unless the denomination is one with an unpaid local clergy (for example, The Church of Jesus Christ of Latter-day Saints), money can be made in ministry. A healthy demographic as part of a separate church can easily generate a living for a pastor, despite the fact that an estimated 80 percent of new churches fail within the first five years.[47] From the earliest days of Christianity, it was not unusual for clergy to become quite wealthy from their ecclesiastical duties, even helping family members benefit from their positions. This tradition has carried over to the modern day, when it is possible for a minister to make a modest, and sometimes robust, living from leading a church. For example, according to the *2009 Compensation Handbook for Church Staff*, the average senior pastor in the United States makes $81,113 of total annual compensation, with those holding advanced academic degrees making significantly more.[48] The Bible both supports and discourages a paid ministry, leading some to starting their own churches thus increasing the number of Christian denominations.

Called by God

Some pastors feel called by God to start new churches; therefore, one must consider the possibility that denominational proliferation is partially the result of divine intervention. Although this is certainly a possibility, it is difficult to imagine on a large scale. One philosophy might be that God will do whatever it takes to reach his children through his Son Jesus Christ, and if that means forming a separate church, then "so be it!" Another philosophy might be that God wants a unity of faith (Ephesians 4:13), and anything that inhibits that (like the proliferation of denominations) is not of him. I will leave the discerning of this thought to the reader for his or her own conclusion.

CONCLUSION OF THE HISTORY OF CHRISTIANITY

It cannot be stressed enough that the history of Christianity provided in this section is meant to be a summary and is by no means exhaustive. That which is provided is meant to familiarize the reader with key events and dynamics that shaped Christianity into what it is today. If you have ever wondered about the ecclesiastical genealogy of your own Christian faith, then it is hoped that this chapter shed some light on that for you.

The evangelization and formation period (up to AD 299) delivers the prophecies and teachings of Jesus Christ and the details of his ministry and atoning sacrifice that would forever change the world, and demonstrates how the power of a small group of believers with faith and perseverance can overcome bigotry and persecution. The legitimacy and codification period (AD 300 to 999) reveals the explosive growth of Christianity from an obscure fringe movement to a dominant world religion both spiritually and politically. The corruption and division period (1000 to 1499) exposes how human frailty and evil crept into the Church, distorting its mission in an attempt to destroy the work of God. The reform and denominational proliferation period (1500 to the present) illustrates that despite man's corruptive nature and imperfection, God always finds a way to move his kingdom forth.

The history of Christianity is filled with beauty, wonder, miracles, politics, intrigue, and war—something for everyone! The history is complex and is shaped by perspectives, influenced by a host of different characters and events both internal and external, and not always logical. Those who seek to find simplicity and purity can find it. Those who seek to find imperfection and corruption can find it. However, those who attempt to use Christianity's history to prove its failings and absence of divinity must do so by overlooking the overwhelming evidence of God's hand in leading and guiding the Church of Jesus Christ toward preservation against overwhelming odds.

HOW HISTORY SHAPES OUR OWN CHRISTIANITY

Like it or not we Christians of today are influenced by the past and are products of our own history. It is a history that produced the best and worst of humanity over a two-thousand-year period. Our faith walk in the modern day is affected by and reflects the four periods of

Christian history. As adherents of Christianity we are *evangelizers* and *builders*, called to teach the gospel and realize the Lord's kingdom on earth. As followers of truth, we crave *legitimization* in our spiritual choices and *codification* of theology that leads to doctrinal clarity. As children of God, we are vulnerable to *corruption* and *divide* ourselves by nature according to that which we are most comfortable with. And as disciples of Christ, we are challenged to *reform* ourselves and stand up for truth and righteousness amid a community of believers that are *scattered* and broken. As Christians, we are susceptible to all of these characteristics to one degree or another; therefore, if you think the history of Christianity doesn't affect you, think again.

We need not apologize for the past, nor become a slave to it. Ultimately our own choices will magnify or limit the effect of these dynamics in our spiritual lives. Having a better understanding of where we came from as a Christian people, we are now ready for the next leg of our spiritual expedition taking on the question: "What is a Christian?"

WHAT IS A CHRISTIAN?

A Definition

"Being a Christian is more than just an instantaneous conversion—it is a daily process whereby you grow to be more and more like Christ."

—Billy Graham

NOW THAT WE KNOW WHO THE CHRISTIANS WERE AND HOW CHRISTIANITY arrived at this point in time, we will now turn our attention to *what* a Christian is today. If you think it is an easy task to define a Christian, think again. This section is full of unexpected twists and turns that will surprise you.

The world has always had its writers, philosophers, and speakers who have sought to define everything from the mundane to the profound. Whether it is a speech given by an ancient Greek orator or an article written in the *New York Times*, the world has never been deprived of opinions—especially when it comes to politics and religion. In few areas of the contemporary period is this truer than in the ongoing battle to define a Christian.

With the advent of blogging and social media, basically anyone with a computer can publish an opinion on the Internet. Public conversations à la keyboards rage every minute in online forums around the globe. While most of the world's bloggers and web enthusiasts are unknown and lack credibility in the reputable circles of religious dialogue, there are numerous publications that have already established a standing among the intellectual and academic influencers of the world today. But what is credible? Who decides what truth is and what is fiction?

THE TRINITY AND ITS CREEDS

Before addressing the above questions a bit of preparation on the Trinity and its related creeds is in order to help us more effectively navigate the conversation. As you will soon learn, the doctrines of the Trinity, the Nicene Creed, the Apostles' Creed, and the Athanasian Creed (identified in the previous section on the history of Christianity) will appear from time to time as being critical components in various statements of faith. An aggregate of the books written about the Trinity, and the creeds that support the Trinity, can likely fill an entire library and more. The intent of this book is not to provide an extensive review of Trinitarian doctrine and its related creeds; however, a brief summary on the doctrine of the Trinity and the three aforementioned creeds will be necessary for you to have a basic understanding of these concepts so as to recognize them when they are referenced.

Trinity and the Nicene Creed

Although not directly found as an explicit doctrine in the New Testament, the theology of the Trinity is the result of exhaustive studies of the scriptures by the early church and divine inspiration, resulting in extensive debate and treatises.[1] The word Trinity comes from the Latin noun *trinitas*, which literally means "three are one." The Trinitarian concept was expressed in early writings from the beginning of the second century, but the Trinity did not become a formal doctrine until AD 325 at the First Council of Nicaea. With the Council of Nicaea, "the Church had taken her first great step to define doctrine more precisely in response to a challenge from a heretical theology."[2] The key deliverables from the Council were the Nicene Creed, along with approximately twenty decrees, or canons. (See chapter 2 for a complete text of the Nicene Creed.)

The key phrase in the Nicene Creed is that the Trinity is "one in Being," referring to the concept of consubstantiality. The concept of consubstantiality comes from Latin Christology. Consubstantiality describes the relationship between the divine persons of the Trinity—defining God the Father, God the Son, and God the Holy Spirit being of one substance. Three separate persons (God, Jesus Christ, and the Holy Spirit), who are one in being in order to maintain the monotheistic pattern of the Old Testament.

The Trinity from a Biblical Perspective

Although the Bible itself does not include the word *Trinity*, a number of scriptural passages when combined and interpreted can support the doctrine of the Trinity. Biblical support for the Trinity includes, but is not limited to, the following:

- **The Existence of Only One God**: Deuteronomy 4:35, Isaiah 44:6, Romans 3:30

- **God is More than a Single Being**: Genesis 1:26, Genesis 3:22,

- **The Existence of God the Father**: 2 Corinthians 1:3, Ephesians 1:3,

- **The Existence of God the Son (Jesus)**: John 1:1, John 20:28, Titus 2:13, 2 Peter 1:1

- **The Existence of God the Holy Spirit**: Acts 5:3–4, 2 Corinthians 3:17–18

- **The Father, Son and Holy Spirit are distinct and separate**: Matthew 28:19, John 3:17, Romans 1:7, John 15:26, John 16:7, Romans 8:26–27, Luke 3:21–22

- **Jesus and the Father are One**: John 10:30, 1 John 5:7

There are variations of belief with respect to the Trinity. Those that place more emphasis on the oneness of the Father, the Son, and the Holy Spirit and less in their separate and distinct nature are often referred to as modalists. Modalism is a form of belief that God is a single being who reveals himself in three modes, or forms: Father, Son, and Holy Spirit. There are those who consider true belief in the Trinity to be God as three eternal coexistent, coequal persons being referred to as the Father, the Son, and the Holy Spirit. In nearly all cases, some amount of "mystery" is attributed to belief in the Trinity.

Departing from traditional belief in the Trinity is The Church of

Jesus Christ of Latter-day Saints (LDS/Mormon). The LDS faith believes in what it refers to as the Godhead, a term used three times in the New Testament—Colossians 2:9, Acts 17:29 and Romans 1:20. The LDS doctrine of the Godhead teaches that God the Father, God the Son, and God the Holy Ghost are three separate beings but are one in perfect and united purpose as described in John 17:21–22. The LDS doctrine of the Godhead is considered by some Christians to be polytheistic.

Apostles' Creed

The Apostles' Creed reads like a condensed version of the Nicene Creed, but its origins are much less understood. Modern versions of the creed are similar in nature to the baptismal confessions of the Church of Southern Gaul, while some scholars believe it was derived from "the Old Roman Symbol" of the first or second centuries—later influenced by the Nicene Creed.[3] Some historians date the Apostles' Creed as far forward as the fifth century. Like the Nicene Creed, several translations are in use.

Athanasian Creed

Perhaps the most ardent defender of Trinitarian doctrine in the written word is the Athanasian Creed. Written in response to charges of polytheism, the Athanasian Creed goes to great lengths to define the Trinity, without attempting to define the terms "person" and "substance" philosophically. The majority of today's historians date the creation of the 660 word Athanasian Creed to around AD 500, resembling the writing of Western theologians—in particular those of Saints Ambrose of Milan, Augustine of Hippo, and Vincent of Lérins.[4]

Summary of the Trinity

The doctrine of the Trinity generally, and the content of the creeds specifically, have become cornerstones of theological belief among a majority of Christian denominations for centuries. The theology of the Trinity attempts to be exact in directing an unambiguous belief in the nature and relationship of the God the Father, his Son Jesus Christ, and the Holy Ghost so as to avoid perceived heretical practices and worship that might otherwise come from a belief in three separate gods.

Chapter 5

IT'S CONFUSING ACCORDING
TO THE WORLD

ACCORDING TO RESPECTED
SECULAR PUBLICATIONS

A NATURAL PLACE TO START IN DEFINING A CHRISTIAN IS TO SEARCH well-respected and credible nonreligious publications. These unbiased publications have stood the test of time and are highly regarded sources of truth and reliable information on a variety of subjects. In this case, we will select two such enduring publications: *Webster's Dictionary* and the *Encyclopedia Britannica*. Although some may not consider these sources to be "scholarly," both of these centuries-old publications are known across the globe and turned to by millions on a daily basis.

Webster's Dictionary defines a Christian as "one who professes belief in the teachings of Jesus Christ,"[1] and, "adhering to the religion based on the teachings of Jesus Christ."[2] These definitions seem simple and to the point. So let's move on.

The *Encyclopedia Britannica* has been in continuous publication since 1768 and is often regarded as a beacon of academic information for the young and old alike. There is a plethora of content regarding Christianity in the *Encyclopedia Britannica* making it difficult to pin down a single definition of a Christian. However, a few key passages from the 2006 online edition offer a glimpse into the components that may lead to a reliable definition.

The *Encyclopedia Britannica* discusses Christianity as a faith tradition with accompanying culture, ideas, method of living, practices, and relics passed down from one generation to another since the time of Christ. It goes on to explain that although simple in nature, Christianity is complex as a result of thousands of different Christian denominations that make up the composite of modern Christianity. The breathtaking variety makes for extreme diversity in the very core of traditions such as prayer and worship. The essence of Christianity is said to be contained in the four Gospels of the New Testament, having recorded the thoughts of the earliest Christians in what was being taught and believed about Jesus Christ.

Perhaps the most revealing of the Christian content in the *Encyclopedia Britannica* relates to a short passage that identifies Christians in more general terms:

> Christianity is the faith tradition that focuses on the figure of Jesus Christ. In this context, faith refers both to the believers' act of trust and to the content of their faith. As a tradition, Christianity is more than a system of religious belief. It also has generated a culture, a set of ideas and ways of life, practices, and artifacts that have been handed down from generation to generation since Jesus first became the object of faith. Christianity is thus both a living tradition of faith and the culture that the faith leaves behind. The agent of Christianity is the church, the community of people who make up the body of believers.[3]

Summary of Secular Publications

The definition of a Christian from *Webster's Dictionary* suggests a wide and inclusive swath by which Christians can be defined and identified. Such a definition would include anyone who claims a belief in Jesus Christ or a loyalty to a Christian religion. In the same vein, the *Encyclopedia Britannica* focuses its Christian-related content on historical records, traditional writings, and scholarly feedback, resulting in a definition that is more inclusive than narrow. One might conclude that a Christian is one who believes in Jesus Christ; aligns with the traditions, cultures, and precepts of Christianity; subscribes to the scriptural content associated with the four Gospels in the New Testament; and calls himself or herself a Christian.

ACCORDING TO RESPECTED
RELIGIOUS ORGANIZATIONS

The staggering array of Christian churches in the world today has given birth to a number of organizations that attempt to globally represent interests and facilitate ecumenical relationships. These organizations often conduct their affairs as councils and alliances, providing support under the umbrella of worldwide Christian or religious unity. As the author of the present work, I engaged with each organization by way of email and written letter requesting their definition of a Christian. Some organizations responded and others did not, perhaps suggesting the level of difficulty in defining a Christian and the political sensitivities that surround it.

National Council of Churches

The National Council of Churches (NCC) was founded in 1950 with the vision of becoming a driving force for ecumenical cooperation among Christians in the United States. Member faith groups within the NCC include a wide range of Christian denominations totaling an estimated "45 million people in more than 100,000 local congregations in communities across the nation."[4]

The NCC would not offer an official definition of a Christian, but its Statement of Faith includes the phrase: "The National Council of Churches is a community of Christian communions, which, in response to the gospel as revealed in the Scriptures, confess Jesus Christ, the incarnate Word of God, as Savior and Lord."[5] The NCC Statement of Faith goes on to acknowledge that member communions have common and differing beliefs and religious traditions, reflecting diversity among Christians in America.

The NCC delivered a policy statement in 1999, which provided guidelines and guidance for churches of the NCC in the ongoing dialogue regarding Christian diversity. Section 31 and 34 of the document states:

> "31. The revelation of God's love in Jesus Christ is the center of our faith. Incarnating both the fullness of God and the fullness of humanity, Jesus Christ initiates a new creation, a world unified in relationship as God originally intended. We believe that Jesus Christ makes real God's will for a life of loving community with God, with the whole

WHERE ARE THE CHRISTIANS?

human family and with all creation. Through Jesus Christ, Christians believe God offers reconciliation to all. "In Christ God was reconciling the world to [God]self" (2 Corinthians 5:19) . . .

34. As Christians we recognize that Jesus is not central to other religious traditions. For men and women in other communities, the mystery of God takes many forms. Observing this, we are not led to deny the centrality of Christ for our faith, but to contemplate more deeply the meaning of St. Paul's affirmation: "Ever since the creation of the world, (God's) eternal power and divine nature, invisible though they are, have been understood and seen through the things [God] has made" (Romans 1:20). Christians disagree on the nature and extent of such "natural revelation" and its relation to salvation. No matter what our view on this may be, we can be open to the insights of others"[6]

The NCC statement of faith, along with its policy statement, suggests that a Christian is defined as one who professes Jesus Christ to be the center of their faith; their personal Savior; their Lord, and the Word of God made flesh with a consequent way of life. At the same time the NCC allows for a range of ancillary beliefs and traditions among Christians outside a core belief in Jesus Christ.

World Council of Churches

The World Council of Churches (WCC), founded in 1948, claims to have the broadest and most inclusive ecumenical association among the Christian unity movement. Tracing its origins to the 1910 World Missionary Conference in Edinburgh, Scotland,[7] as of 2012 the WCC includes 349 churches and denominations in more than 110 countries and territories constituting over 560 million Christians.[8]

The WCC directed the question of defining a Christian to various published documents, which, instead of defining a Christian directly, were more like statements of faith. From the WCC document *Called to be the One Church*[9] come the following statements:

We are "a fellowship of churches which confess the Lord Jesus Christ as God and Saviour according to the scriptures, and therefore seek to fulfill their common calling to the glory of the one God, Father, Son, and Holy Spirit." (Section I)

Holy scripture describes the Christian community as the Body of Christ whose interrelated diversity is essential to its wholeness: "Now there are varieties of gifts, but the same Spirit; and there are varieties of services, but the same Lord; and there are varieties of activities, but it is the same God who activates all of them in everyone. To each is given the manifestation of the Spirit for the common good" (1 Corinthians 12:4–7)." (Section II)

There are some who do not observe the rite of baptism in water but share in the spiritual experience of life in Christ. (Section III)

"The membership of the church of Christ is more inclusive than the membership of their own church body. They seek, therefore, to enter into living contact with those outside their own ranks who confess the Lordship of Christ." (Section III, sourcing the Toronto Statement, IV.3)

The statement from Section I implies a Christian is one who professes Jesus Christ to be God and Savior referring to "one God, Father, Son and Holy Spirit"—two references that would suggest a Trinitarian belief system. However, the statements from section II and III suggest a much broader definition of a Christian using such words as "diversity," "varieties," and "inclusive." This suggests a disciple within the Body of Christ transcends any affiliation that disciple may have to a particular church.

World Evangelical Alliance

The World Evangelical Alliance (WEA) was established in 1951 under the name of World Evangelical Fellowship, with the vision of expressing unity among different Christian churches. In 2012, the WEA included a network of churches in 129 nations, among 600 million evangelical Christians[10] with the mission to "foster Christian unity and to provide a worldwide identity, voice and platform to Evangelical Christians."[11]

From the WEA's statement of faith, one can produce a basic definition of a Christian for working purposes. The WEA believes the holy scriptures to be "infallible" and the "supreme authority in all matters of faith and conduct." That God is one in the Trinity. That Jesus Christ was born of a virgin as God in the flesh; was sinless in human life; atoned for the sins of the world; was resurrected; and will return in glory. That man can be saved through the blood of Christ, and not by works. And that all mankind will be resurrected—both the saved and the damned.[12]

The WEA statement of faith suggests a Christian is one that fully embraces the Bible as the supreme word of God, embraces a Trinitarian belief, accepts Jesus Christ as their Savior as the way to salvation, and believes in the resurrection of all men.

American Council of Christian Churches

The American Council of Christian Churches (ACCC) was established in 1941, reportedly in response and opposition to the then Federal Council of Churches (which is today the National Council of Churches). This opposition continues in that ACCC membership is prohibited if a church belongs to other religious organizations according to Article III, section 4 of the ACCC's Articles of Membership.[13]

In response to a request for a definition of a Christian, the following was provided by the ACCC:

> Simply put, a Christian is one who has been saved from his sins and their eternal consequences by means of faith in Jesus Christ. One who believes thus in Jesus Christ may not be aware of the truths regarding God and Christ that are included in the doctrinal statement. But when shown these truths from Scripture, he will believe them.[14]

Despite the simple definition offered by the ACCC, the reference to "the doctrinal statement" made it necessary to review that statement. The doctrinal statement of the ACCC puts forth a number of beliefs including the divine inspiration of the scriptures; the Triune God; the birth, nature, Atonement, and Resurrection of Jesus Christ; the nature and salvation of man; and the need to maintain purity in the church.[15] Wow, what a difference! The ACCC offers a simplistic definition of a Christian, acknowledging a Christian may not be familiar with the theology behind God and Jesus Christ and asserts if they were made aware of such theology they would accept it. While this definition makes sense, one might ask if a Christian does not accept the tenets put forth in the ACCC doctrinal statement after being made aware of it would they still be considered a Christian?

National Association of Congregational Christian Churches

The National Association of Congregational Christian Churches (NACCC) was formed in 1955 as a result of concerns in the formation of the United Church of Christ through the merging of the Evangelical and Reformed Church.[16] The NACCC was formed by former clergy and laypeople of the Congregational Christian Churches and as of 2012 included membership of approximately 400 churches. In response for a definition of a Christian, the NACCC offered the following:

As an association of Congregational Christian Churches you would find that our primary clients and churches would have different definitions of what a Christian is. Since we do not set policy, make social or political statements on behalf of our churches, it would be difficult for me to give you the definition you seek. The website pages, in the broadest sense, would give you some direction. When any church joins the Association they know that above all considerations is the fact that we believe Christ is the only head of the church. How churches and individuals within them go on to define that is part of the blessing of being an Association which respects the congregations and individuals within to define how they live and what they believe as Christ's covenant people.[17]

A review of the NACCC website regarding membership explains it does "not seek to be led by a creed, but by the Spirit" including studying of the Bible and being open to the Holy Spirit and prayer. The NACCC stresses fellowship among members of the Church to strengthen one another in Jesus Christ. Finally, the NACCC describes a "freedom of conscience in following Christ," being "bound by love, not law, to other members of our local church, and not to other churches," recognizing the accountability of churches to God.[18]

The Council on Christian Unity

With its origins from the 1910 National Convention of the Disciples, the Council of Christian Unity (CCU) is focused on bringing together Christians and Christian Churches through ecumenical evangelism. The simplicity of its ministry makes the CCU a refreshing voice in an era of divisive denominational movements throughout Christianity. Dr. Robert Welsh, president of the CCU, offered the following thoughts on the definition of a Christian:

In one way, I would have a very simplistic definition: that is, to be Christian is to seek to follow Christ. In relation to the title of my organization (Council on *Christian* Unity), I would see the term meaning that we are seeking a unity that is centered upon the person of Jesus Christ (not a unity in belief or practice or creed or structure)—but a unity that witnesses to Christ's love for all persons, and a unity that is discovered as persons come together to receive the bread and cup of the Lord's Supper as a sign and symbol of God's grace and welcome extended to all.[19]

The statement clearly reflects the ministry of the CCU in that it provides an inclusive tone of inviting many to the table of Christianity.

Summary of Respected Religious Organizations

Unlike the definitions of a Christian offered by *Webster's Dictionary* and the *Encyclopedia Britannica*, which were wider in nature, the definitions offered by half of the national and international religious organizations studied tended to be narrower in scope. The NCC, NACCC, and CCU focus their statements on faith in Jesus Christ, the love of God, the inspiration of the Holy Spirit and the Bible being the word of God—much along the same lines as Webster's and Britannica. The WCC, WEA and ACC have similar statements of faith; however, each includes an implied requirement of Trinitarian belief as a qualification for inclusion.

ACCORDING TO AMERICA'S LARGEST CHRISTIAN CHURCHES

While religious organizations and councils aggregate the teachings of multiple Christian denominations to formulate integrated statements of faith, specific Christian denominations offer less complex statements focused on their interpretations of core Christian doctrine. Having a more native perspective on the definition of a Christian is essential in developing our ultimate definition of a Christian. The Christian denominations selected for this exercise were required to meet the following two key criteria:

- Categorized as Christian by the *World Christian Encyclopedia* (WCE)

- Included in the 2012 *Yearbook of American and Canadian Churches* (YACC) published by the National Council of Churches[20]

Conveniently the ten largest churches in the United States according to the YACC are all categorized as Christian by the (WCE). Accordingly, the ten largest Christian Churches in America (as of 2012) are the following:

1. The Catholic Church, 68,202,492 members

2. Southern Baptist Convention, 16,136,044 members

3. The United Methodist Church, 7,679,850 members

4. The Church of Jesus Christ of Latter-day Saints, 6,157,238 members

5. The Church of God in Christ, 5,499,875 members

6. National Baptist Convention, USA, Inc., 5,197,512 members

7. Evangelical Lutheran Church in America, 4,274,855 members

8. National Baptist Convention of America, Inc., 3,500,000 members

9. Assemblies of God, 3,030,944 members

10. Presbyterian Church (USA), 2,675,873 members

A brief study of these Christian denominations produces another varied selection of definitions of a Christian to consider. For each of the churches studied above, I will include a brief outline of its core beliefs followed by a provided or derived definition of a Christian. Note that "core beliefs" covers a basic belief system and does not seek to be comprehensive or exhaustive in its content.

The Roman Catholic Church

The Roman Catholic Church is the oldest and largest Christian denomination in the world, with Catholicism in general being the largest in the United States. One in every four Christians in the US claims Catholicism as their religion. Core beliefs of the Roman Catholic Church include, but are not limited to, the following statements:

- **The Triune God:** The Nicene Creed is an integral part of the liturgy, spoken out loud, word for word, during mass by those in the congregation. The Apostles' Creed and Athanasian Creed are also accepted as outlining Trinitarian doctrine.

- **The Bible:** The Bible is considered the word of God. The Roman Catholic Church includes books not found in Protestant Bibles, which are often referred to as Deuterocanonical books.

- **Baptism**: The sacrament of baptism is necessary for salvation, although there are provisions for salvation for "those who die for the faith, those who are catechumens, and all those who, without knowing of the Church but acting under the inspiration of grace, seek God sincerely and strive to fulfill his will" (CCC 1281).

- **The Lord's Supper**: The sacrament of the Lord's Supper, referred to by Catholics as the Eucharist or Holy Communion, is the substance of the body and blood of Jesus Christ made possible through the process of transubstantiation.

- **Authority**: The Roman Catholic Church believes it is God's church on earth, having the authority of the priesthood through full apostolic succession and sacred (or holy) tradition.

- **Salvation**: The salvation of man comes by way of faith and consequent works.

Because of the abundance of information published by the Roman Catholic Church on doctrine, mainly its Catechism, it is not difficult to locate a definition of a Christian. The *Catechism of the Catholic Church* (CCC) 1229 describes the steps required to become a Christian:

> From the time of the apostles, becoming a Christian has been accomplished by a journey and initiation in several stages. This journey can be covered rapidly or slowly, but certain essential elements will always have to be present: proclamation of the Word, acceptance of the Gospel entailing conversion, profession of faith, Baptism itself, the outpouring of the Holy Spirit, and admission to Eucharistic communion.[21]

CCC 1229 defines clearly that a Christian is one who has accepted Jesus Christ and his gospel, is baptized, receives the Holy Spirit, and has partaken of the Eucharist. Furthermore, the Catechism of the Catholic Church, in harmony with historic statements made by the early church fathers, refers to the Catholic Church as "the universal sacrament of salvation" (CCC 776).[22] Firmianus Lactantius, an early Christian author (AD 240–320) and advisor to Constantine I wrote, "It is only the Catholic Church that keeps true worship. It is the source of truth, the home of faith and the temple of God: anyone who does not enter it, or who walks out from it, is estranged from hope of life and salvation."[23]

Since partaking of the Eucharist is strictly for those who are Catholic, or those who hold and accept the Catholic belief of the Eucharist; and the Catechism of the Catholic Church states, "outside the Church there is no salvation,"[24] one might conclude that the Catholic definition of a Christian is one who is Catholic. However the Catechism also includes the following statement:

> "The Church knows that she is joined in many ways to the baptized who are honored by the name of Christian, but do not profess the Catholic faith in its entirety or have not preserved unity or communion under the successor of Peter." Those "who believe in Christ and have been properly baptized are put in a certain, although imperfect, communion with the Catholic Church." *With the Orthodox Churches*, this communion is so profound "that it lacks little to attain the fullness that would permit a common celebration of the Lord's Eucharist." (CCC 838)[25]

This statement suggests the Roman Catholic Church recognizes there are other Christians in the world who are not Catholic, but that the form of Christianity they ascribe to is in an "imperfect communion" with Catholicism.

Southern Baptist Convention

The Southern Baptist Convention (SBC) was established in 1845 in Augusta, Georgia and has since grown to over sixteen million members across more than 45,000 churches in the United States as of 2012,[26] making it the second largest Christian congregation in North America according to the 2012 YACC. Core beliefs of the SBC include, but are not limited to, the following statements[27]:

- **The Triune God**: There is only one true and living God revealed to man as the eternal Triune God in God the Father, God the Son, and God the Holy Spirit—having distinct attributes but being one in nature, essence, and being.

- **The Bible**: Although written by men, the Bible is the divinely inspired word of God.

- **Baptism**: Baptism is an act of obedience that symbolizes a believer's faith and is a prerequisite of membership and to partaking of the Lord's Supper.

- **The Lord's Supper**: The Lord's Supper is a symbolic act of obedience in taking of the bread and fruit of the vine memorializing the death of Jesus Christ and the anticipation of his Second Coming.

- **Authority**: There is not one authoritative single church, but rather members are accountable to the Lord themselves and the church as part of a congregational form of government.

- **Salvation**: The salvation of man comes by faith alone through the grace of God.

The SBC did not offer an official definition of a Christian; however, it does offer on its website a page on "How to Become a Christian" as a sort of profession of faith:

> I acknowledge I am a sinner in need of a Savior—this is to repent or turn away from sin; I believe in my heart that God raised Jesus from the dead—this is to trust that Jesus paid the full penalty for my sins; I confess Jesus as my Lord and my God—this is to surrender control of my life to Jesus; I receive Jesus as my Savior forever—this is to accept that God has done for me and in me what He promised [28]

A synthesis of these statements from the SBC website suggests Christians to be those who repent of their sins and confess Jesus Christ to be their Lord (God) and their personal Savior, putting their trust in him.

United Methodist Church

The United Methodist Church (UMC) was established in 1968 with the joining together of the Evangelical United Brethren Church and the Methodist Church. However, the origins of the Methodist faith date back to the 1700s under the ministry of John Wesley (1703–1791) and his brother Charles (1707–1788), with the church gaining prominence during the Second Great Awakening in the first half of the nineteenth century. Today the United Methodist Church is the third-largest Christian denomination in the US according to the 2012 YACC. Core beliefs of the UMC include, but are not limited to the following[29]:

- **The Triune God**: God is in three persons: Father, Son, and Holy Spirit as the threefold nature of God.

- **The Bible**: The Bible is God's word, the primary authority of faith and practice, and should be studied by all Christians.

- **Baptism**: Baptism joins the baptized with the church and other Christians as a symbol of new life and of God's love and forgiveness of our sins.

- **The Lord's Supper**: The Lord's Supper is a holy meal that symbolizes the body and blood of Christ, recalling the life, death, and Resurrection of Jesus, helping the partakers to celebrate the unity of all members.

- **Authority**: There is no authoritative single church, but rather the holy scriptures are the authority.

- **Salvation**: "Salvation cannot be earned" through "behavior, no matter how holy or righteous . . . Rather, [salvation] is the gift of a gracious God."[30]

In response to a definition of a Christian, the UMC indicated there is no official definition and that the general conference is the only body who has the authority to speak for the UMC. The UMC has policies regarding the acceptance of baptisms from other Christian churches, indicating a somewhat broad recognition of Christian beliefs and practices from such faith traditions as Presbyterianism.

The Church of Jesus Christ of Latter-day Saints (LDS/Mormon)

The Church of Jesus Christ of Latter-day Saints (LDS/Mormon), categorized as a "marginal Christian"[31] denomination by the WCE for its nontraditional Christian doctrines, was founded in 1830 under the direction of Joseph Smith its first Prophet and President. The LDS/Mormon Church claims to be the restored Church of Jesus Christ on the earth today. As of 2012, there were 14.4 million Latter-day Saints worldwide,[32] with over 6 million residing in the US, making The Church of Jesus Christ of Latter-day Saints the fourth-largest Christian denomination according to the 2012 YACC. Core beliefs of the LDS Church include, but are not limited to, the following[33]:

- **The Triune God**: There is not a Triune God but rather a Godhead consisting of God the Father, God the Son, and God the

Holy Ghost—three distinct beings with a perfect unity of purpose (not in being).

- **The Bible**: The Bible is the word of God as far as it is translated correctly. The Book of Mormon is another Testament of Jesus Christ and is also considered the word of God as part of an open canon.

- **Baptism**: Baptism is considered the first saving ordinance of the gospel and is a necessity for Church membership and eternal salvation.[34]

- **The Lord's Supper**: Referred to as "the sacrament," the Lord's Supper as an ordinance is an essential part of worship and spiritual development through which church members renew covenants made with God when they were baptized.[35]

- **Authority**: While there is truth in all Christian Churches, the LDS/Mormon Church is the only Christian Church on the earth today with the fullness of the gospel and the authority of the priesthood.

- **Salvation**: All mankind may be saved through the Atonement of Jesus Christ by exercising faith and obedience to the laws and ordinances of the gospel. The Atonement includes the suffering in the Garden of Gethsemane, the shedding of the blood of Christ, his death, and his Resurrection.

The LDS/Mormon definition of a Christian can be gleaned from an address given by the Apostle M. Russell Ballard, who said, "We accept as fellow Christians all who believe Jesus Christ to be the Son of God and the Savior of all mankind."[36]

Church of God in Christ

The Church of God in Christ (COGIC) was established in 1907 by Bishop Charles Harrison Mason (1866–1961), who did so after being expelled from the Baptist Church he attended because his views and teachings were thought of as being out of the mainstream for the day.[37] The COGIC is said to be the largest Holiness-Pentecostal and African-American Christian denomination in the US today and is the fifth-largest Christian congregation in North America according to the 2012 YACC. Core beliefs of the Church of God in Christ include, but are not limited to, the following:[38]

- **The Triune God**: There is a Triune Godhead that includes three persons: The Father, the Son, and the Holy Ghost.

- **The Bible**: The Bible is the inspired and only infallible written Word of God.

- **Baptism**: Water baptism is necessary as instructed by Christ, but baptism alone is not a means of salvation but an outward demonstration of faith and conversion to the Lord Jesus Christ.

- **The Lord's Supper**: The Lord's Supper is a symbolism of the suffering and death of Jesus Christ for the benefit of his people, allowing believers to participate in the crucified Lord.

- **Authority**: There is no one authoritative church, but rather authority is delivered in the written word of God.

- **Salvation**: Salvation comes as a result of the application of the work of redemption to the sinner with his restoration to divine favor and communion with God by the redemptive operation of the Holy Ghost through repentance and faith in Jesus Christ.

The COGIC did not respond to numerous written and oral requests for a definition of a Christian, nor are there any statements of faith that can be used to derive one. Therefore, the reader is left to glean his or her own thoughts from the belief system outlined above.

The National Baptist Convention, USA, Inc.

The National Baptist Convention (NBC), USA, Inc. (NBCUSA) was founded in 1886 and is the oldest and, with a membership of 5.1 million, the largest African-American religious convention in America,[39] making it the sixth-largest Christian congregation in North America according to the 2012 YACC. The core beliefs of the NBCUSA include, but are not limited to, the following[40]:

- **The Triune God**: "There is only one . . . living and true God, an infinite, intelligent Spirit, . . . Jehovah" consisting of three persons in the Godhead (the Father, the Son, and the Holy Ghost) equal to one another in divine perfection executing distinct but harmonious offices.

- **The Bible:** Although written by men, the Bible is the divinely inspired word of God.

- **Baptism:** Baptism is a solemn and beautiful emblem of a believer's faith and is prerequisite to membership and to partaking of the Lord's Supper.

- **The Lord's Supper:** The Lord's Supper is a communal commemoration, using bread and wine, of the dying love of Christ.

- **Authority:** There is not an authoritative single church, but rather the scriptures are the supreme standard by which all human conduct, creeds, and opinions shall be tried.

- **Salvation:** "The salvation of [man] is wholly of grace; through the mediatorial offices of the Son of God."

The NBCUSA did not respond to numerous written and oral requests for a definition of a Christian; however, as part of its statement of religious freedom the NBCUSA proclaims "religious liberty is a gift from God. We support the freedom of the individual conscience to choose to worship God according to the dictates of one's heart."[41] Such a statement suggests a more inclusive definition of a Christian.

Evangelical Lutheran Church of America

The Evangelical Lutheran Church of America (ELCA) was formed in 1988 with the merging of the American Lutheran Church, the Association of Evangelical Lutheran Churches, and the Lutheran Church in America. As of 2012, the ELCA purports a membership of 4.8 million members across nearly 10,500 congregations in the US and Caribbean,[42] making it the seventh-largest Christian congregation in America according to the 2012 YACC. Core beliefs of the ELCA include, but are not limited to, the following:[43, 44]

- **The Triune God:** The Father, the Son, and the Holy Spirit form the Triune God as outlined and fully accepted in the Apostles', Nicene, and Athanasian Creeds.

- **The Bible:** The Bible (Old and New Testament) is the written Word of God authored by those who were inspired by God's Spirit to record God's revelations focused on Jesus Christ.

- **Baptism**: Baptism is the entry rite into Christian faith, instituted by God, whereby the baptized are united with Christ.

- **The Lord's Supper**: The Lord's Supper (that is, Eucharist) represents a remembrance of the saving acts of God in his Son Jesus Christ by partaking of the Lord's body and blood (no elaboration) in the form of bread and wine, respectively.

- **Authority**: The ELCA does not offer a statement on the authority of the Church, instead it looks to scripture as the ultimate authority.

- **Salvation**: Jesus Christ as Lord and Savior and the gospel are the power of God with the authority to save all who believe.

The ELCA responded to a request for a definition of a Christian, supplying the following: "The ELCA's definition of 'Christian' would be the same as that in any dictionary: A person who believes in Jesus Christ."[45] This definition is consistent with the ELCA's website definition of "Christians believe in Jesus Christ and follow his teachings. We believe Jesus is God's own son, sent by God to become human."[46]

National Baptist Convention of America, Inc.

The National Baptist Convention of America, which is now called the National Baptist Convention of America, Incorporated International (NBCA), established its roots in 1895 as the National Baptist Convention of the United States of America and then incorporated in 1987 under the NBCA. Controversy ensued in 1988 during the 104th annual session with the National Baptist Convention USA, Inc., leading to the NBCA body voting to operate its own National Congress.[47] The NBCA has approximately 3.5 million members, making it eighth-largest Christian congregation in America according to the 2012 YACC. The NBCA did not respond to numerous written requests and phone calls over a two-year period for information on core beliefs and its definition of a Christian. The National Council of Churches indicated the NBCA belief system is likely similar to that of the NBCUSA; however, it was not possible to verify this and therefore it is left up to the reader to discern.

Assemblies of God (USA)

The Assemblies of God (AOG), also known as the General Council of the Assemblies of God (USA), was organized in 1914 and is one of the largest Pentecostal denominations in the United States. Long before that, however, the Pentecostal movement took shape during the First and Second Great Awakenings (1730–1740 and 1800–1870, respectively), with individuals involved in the movement identifying themselves with reformers and revivalists such as Martin Luther, John Wesley, and Dwight L. Moody.[48] The AOG is the ninth largest Christian congregation in North America according to the 2012 YACC. Core beliefs of the AOG include, but are not limited to, the following:

- **The Triune God**: "There is only One True God—revealed in three persons . . . Father, Son, and Holy Spirit."

- **The Bible**: "The scriptures are inspired by God and declare his design and plan for mankind."

- **Baptism**: Baptism is performed by immersion after repentance and receiving salvation through Jesus Christ. As a side note: the AOG places a great deal of emphasis on baptism of the Holy Spirit, whereby an individual has the ability to speak in tongues.

- **The Lord's Supper**: The Lord's Supper (that is, Holy Communion) is a symbolic remembrance of Christ's suffering and death for the salvation of man.

- **Authority**: There is not one authoritative church; "'the church' is the Body of Christ and consists of people who, throughout timr, have accepted God's offer of redemption . . . through . . . Jesus Christ."

- **Salvation**: Salvation comes through "trusting [Jesus] Christ, through faith and repentance, to br our personal Savior."[49]

In response to my request, the AOG provided the following definition of a Christian:

For the Assemblies of God, a true Christian is a person who accepts the Bible as God's Word for mankind and has made a mind and heart commitment to Jesus Christ as the source of our salvation and eternal life. He or she must believe that "God so loved the world that He gave

His only begotten Son, that whosoever believes in Him should not perish but have eternal life" (John 3:16, paraphrased). After taking that step, a true Christian seeks to follow the New Testament teachings and examples, including the Old Testament Ten Commandments, nine of which are re-articulated in the New Testament. The rest of the Old Testament portrays a God who relates personally to those who choose to follow Him and His design for meaningful human life.[50]

Presbyterian Church (USA)

The Presbyterian Church (USA)—PCUSA—was formed in 1983 combining the Presbyterian Church in the US (PCUS) and the United Presbyterian Church in the USA (UPCUSA). Presbyterianism has experienced a number of splits and reunions within its denominations with its faith tradition dating back to the *Westminster Confession of Faith and Catechisms* inspired by John Calvin in 1647.[51] With its approximately 2.6 million members the PCUSA is the tenth-largest Christian congregation in the US according to the 2012 YACC. Core beliefs of the PCUSA include, but are not limited to, the following:

- **The Triune God**: There is one Triune God consisting of God the Father, Jesus Christ—"fully human and fully God"—and the Holy Spirit as "the giver and renewer of life."[52]

- **The Bible**: The scriptures are the word of God written, witnessing to God's self-revelation.[53]

- **Baptism**: "Baptism is the sign and seal of incorporation into Christ."[54] "Being washed with the water of baptism, Christians [receive] new life in Christ and [present] their bodies to be living sacrifices to God."[55]

- **The Lord's Supper**: "The Lord's Supper is the sign and seal of eating and drinking in communion with the crucified and risen Lord."[56] The partaker "receive[s] the sustaining presence of Christ, remember[s] God's covenant promise, and pledge[s] [his or her] obedience anew."[57]

- **Authority**: There is not one supreme and authoritative church, the gospel of Jesus Christ, and Jesus Christ himself, is the ultimate authority.[58]

- **Salvation**: God, through Jesus Christ, has broken the power of sin and evil, delivering the faithful from death to life eternal.[59]

Charles Wiley, coordinator of the Office of Theology and Worship General Assembly Council, responded to a request for a definition of a Christian with a number of passages from the Book of Order, which is Part II of the Constitution of the PCUSA. The 2009–2011 Book of Order contains the Form of Government, Directory for Worship, Rules of Discipline, and the Formula of Agreement. Mr. Wiley focused his response in defining a Christian on three passages from the PCUSA Book of Order:

1. "One becomes an active member of the church through faith in Jesus Christ as Savior and acceptance of his Lordship in all of life. Baptism and a public profession of faith in Jesus as Lord are the visible signs of entrance into the active membership of the church." (Book of Order G-5.0101a)

2. "Those desiring the Sacrament of Baptism for their children or for themselves shall make vows that profess their faith in Jesus Christ as Lord and Savior, renounce evil and affirm their reliance on God's grace, declare their intention to participate actively and responsibly in the worship and mission of the church." (Book of Order W-3.3603)

3. "Membership as Ministry: A faithful member accepts Christ's call to be involved responsibly in the ministry of his Church. Such involvement includes: proclaiming the good news, taking part in the common life and worship of a particular church, praying and studying Scripture and the faith of the Christian Church, supporting the work of the church through the giving of money, time, and talents, participating in the governing responsibilities of the church, demonstrating a new quality of life within and through the church, responding to God's activity in the world through service to others, living responsibly in the personal, family, vocational, political, cultural, and social relationships of life, and working in the world for peace, justice, freedom, and human fulfillment." (Book of Order G-5.0102 a-i)

These three passages define a member of the Church and thus define a Christian as one who professes faith in Jesus Christ as Lord and Savior. After making such a profession the Christian is then invited to participate in baptism and become an active member of the ministry of Christ in spreading the gospel, living an active spiritual life, and serving God— providing a tangible expression of the love of God to the betterment of others.

Summary of America's Largest Christian Churches

If you're feeling no closer to a definition of a Christian, don't feel bad. This exercise, although revealing and interesting, demonstrates the confusion among Christian churches in providing a clear and useful definition of a Christian. Outside of a common theme of professing Jesus Christ as Savior, there are churches that require baptism by water, another church that adds the necessity of conversion via the Holy Spirit, one that requires acceptance of the three Creeds, another that requires acceptance of the Bible, and those that look to a demonstration of personal commitment to the gospel. There are both inclusive and exclusive definitions of a Christian offered, allowing the reader to draw his or her own conclusions.

THE INTERNET AT LARGE

The Internet offers a dizzying array of content on a limitless number of topics with the definition of a Christian being no exception. Just type the phrase "Define Christian," or several variations of that term, into Google, and thousands of selections appear. So emotionally charged is the process of defining a Christian that religioustolerance.org, a website dedicated to promoting religious dialogue of multiple faiths, makes the following statement on their website:

> The definition of the term "Christian" probably triggers more irate emails from visitors to this site than any other topic. . . . It seems that countless people have their own specific definition of "Christian." They differ greatly from each other. But . . . many Christians believe that their definition is the only true one, and is the only one defined in the Bible.[60]

In their attempt to define a Christian, religioustolerance.org mentions the two most popular definitions are (1) A person who follows Yeshua of Nazareth's (Jesus Christ's) teachings, or (2) A person who attempts to be like Yeshua. The definition of a Christian eventually put forth by relioustolerance.org is the following:

> We accept as Christian any individual or group who devoutly, thought-fully, seriously, and prayerfully regards themselves to be Christian. That is, they honestly believe themselves to be attempting to follow the teachings of Yeshua of Nazareth (a.k.a. Jesus Christ) as they interpret those teachings to be.[61]

The following are a number of other organizations, websites and individuals who have likewise put forth their own definition of a Christian for consideration:

The Christian Apologetics and Research Ministry (CARM) defines a Christian as "knowing the true Christ and following Him in truth." This definition is then supported by host of interpreted biblical passages to qualify what the "true Christ" is and what the corresponding "truth" is.[62]

Got Questions.org defines a Christian as being "a person who has put faith and trust in the person and work of Jesus Christ, including His death on the cross as payment for sins and His resurrection on the third day. . . . The mark of a true Christian is love for others and obedience to God's Word. . . . A true Christian is indeed a child of God, a part of God's true family, and one who has been given new life in Jesus Christ."[63]

Dr. Ray Pritchard, Author, Speaker, and President of Keep Believing Ministries on Christianity.com, provided a lengthy explanation to qualify his eventual definition, which is: "A Christian is a person who has been truly converted to Jesus Christ." Dr. Pritchard's support points include: (1) It begins with God and his choice of us; (2) It requires the true preaching of the gospel; (3) It leads to a heartfelt acceptance of Christ as Lord and Savior; (4) It results in a changed life that changes other lives; and (5) It means that we go "all in" on Jesus.[64]

Mark M. Mattison of True Grace Ministries defines a Christian as "a disciple, a follower of Christ, a spiritual brother or sister to others—one who strives to be like Jesus, regardless of denominational background or creedal preference."[65]

About.com defines a Christian as "a follower of Christ; one who professes belief in Jesus as the Christ and follows his teachings."[66]

Archbishop Paul of Finland defines a Christian as one who

belongs to the Body of Christ, the Church of Christ . . . has been baptized in the name of the Holy Trinity and follows the ideals and beliefs of both the Scriptures and Sacred Tradition. He believes in a living and loving God, Whose Grace protects and guides him in the path of redemption. He believes that God has revealed Himself in the Bible through the Prophets and especially in the Person of Jesus Christ, His only begotten Son who is man's Savior. He especially believes in the Incarnation of Christ as God-Man, in His Crucifixion and Resurrection, in His Gospel and Commandments, and in the world to come.[67]

As with religious organizations and Christian churches, the definitions from the internet at large are broad and wide ranging leaving us unsatisfied in an attempt to define a Christian. More satisfying would be a large number of definitions sharing common elements that could be synthesized into a consolidated definition; however, even that does not exist, and we are all left to ponder.

CONCLUSION OF THE WORLD'S DEFINITION OF A CHRISTIAN

Wilfred Cantwell Smith in his book *The Meaning and End of Religion* cautioned those who embark on a study of religion that "there is much to be said for approaching not merely with caution but with hesitation and even something akin to awe."[68] Smith warns that attempts to understand and explain religion are ripe with challenges that are not easily overcome—something we are catching a glimpse of in our search for the definition of a Christian.

This qualitative exercise to define a Christian has likely left most readers bewildered and confused. Don't worry, it left me bewildered and confused as well! While *Webster's Dictionary* and the *Encyclopedia Britannica* provide straightforward and more inclusive definitions of a Christian, religious organizations and denominations offer a greater variety of more constricted definitions, with the Internet at large being varied. Is it any wonder why the debate over defining a Christian rages on today?

When confusion reigns it is common to turn to one with authority to resolve the confusion. In this case, the world is full of experts—individuals with doctorates of theology and divinity and institutions of religions that have been around for centuries. Despite the existence of such experts and organizations, there is still no agreement on the definition of a Christian. There are small threads of commonality among the many competing definitions, but even then the final definition of a Christian eludes us.

This confusion around defining a Christian is reminiscent of the reasons Constantine called for the gathering of the First Ecumenical Council in Nicaea to resolve differences and create a common belief by way of committee—the result being the Nicene Creed. Can there be a greater challenge than reaching consensus on one or more spiritual matters among learned individuals with divergent opinions, with compromise and political correctness lurking in the corridors? Without the inspiration of the Holy Ghost and humility among the participants such consensus in alignment with God the Father is virtually impossible.

Can passionate, well-meaning individuals who have aligned themselves to particular Christian denominations—either as employed ministers or laypeople—offer objective views on this sensitive topic? While the answer is a reluctant yes, what then are the true motivations of narrowing the definition of a Christian as opposed to broadening that definition in hopes of greater unity among the Christian world?

After evaluating the many definitions and content outlined in this chapter, five definitions of a Christian should be considered:

1. A Christian is one **who believes he or she is a Christian**: This is the broadest of all definitions and would allow any person who self-describes as a Christian to be considered a Christian. According to the American Religious Identification Survey in 2008, 76 percent of the US population identifies as being Christians.[69]

2. A Christian is one **who believes in and follows Jesus Christ**: This is also a broad definition and removes most doctrinal requirements associated with Jesus Christ. Typically those who believe in and follow Jesus Christ accept him to be the Son of God and the Savior of the World.

3. A Christian is one **who embraces a particular set of beliefs**: Several organizations and churches have statements of faith (or the equivalent) that define a Christian as part of their particular profession of faith. Examples might be a belief in the Trinity and acceptance of the Bible as the word of God.

4. A Christian is one **who is born again**: This is a definition that is typically found among Fundamentalists and Evangelicals. According to a Barna Research Group survey in 2001, only 41 percent of Christians in the US consider themselves to be born again.[70]

5. A Christian is one **who is a member of a particular church**: This is the narrowest of definitions and would limit the number of Christians to a very small number depending on the denomination.

Although these five definitions are helpful to consider, the degree in variation between the definitions makes them unsuitable for practical use. In fact, these five definitions clearly demonstrate the confusion in our world today in defining a Christian. With the world in confusion about the definition of a Christian we must turn to a more native and reliable source to gain understanding—the Bible.

Chapter 6

IT'S CLEAR ACCORDING TO
THE BIBLE

THE TITLE OF THIS CHAPTER SUGGESTS ONE NEED ONLY PROCEED TO Acts 11:26, Acts 26:28, or 1 Peter 4:16 (the three places in the New Testament where the word *Christian* can be found) and read a sentence that begins with "a Christian is . . ." Unfortunately, it will not be that easy. Most matters of faith usually aren't. Jesus taught that we must "search the scriptures" (John 5:39)—the word "search" translated in this case to mean to search diligently or anxiously. The clarity the chapter title suggests comes when one diligently searches the Bible, systematically piecing together the words of Christ and his Apostles, while seeking divine inspiration. This is exactly what I did after finding little satisfaction in the previous chapter's effort, and I will share my scriptural journey with you. If you have a Bible handy, great! If not, this chapter will open up the Bible to you to more clearly answer the question "What is a Christian?"

FROM THE WORDS OF JESUS CHRIST
AS RECORDED IN THE BIBLE

Jesus Christ was not one to be exclusive. Jesus hung out with sinners and saints and recognized the efforts of all those with well-intentioned hearts, while scoffing at attempts to create an elite religious class. When the Apostle John complained "Master, we saw one casting out devils in thy name, and he followeth not us: and we forbad him, because he followeth not us," Jesus responded, "For he that is not against us is on our part" (Mark 9:38–40). In this scripture, John appears jealous that another individual, who was not part of their group, was serving in the name of Jesus Christ, to which the Savior immediately rebuked him for his exclusive attitude, reminding him they are all on the same team. Knowing Christ's orientation of inclusiveness helps us to define a Christian first using HIS words.

Being a Christian Starts with Belief in Jesus Christ

Everlasting, or eternal life is the ultimate goal of every Christian and is therefore often associated with being a Christian. According to Jesus Christ one must *believe* in him to gain *eternal life* or *everlasting life*, otherwise he is condemned (see John 3:18, John 3:36 and John 8:24). Consider the following passages with Jesus Christ speaking, each adding emphasis to the operative terms of interest:

- "And this is the will of him that sent me, that every one which seeth the Son, and *believeth* on him, may have *everlasting life*: and I will raise him up at the last day." (John 6:40)

- "Verily, verily, I say unto you, He that heareth my word, and *believeth* on him that sent me, hath *everlasting life*. . ." (John 5:24)

- "For God so loved the world, that he gave his only begotten Son, that whosoever *believeth* in him should not perish, but have *everlasting life*." (John 3:16)

- "He that *believeth* on the Son hath *everlasting life*. . ." (John 3:36)

- "Verily, verily, I say unto you, He that *believeth* on me hath *everlasting life*." (John 6:47)

- "Jesus said unto her, I am the resurrection, and the life: he that *believeth* in me, though he were dead, yet shall he live: And whosoever liveth and *believeth* in me *shall never die*." (John 11:25–26, see also John 11:25)

- "Verily, verily, I say unto you, He that heareth my word, and *believeth* on him that sent me, hath *everlasting life*." (John 5:24)

- "But these are written, that ye might *believe* that Jesus is the

Christ, the Son of God; and that *believing* ye might *have life* through his name" (John 20:31)

Other scriptural passages include John 6:27, John 9:35, John 13:19, and John 12:36. Note that "eternal life" and "everlasting life "can be used interchangeably since both come from the same Greek word *aiwvios* (*aionios*), meaning "perpetual."[1]

Two New Testament passages attributed to Christ that are akin to those above involve the word "faith" as opposed to "belief," and "saved "as opposed to "everlasting (or eternal) life." To the sinful woman and to the blind man Jesus said, "thy *faith* hath *saved* thee" (Luke 7:50 and Luke 18:42 respectively, emphasis added). The differences between the words faith and belief are either great or subtle according to various biblical scholars. Belief and faith come from the same word in Greek, *pistis*, suggesting belief and faith can be used interchangeably and generally mean the same thing. This is confirmed when Jesus speaks to the centurion who desires his servant to be healed and tells the Savior, "but speak the word only, and my servant shall be healed" (Matthew 8:8), to which the Savior responds, "I have not found so great *faith*, no, not in Israel" (Matthew 8:10, emphasis added). Three verses later, the Savior tells the centurion "Go thy way; and as thou hast *believed*, so be it done unto thee" (Matthew 8:13, emphasis added). Was it the centurion's faith or belief that healed his servant? The answer is the centurion's faith and belief in Jesus are both fundamentally the same.

More challenging from a theological perspective is the difference between the gift of everlasting (or eternal) life and the gift of salvation. Although different Christian denominations may have different definitions, in general salvation means to be saved from physical and spiritual death, where everlasting (or eternal) life means to live in God's presence forever. Desiring to defer a more complex explanation at this juncture, it suffices to say that belief or faith in Jesus Christ brings about the desired effect the Christian seeks.

Belief Means to Believe in the Divinity and Calling of Jesus

If one is to believe in Jesus Christ, what are they to believe about him? The Savior was clear in telling those around him who he was either directly or by confirming what others said about him. To make this clear, we will place a particular emphasis on those scriptures that are qualified with the words "I am" as spoken by or referenced by Jesus:

Jesus is the Christ—the Messiah: Jesus confirmed that he is the Christ when he asked the Apostles who they believed him to be. Peter answered, "Thou art the Christ, the Son of the living God" (Matthew 16:16; see also Mark 8:29–30 and Luke 9:20–21). Sometime later after being captured and questioned, the high priest asked Jesus, "Art thou the Christ, the Son of the Blessed?" to which Jesus responded, "I am" (Mark 14:61–62). The word "Christ" comes from the Greek word *Khristós*, which is a translation of the Hebrew *Māšíaḥ*, meaning the Messiah.[2] The word "messiah" means the anointed one.

Jesus is the Son of God (qualified as the "Only Begotten" Son of God): On numerous occasions, Jesus referred to himself as the "son of man," meaning the Messiah in human form. Jesus confirmed he is the Son of God (Luke 22:70 and John 10:36), qualifying that he is the "only begotten son" of God in John 3:16–18. This fact was further reinforced by those who testified of the words from God the Father who spoke from heaven, saying, "This is my beloved Son, in whom I am well pleased" (Matthew 3:17; see also Luke 3:22, Mark 1:11, 2 Peter 1:17, and Matthe w 17:5). While all believers may become the "sons of God" (John 1:12), there is only one "begotten" son of God—Jesus Christ. The Greek word for "begotten" is *monogenes* which means "only generated;"[3] however, the Greek meaning goes even further to imply Jesus was 100 percent the Father's Son and as such there is 100 percent continuity and connectivity between the two.

Jesus is the Light of the World: Jesus told his disciples "I am the light of the world" (see also John 8:12, 9:5).

Jesus is the Forgiver of Sins: Jesus proclaimed he had the power to forgive sins (Mark 2:10; see also Matthew 9:6)

Jesus is the Good Shepherd: Jesus described himself as "the good shepherd" (John 10:11, 14), one who takes care of those whom he has stewardship over, even giving up his life for them.

Jesus is the Only Way to the Father and everlasting life (salvation): Jesus said, "I am the way, the truth, and the life: no man cometh unto the Father, but by me" (John 14:6). Further proclamations of a similar nature by Jesus included calling himself the "bread of life" (John 6:35, 48), "the resurrection and the life" (John 11:25), and he who was prepared to give his life so that his sheep might live calling himself "the door of the sheep" (John 10:7, 9).

Jesus is one with the Father: Jesus said, "I am in the Father, and the Father in me" (John 14:10–11, 20), meaning that he is one with God the Father. This was further clarified during his intercessory prayer when he cried, "That they [speaking of his disciples] all may be one; as thou, Father, art in me, and I in thee" (John 17:21; see also John 17:11 and John 17:22), revealing a perfect oneness between Jesus Christ and God the Father. Christ prayed that we would pattern our own relationships with God after this oneness ("that they all may be one").

Belief in Christ Can Bring about Great Things

The first stage of believing in Jesus Christ can bring about great things in this life (mortality). The centurion referenced earlier believed in Jesus Christ, calling him Lord (although we have no knowledge of what he believed in terms of theology or his level of conversion), and as a result of this belief, his servant was healed. The father of a child with a dumb spirit believed in Jesus Christ, albeit a very fragile belief, and because of that belief his son was healed (Mark 9:24). Two blind men believed in Jesus Christ as being the "son of David" and as a result were healed (Matthew 9:28–29).

One is left to ponder in these applications of belief if the believer had a full understanding of who Jesus Christ was, or was it simply a belief that Jesus had the power to heal. Nonetheless, belief in Jesus Christ alone can bring about marvelous things in our earthly life.

However, Belief in Christ Alone May Not Be Enough

Although belief in Christ is the first stage in becoming a Christian, and belief alone can bring about miracles in the life of the believer, Jesus Christ made it clear that belief alone may not be enough. Consider what the Savior told his disciples in making this point understood:

> Not every one that saith unto me, Lord, Lord, shall enter into the kingdom of heaven; but he that doeth the will of my Father which is in heaven. Many will say to me in that day, Lord, Lord, have we not prophesied in thy name? and in thy name have cast out devils? and in thy name done many wonderful works? And then will I profess unto them, *I never knew you*: depart from me, ye that work iniquity. (Matthew 7:21–23, emphasis added)

There may be those who believe in Jesus Christ, and even supposedly perform mighty works in his name, but for belief to manifest itself into salvation as a Christian means Jesus Christ must *know* the believer. The word used for "knew" in the above scripture comes from the Greek word *égnon*, the past tense of the verb meaning "to know well," even "to understand" or "to have experienced." Therefore, even though we fully understand the Lord knows us intimately (Isaiah 43:1), in the aforementioned passage the Lord is saying he did not have experiences with those who claim to have done his work.

The believer becomes known to the Savior through the experiences of prayer, sincere belief, and service to him in love (discussed in later sections). In the case of Matthew 7:21–23, the Savior not having those experiences with those who supposedly called upon his name were denied a place in the kingdom of heaven. After all, even the evil spirits believe in Jesus Christ as "the Holy One of God" (Mark 1:23–24), and how does that benefit them? One can conclude that belief, or faith, in Jesus Christ is a *first step* in the process of being given the gift of salvation or everlasting (or eternal) life.

The question then becomes "What does it mean to truly believe or to have faith?" The Savior commented that "Except ye be converted, and become as little children, ye shall not enter into the kingdom of heaven" (Matthew 18:3). To convert means to change or transform. To be as a child means to always be looking to the parent for guidance and to be inherently teachable or humble. The opposite would be what the Savior described as "this people's heart is waxed gross, and their ears are dull of hearing, and their eyes they have closed," telling his disciples "lest at any time they should see with their eyes, and hear with their ears, and should understand with their heart, and should be converted, and I should heal them" (Matthew 13:15; see also John 12:40).

We can conclude the kind of belief that brings about salvation and everlasting life is that which causes one to be transformed fully to Christ, looking to their Heavenly Father and his Son Jesus Christ for guidance, being moldable in the gospel, and having experiences with the Lord that cause him to "know" the believer.

Repentance is Essential in Becoming a Christian

Besides urging people to believe in him, Jesus preached repentance, saying, "the kingdom of God is at hand: repent ye, and believe the gospel" (Mark 1:15; see also Matthew 4:17). The Savior added that unless one repents of their sins, he or she will perish (Luke 13:3–5).

Baptism is Part of Becoming a Christian

On one occasion Jesus added something more onto the need to believe in order to be saved, saying, "He that believeth *and* is baptized shall be saved" (Mark 16:16, emphasis added). Jesus himself was baptized (Matthew 3:13–17; Mark 1:9–11; Luke 3:21–22) and commissioned his disciples to "Go ye therefore, and teach all nations, baptizing them in the name of the Father, and of the Son, and of the Holy Ghost" (Matthew 28:19).

How important is baptism? Jesus told Nicodemus, "verily, I say unto thee, Except a man be born of water and of the Spirit, he cannot enter into the kingdom of God" (John 3:5). The phrase "kingdom of God" is interpreted in various ways with a common interpretation being "the Lord's Church." Using this interpretation, baptism is therefore not only a saving ordinance as taught by Jesus Christ, but it is also a means of entering into a covenant as a member of the Lord's Church.

The Lord's Supper as Part of Becoming a Christian

On yet another occasion Jesus proclaimed, "Whoso eateth my flesh, and drinketh my blood, hath *eternal life*" (John 6:54, emphasis added; see also John 6:51, 53, and 56). Although Jesus does not say partaking of his flesh (that is, Holy Communion, the Lord's Supper, the Sacrament, and so on) is a requirement to obtain eternal life, he does make it clear that those who do have eternal life.

Following Jesus is Part of Becoming a Christian

Although believing, repenting, being baptized, and partaking of the Lord's flesh and blood take effort, *following* Jesus Christ takes a little more effort and can be seen as another step in the process of becoming a Christian (that is, a disciple of Christ). Jesus said, "My sheep hear my voice, and I know them, *and they follow me*" (John 10:27, emphasis added), meaning those of the fold of Jesus Christ are those who follow him. The Savior commented, "If any man serve me, *let him follow me*" (John 12:26, emphasis added), meaning to follow Jesus Christ is to serve him, and to serve is the greatest of all callings in the kingdom (Luke 22:26).

Following Jesus Christ as a Christian Means Making Sacrifices

Jesus said, "If anyone would come after me, let him *deny himself* and take up his cross daily *and follow me*" (Luke 9:23, emphasis added; see also Mark 8:34). The insinuation here is that following the Savior is likely to result in making sacrifices. Demonstrating the practical application of this counsel Jesus told the rich young man to "go and sell that thou hast, and give to the poor, and thou shalt have treasure in heaven: and come and follow me" (Matthew 19:21; see also Luke 18:22 and Mark 10:21). In some cases, the sacrifice can be tremendous!

In following Jesus, the Apostle Peter commented he and the other Apostles had "forsaken all" (Matthew19:27), to which Jesus replied, "And every one that hath forsaken houses, or brethren, or sisters, or father, or mother, or wife, or children, or lands, for my name's sake, shall receive an hundredfold, and shall inherit *everlasting life*" (Matthew 19:29, emphasis added). The Savior was teaching the rewards of making sacrifices in following him are both temporal and eternal and are the cost of true discipleship as a Christian.

The principle of sacrifice as a progression from believing and following the Savior is further reinforced by Jesus when he told his disciples "For whosoever will save his life shall lose it: but whosoever will lose his life for my sake, the same shall save it" (Luke 9:24; see also Mark 8:35, Luke 17:33 and Matthew 16:25). Because following Jesus Christ may mean a lifetime of sacrifice the Savior assures his followers, "he that shall endure unto the end, the same shall be *saved*" (Matthew 24:13; see also Matthew 10:22, emphasis added). Once again, Jesus makes clear the reward for sacrifice is salvation.

Believers Who Follow Jesus Christ Must Love

Love was a central theme to the public ministry of Jesus Christ proclaiming the great commandments to be "Thou shalt love the Lord thy God with all thy heart, and with all thy soul, and with all thy mind. This is the first and great commandment. And the second is like unto it, Thou shalt love thy neighbour as thyself" (Matthew 22:37–39; see also Mark 12:30–31 and Luke 10:27). The Savior added to this that his true disciples will be known by their love for one another (John 15:12, 17). The principles of believing in Jesus Christ and loving Jesus Christ are inseparable (John 16:27), as are the principles of love and forgiveness (Luke 7:47).

Loving the Lord Means Keeping the Commandments

Given the importance of loving the Lord as part of the Christianization process, how are we to "love the Lord"? This question is soundly answered by Jesus when he told his followers "if ye love me, keep my commandments" (John 14:15). In this same chapter of John, Jesus expounds further that keeping his commandments translates into having the love of the Father and abiding in the Father and the Son (John 14:21, 23 and John 15:10).

Summary of Defining a Christian Using the Words of Jesus Christ

In this section, we focused solely on the words of Jesus Christ in the Bible in what he urged his followers to do, focusing on the ultimate objective of every Christian in being given eternal life. By doing so, we are able to gain a unique and solid perspective in defining a Christian. The pattern we learn from the words of Christ in becoming a Christian, and not necessarily in this order, is one who

- **Believes in Jesus Christ** as the only begotten Son of God, the one true Messiah, and the only path to salvation

- **Is transformed through belief in Jesus Christ** in one's heart and life

- **Repents, is baptized, and partakes of the Lord's Supper in the name of Jesus Christ** as a profession of belief and act of obedience

- **Is known by Jesus Christ** through having experiences with the Savior

- **Follows Jesus Christ** by following his teachings and his example

- **Sacrifices for Jesus Christ** in serving others

- **Loves God and Jesus Christ** and extends that love to others

- **Keeps the commandments of Jesus Christ** as a demonstration of his or her love for Jesus Christ

This is not a definition of a Christian but rather components of a framework that can help us define a Christian. These components relate to both believing (faith) and doing (works). This framework built on the words of Christ toward defining a Christian takes much greater shape than relying on religious organizations, churches, and the Internet as a whole. Simply put—we are on to something here! Although religious organizations, churches, and individuals have also used the Bible in creating their statements of faith and definitions of a Christian examined earlier, we are returning to the native source to reconstruct our own. Think of this as returning to the original Greek manuscripts of the Bible to search for a more native understanding of scripture. We are simply digging into the Bible to identify the native sources of the definition of a Christian for ourselves.

It was mentioned earlier that Christ was inclusive in his ministry, thus this emerging definition of a Christian from our exercise appears wider than many of those previously studied. The exclusiveness of Christianity is dictated by individual choice. Jesus Christ told his disciples: "Enter ye in at the strait gate: for wide is the gate, and broad is the way, that leadeth to destruction, and many there be which go in thereat: Because strait is the gate, and narrow is the way, which leadeth unto life, and few there be that find it." (Matthew 7:13–14). It is up to individuals to enter into the gate and find the narrow path to life by exercising their own free will to do so. Jesus Christ makes it possible for all to enter into the gate (inclusive), and those who choose not to enter into the gate are those who are excluding themselves.

THE WORDS OF THE NEW TESTAMENT AUTHORS

You might be asking yourself, "Why divide the definition of a Christian between the words attributed to Jesus Christ himself (as recorded in the Bible) and the words of those who authored the New Testament? Shouldn't they be the same?" Although the answer to that question should be yes, the more practical answer is no because the Bible after the four Gospels and the first chapter of Acts transitions from our being taught by Jesus Christ in the flesh to being taught by God's chosen through the Holy Ghost. Think of it this way: the words of Jesus Christ are pure divine revelation, and the words of the New Testament authors are theology about

God inspired through the Holy Ghost. In that respect, we compare God (Jesus Christ as God the son) teaching man about God, compared to man (Paul, James, Peter, and so on) teaching man about God. The differences produce subtle differences worth examining.

Belief Still Stands with Eternal Life Replaced by Salvation

The New Testament authors still emphasize the principle of belief in Jesus Christ. However, notice how the phrases "eternal life" and "everlasting life" used by Jesus Christ to denote a reward for belief in him from the four Gospels are now largely replaced by "saved" and "salvation" in the books of the Bible that follow. Emphasis has been added to each of these scriptural passages to highlight the operative words:

- "And they said, *Believe* on the Lord Jesus Christ, and thou shalt be *saved*, and thy house." (Acts 16:31)

- "For I am not ashamed of the gospel of Christ: for it is the power of God unto *salvation* to every one that *believeth*; to the Jew first, and also to the Greek." (Romans 1:16)

- "But we are bound to give thanks alway to God for you, brethren beloved of the Lord, because God hath from the beginning chosen you to *salvation* through sanctification of the Spirit and *belief* of the truth:" (2 Thessalonians 2:13)

- "These things have I written unto you that *believe* on the name of the Son of God; that ye may know that ye have *eternal life* . . ." (1 John5:13)

- "That if thou shalt confess with thy mouth the Lord Jesus, and shalt *believe* in thine heart that God hath raised him from the dead, thou shalt be *saved*" (Romans 10:9)

What are the differences between eternal life and salvation? The linguistic differences between the two from a Greek perspective are slight. When examining the New Testament, the phrases "eternal life" and everlasting life" are used in twenty-seven passages of the four Gospels and in nineteen thereafter and the words "saved" and "salvation" are used in sixty-two passages of the four Gospels and in 102 thereafter. The post-gospel authors of the New Testament appear fonder of the words "saved" and "salvation." To some, salvation is a prerequisite of eternal life; to others there is no difference. I will defer the theological debate of discerning between these words and terms for another book. The point here is that beyond the four Gospels, the principle of belief in Christ leading to salvation (or eternal life) is continued as being the first step in becoming a Christian.

Grace Enters the Picture

A word scarcely used in the four Gospels that finds a prominent role in the remaining books of the New Testament is "grace." "Grace" appears in 122 passages of the New Testament. Jesus Christ never used the term himself, perhaps because he himself was grace and demonstrated to all what it looks like. In the four Gospels, the word "grace" is used in only four passages—three of which are in the first chapter of the Gospel of John.

Grace, or *charis* in Greek, has more than one biblical meaning. For example, Proverbs 22:11 uses the word "grace" as a noun to mean beauty in referring to lips, while in Genesis 6:8 it is used to denote Noah finding favor with God. Although a variety of meanings may be attributed to the word, it is most prominently used in the New Testament to signify "the unmerited goodness or love of God to those who have forfeited it, and are by nature under a sentence of condemnation."[4] Consider these scriptural passages with emphasis being given to the word grace in this manner:

- "Even when we were dead in sins, hath quickened us together with Christ, (by *grace* ye are saved)." (Ephesians 2:5)

- "But we believe that through the *grace* of the Lord Jesus Christ we shall be saved, even as they." (Acts 15:11)

- "For the *grace* of God that bringeth salvation hath appeared to all men." (Titus 2:11)

- "That being justified by his *grace*, we should be made heirs according to the hope of eternal life." (Titus 3:7)

- "That as sin hath reigned unto death, even so might *grace* reign through righteousness unto eternal life by Jesus Christ our Lord." (Romans 5:21)

Grace is made available through the Atonement of Christ (his suffering in Gethsemane, the Crucifixion, and his Resurrection—one or move of these events depending on the doctrinal belief of the Christian denomination). The Atonement is a great and freely given gift of God the Father as a result of his mercy, love, and condescension toward man with the power to deliver him from his sins and provide a pathway for salvation and eternal life.

Paul explains that grace is made available to us through our faith writing "For by *grace* are ye saved *through faith*; and that not of yourselves: it is the gift of God" (Ephesians 2:8, emphasis added). So while grace is something that all Christians enjoy freely and is an essential characteristic of Christianity, grace is activated as a result of faith in Jesus Christ, hence belief is still the first step in becoming a Christian.

Following Christ and Following after His Characteristics

Where Christ used variations of the phrase "follow me" on multiple occasions, the phrase is used sparingly beyond the Gospels. Peter reminds us that Christ left "us an example, that ye should follow his steps" (1 Peter 2:21) and the book of Revelation makes it clear at the final judgment those who "follow the Lamb whitersoever he goeth . . . [are those] redeemed from among men, being the first fruits unto God and to the Lamb" (Revelation 14:4). Although these verses point to the need to follow Christ and his example, the direct phrases to follow Christ in the Gospels are replaced by admonitions to "follow after" the characteristics of Christ. Consider the following scriptural passages with emphasis given on following Christlike characteristics:

- "But thou, O man of God, flee these things; and *follow after* righteousness, godliness, faith, love, patience, meekness." (1 Timothy 6:11)

- "Let us therefore *follow after* the things which make for peace, and things wherewith one may edify another." (Romans 14:19)

- "*Follow after* charity, and desire spiritual gifts, but rather that ye may prophesy." (1 Corinthians 14:1)

- "Flee also youthful lusts: but *follow [after]* righteousness, faith, charity, peace, with them that call on the Lord out of a pure heart." (2 Timothy 2:22)

- "Beloved, *follow [after]* not that which is evil, but that which is good. He that doeth good is of God: but he that doeth evil hath not seen God." (3 John 1:11)

Sacrifices in Following Christ Still Stands

The Gospels record Jesus explaining that following him requires self-denial and taking up one's cross—sacrifices that result from discipleship in the gospel of Christ. The same principle holds true beyond the Gospels that salvation can only come through Christ (Acts 4:12), reinforcing the teaching that the road to salvation and eternal life is not easy. The authors explain that salvation comes through faith (2 Timothy 3:15, 1 Peter 1:5, 9), adding godly sorrow and repentance (2 Corinthians 7:10), obedience (Hebrews 5:9 and Philippians 2:12), and even suffering (Romans 8:18, 2 Corinthians 1:6, Philippians 1:28–29, 1 Peter 4:13) are a part of the journey.

Works Are Important but Alone Are Not Enough

In the Gospels, Jesus urges his disciples to be examples to others by allowing them to see their "good works" (Matthew 5:16), letting his disciples know that each will be rewarded "according to his works" (Matthew 16:27). Jesus also used the word "fruit" on many occasions to figuratively reference that which proceeds forth from a man—either good or evil—including works. *Vine's Expository Dictionary of New Testament Words* defines fruit as "being the visible expression of power working inwardly and invisibly, the character of the 'fruit' being evidence of the character of the power producing it."[5] What makes fruit or works good is not the fruit itself but how it glorifies God while exemplifying discipleship in Jesus Christ.

Jesus uses the analogy of a tree and its fruit in Matthew 7:17–20, teaching that a good tree brings forth good fruit and a corrupt tree brings forth corrupt fruit, ending the lesson with "Wherefore by their fruits ye shall know them." In reading the Gospels alone, one might conclude the Savior felt strongly about works, to the point of letting his disciples know that those who show forth good works, or good fruit, are righteous and worthy of the kingdom provided the Lord *knows* them as explained earlier (Matthew 7:21–23). Beyond the four Gospels, however, Paul goes to great lengths to warn readers that works alone will not be enough to save, including the following passages with emphasis added to the operative phrases:

- "For by grace are ye saved through faith; and that *not of your-selves*: it is the gift of God: *Not of works*, lest any man should boast." (Ephesians 2:8–9)

- "Who hath saved us, and called us with an holy calling, *not according to our works*, but according to his own purpose and grace, which was given us in Christ Jesus before the world began." (2 Timothy 1:9)

- "Knowing that a man is *not justified by the works* of the law, but by the faith of Jesus Christ, even we have believed in Jesus Christ, that we might be justified by the faith of Christ, and *not by the works* of the law: for by the works of the law shall no flesh be justified." (Galatians 2:16)

- "*Not by works* of righteousness which we have done, but according to his mercy he saved us, by the washing of regeneration, and renewing of the Holy Ghost." (Titus 3:5)

These Pauline passages and others like them are primarily directed at the Jews, who at the time felt their adherence to the law would save them. Although Paul's writings encourage Christians to show forth good works (Titus 2:7), his writings also offer some of the strongest rebuke toward those Christians that overemphasize the need for good works.

In an attempt to balance the discussion, James clarifies the dynamics of faith and works, writing, "Yea, a man may say, Thou hast faith, and I have works: shew me thy faith without thy works, and I will shew thee my faith by my works" (James 2:18). James then went even further when he taught in no unclear terms that "faith without works is dead" (James 2:14–26).

Peter and John also added to the balance reminding Christians that works will have a role in the Final Judgment (1 Peter 1:17, Revelation 20:12–13) and will remain with the Lord's faithful into the eternities (Revelation 14:13). For the Christian, works are a demonstration of faith and a means of laying up for oneself treasures in heaven (Matthew 6:20), treasures that will accompany them into the next life as evidence of a life in Christ at the Final Judgment.

Conversion, Repentance, Baptism, and the Lord's Supper

The books beyond the Gospels reinforce the process of repentance that leads to conversion followed by baptism; however, not always in that order. For example, after Peter spoke on the day of Pentecost, the Bible says, "they were pricked in their heart," signifying conversion to the prompting of the men to ask Peter and the Apostles "what shall we do" (Acts 2:37)? Peter responded, "Repent, and be baptized every one of you in the name of Jesus Christ for the remission of sins," adding if they would do so they "shall receive the gift of the Holy Ghost" (Acts 2:38). Repentance can bring about a mighty change of heart toward conversion or vice versa. After healing a blind man Peter told the crowd "Repent ye therefore, and be converted, that your sins may be blotted out" (Acts 3:19).

Conversion is more deeply explored beyond the Gospels in what Paul describes as becoming a "new creature: old things are passed away; behold, all things are become new" (2 Corinthians 5:17). Conversion is likened to becoming alive again with a "newness of life" (Romans 6:4) or "newness of spirit" (Romans 7:6). As cited earlier from Titus 3:5, conversion is referred to as "regeneration, and renewing of the Holy Ghost," moving one's heart (Acts 11:23, Hebrews 10:22, Romans 6:17) and inspiring the bearing of testimony toward salvation (Romans 10:8–9).

There is a record of Jesus being baptized and at least one Apostle (Paul) being baptized (Acts 9:18), creating a pattern that resulted in thousands being baptized (Acts 2:41). The book of Acts records numerous instances of baptism (for example, Acts 16:29–33, Acts 10:47–48, Acts 16:15, and Acts 22:16), with the typical sequence being belief followed by baptism. Consider the following scriptural passages with emphasis given to the operative terms:

- "And Philip said, If thou *believest* with all thine heart, thou mayest. And he answered and said, I *believe* that Jesus Christ is the Son of God. And he commanded the chariot to stand still: and they went down both into the water, both Philip and the eunuch; and he *baptized* him." (Acts 8:37–38)

- "But when they *believed* Philip preaching the things concerning the kingdom of God, and the name of Jesus Christ, they were *baptized*, both men and women." (Acts 8:12)

- "Then Simon himself *believed* also: and when he was *baptized*, he continued with Philip, and wondered, beholding the miracles and signs which were done." (Acts 8:13)

- "And Crispus, the chief ruler of the synagogue, *believed* on the Lord with all his house; and many of the Corinthians hearing believed, and were *baptized*." (Acts 18:8)

Partaking of the body and blood of Jesus Christ, which was prominently mentioned by Jesus Christ, is mentioned only briefly after the Gospels, exclusively by Paul in two sequential passages. Paul teaches of the "communion" of the body and blood of Christ bringing unity to the faithful (1 Corinthians 10:16–17), while later reminding of how the Lord instituted the communion and cautioning not to take the Lord's Supper unworthily (1 Corinthians 11:24–27).

The Holy Ghost (or Holy Spirit) Assumes a Prominent Role

The presence and workings of the Holy Ghost, or the Spirit of God, is recorded in the Old Testament (Genesis 1:2, Isaiah 11:2, Isaiah 4:4 and Isaiah 61:1). The story of Simeon in the temple demonstrates the inspiration of the Holy Ghost was alive and well while Jesus Christ was on the earth (Luke 2:25–26); however, Jesus Christ told his Apostles, "Nevertheless I tell you the truth; It is expedient for you that I go away: for if I go not away, the Comforter [the Holy Ghost] will not come unto you; but if I depart, I will send him unto you" (John 16:7). The meaning of these two biblical passages is that although the inspiration of the Holy Ghost had been felt by many for centuries, the gift of the Holy Ghost received by man as a constant companion would not be given until Jesus was glorified (John 7:39). Consider the following sequence regarding the Holy Ghost from the New Testament:

- The Holy Ghost is present: Luke 2:25–26

- Christ teaches his Apostles about the Holy Ghost: John 14:26 and 15:26

- Christ teaches the gift of the Holy Ghost cannot come until he departs: John 7:39 and John 16:7

- The resurrected Christ gives the gift of the Holy Ghost to his

Apostles: John 20:22 and teaches his Apostles on using the gift: Acts 1:8

- The Holy Ghost guides the Apostles: Acts 1:2

- The Holy Ghost is poured out on the day of Pentecost: Acts 2:1–4

- The gift of the Holy Ghost is given after baptism by the laying on of hands: Acts 8:15–17, Acts 19:4–6,

- The Holy Ghost comforts those that receive it: Acts 9:31

- Paul teaches that the Holy Ghost dwells within us: 1 Corinthians 6:19 and 2 Timothy 1:14

- Paul informs that the Holy Ghost teaches and brings joy, peace, and hope: 1 Corinthians 2:12–13 and Romans 14:17

Some might wonder what the difference is between the Holy Ghost, the Holy Spirit, and "the spirit" (a term used generously by Paul in his writings). The short answer is there is no difference. The difference between "Ghost" and "Spirit" are purely translational and can be used interchangeably. Paul and Peter perhaps used the shortened version (the Spirit) for matters of expediency and ease of understanding:

- The Spirit dwells within us: 1 Corinthians 3:16 and James 4:5

- The Spirit changes the hearts of men: 2 Corinthians 3:3

- The Spirit guides: Acts 8:29, Acts 10:19, Acts 11:12, Acts 16:7, Acts 20:22, Acts 21:4, and Galatians 5:18

- The Spirit inspires righteousness: Ephesians 5:9 and Galatians 5:22

- The Spirit sanctifies: 2 Thessalonians 2:13 and 1 Peter 1:2

- The Spirit enlightens and reveals: Acts 11:27–28, 1 Peter 3:18, Romans 8:11 1 Timothy 4:1, 1 Corinthians 2:9–10, Romans 8:16, and 1 John 5:6

- The Spirit inspires: Acts 18:5, Acts 18:24–25, Acts 19:21

With the immense emphasis placed on the Holy Ghost (or the Spirit) in the New Testament, and with Paul boldly proclaiming one must have the Spirit to know God (1 Corinthians 2:11) and to be of Christ

(Romans 8:9), it is difficult to imagine a true Christian who is without the Holy Ghost.

This brings up the question that if one receives the Holy Ghost, can they lose it? The Old Testament suggests this is possible with David praying the Holy Spirit would not leave him (Psalm 51:11), while the Spirit of the Lord departed from Samson (Judges 16:20) and Saul (1 Samuel 16:14). The New Testament, however, suggests once the Holy Ghost is received, it abides with the receiver "forever" (John 14:16), sealed as an inheritance (Ephesians 1:13–14), never to be corrupted (1 Peter 1:23). Conversely, Paul makes it clear that if an individual receives the Holy Ghost and transgresses seriously enough, they will be unable to receive forgiveness (Hebrews 6:4–6), reminiscent of the unpardonable sin spoken of by Christ (Matthew 12:31–32, Mark 3:29 and Luke 12:10).

From these scriptures we learn that God chooses with whom his Spirit will dwell, and if it be that someone has the gift of the Holy Ghost and transgresses seriously enough, God will withdraw his Spirit from them. Worse yet, such a transgression invokes the possibility of far worse than just losing the spirit, but rather "If any man defile the temple of God, him shall God destroy; for the temple of God is holy, which temple ye are" (1 Corinthians 3:17).

Other Christian Values the Disciples of Christ Should Embrace

The New Testament in its *entirety* outlines a number of characteristics a Christian should posses and actions a Christian should take. The following are a few examples:

- **Assuming admirable characteristics**: 2 Corinthians 6:4–10, 2 Timothy 2:22, and 1 Peter 3:4

- **Preaching (or confessing) the gospel**: Romans 10:10, Mark 16:15, Luke 9:2, 60, Acts 5:42, Acts 10:42, 2 Timothy 4:2, and 1 Peter 3:15

- **Being pure in heart**: Matthew 5:8, 1 Timothy 1:5, and 1 Peter 1:22

- **Having Gratitude**: Colossians 3:17

- **Turning from sin**: 1 Corinthians 6:18

- **Giving with a cheerful heart**: 2 Corinthians 9:6–7

- **Praising God in the name of Jesus Christ in music and the spoken word**: (Ephesians 5:19–20)

- **Having charity**: 1 Timothy 1:5 and 1 Corinthians 13:3–8

- **Loving one another in kindness**: John 13:34, 1 John 4:7, Romans 12:10, Matthew 22:39, and Mark 12:31

- **Being a good example**: 1 Timothy 4:12 and Matthew 5:16

- **Praying always**: Philippians 4:6, Matthew 6:5–15 and Luke 18:1–14

- **Reading the scriptures**: 2 Timothy 3:16 and John 5:39

- **Serving the poor and needy**: Matthew 19:21, Luke 18:22, James 1:27 and Romans 12:13

- **Serving the Lord** (that is, serving one another): Romans 12:11, Hebrew 12:28, Galatians 5:13, Matthew 25:31–46, and 1 John 3:17–18

- **Fellowshipping with others**: 1 John 1:3

- **Being Humble**: Romans 12:3, Matthew 18:4, James 4:10, and 1 Peter 5:6

- **Seeking after righteousness**: Matthew 5:6 and 1 Timothy 6:11

- **Being merciful**: Luke 6:36 and Matthew 5:7

- **Being a peacemaker**: Matthew 5:9

- **Enduring persecutions**: Matthew 5:10, 2 Thessalonians 1:4, and Romans 12:14

- **Believing without seeing**: John 20:29 and 1 Peter 1:8

Each of these characteristics, or gospel traits, might be summed up into what are called Christian values—principles and ethics becoming of a Christian as defined by Jesus Christ *and* those who preached of Christ and offered inspired words on living a Christian life.

Summary of Defining a Christian Using the Words of the Inspired Authors of the Bible

Focusing on the words of the inspired authors of the Bible provides some validation of the words of Christ and additional considerations in defining a Christian. Summarizing the books beyond the Gospels suggests a Christian is one who

- **Believes in Jesus Christ** as the only begotten Son of God, the one true Messiah, and the only path to salvation
- **Accepts the grace of God** offered through Jesus Christ
- **Is transformed through belief in Jesus Christ** in one's heart and life
- **Repents, is baptized, and partakes of the Lord's Supper in the name of Jesus Christ** as a profession of belief and act of obedience
- **Receives the gift of the Holy Ghost**
- **Follows Jesus Christ** by following his teachings and his example
- **Sacrifices for Jesus Christ** in serving others
- **Exemplifies good works** as a result of faith in Jesus Christ
- **Lives a life that embodies Christian values**

Like the definitional outline offered using exclusively the words of Christ, this is by no means a simple definition and suffers from the same contrast of believing versus doing. However, there is significant crossover between the two perspectives, allowing a more solid definition to take shape.

THE DEFINITION OF A CHRISTIAN

After considering the many definitions of a Christian and the insights offered in chapter 5, and by adding to that our search and review of the words of Jesus Christ and the authors of the New Testament in what constitutes a Christian, we can develop a two-part definition of a Christian of our own addressing the faith-works dynamic:

Believing Christian

A *Believing Christian* is one who believes in and accepts the divinity of Jesus Christ as the only begotten Son of God, the one true Messiah, and the only pathway to the forgiveness of sin, salvation, and eternal life through the grace of God the Father.

Practicing Christian

A *Practicing Christian* is a Believing Christian who commits to living the precepts of the church they belong to, including repentance, baptism, receiving the gift of the Holy Ghost and partaking of the Lord's Supper—motivating them to keep the commandments, follow the example of Jesus Christ, make sacrifices in building and nurturing the kingdom of God, perform good works, and live a life embodying Christian values.

While the Believing Christian meets the criteria mentioned several times by the Savior for the blessings of eternal life, the degree to which a Believing Christian becomes and lives as a Practicing Christian depends on his or her level of conversion to the gospel of Jesus Christ. Those with strong and vibrant conversions will repent, be baptized, receive the gift of the Holy Ghost, and live as disciples of Christ commensurate with the faith community in which they belong according to the scriptures—coming to know God in a personal relationship. Those with weaker conversions to the gospel of Jesus Christ will be less inclined to live as disciples of Christ and therefore become more susceptible to wandering off the narrow path and into the wilderness of disbelief.

Professing in Word and in Deed

One can profess to be a Believing Christian in word, bearing testimony of faith in Jesus Christ and his divine mission. However, becoming a Practicing Christian goes far beyond profession in word only; it must include profession in deed as well showing good works and being a living example in action. Put another way, the Practicing Christian must not just "talk the talk"; they must "walk the walk." Although Christ taught eternal life comes through believing in him, the Savior was equally passionate about active discipleship, saying, "Therefore whosoever heareth these sayings of mine, and *doeth* them, I will liken him unto a wise man, which built his house upon a rock" (Matthew 7:24, emphasis added).

The Christian Discipleship Model

Diagram 1 on the following page introduces the Christian Discipleship Model, a summary of our newly formed definitions of a Christian as explained in this section:

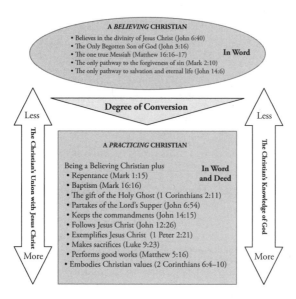

Diagram 1: The Christian Discipleship Model

Is there a greater reward in the eternities for Practicing Christians as compared to Believing Christians? On one hand, the parable of the laborers (Matthew 20:1–16) suggests all will receive a similar or even the same reward. On the other hand, the Savior suggests there may be different rewards according to our works in the "many mansions" of heaven (John 14:2). The reader is left to ponder the possibilities.

Christianity Is Not an Exclusive Club

As mentioned earlier, Jesus Christ was never one to be exclusive and rebuked John for his complaining of others doing works in the name of the Savior who were not of their group (Mark 9:38–40). Translated to modern language, the same scripture might read: "Pastor, we met a group of people claiming to be Christians who were doing good deeds but don't believe in the same things we do and we told them to stop making such claims." Will the pastor rebuke the complaining individual of their jealous remark as Jesus did, or will the pastor provide a theological dissertation as to why these other individuals who don't believe in the same doctrines and theology are not Christians and therefore worthy of such a reproach?

The definition of a Christian offered by this book will not be exclusive enough for some who are likely to complain about its lack of Trinitarian articulation, failing to mention the Bible, its inclusion of aspects that are inconsistent with their own belief system, or the exclusion of those aspects that are. To such individuals I encourage further pondering, keeping in mind the millions of Christians today that are illiterate, of little schooling, or otherwise taught the gospel in simple and meager surroundings: how deeply can such individuals understand complex theological concepts? Jesus Christ preached love (Matthew 22:37–40) and acceptance of the unapparent faithful. Therefore, be careful before judging who is and who is not a Christian.

Chapter 7

IT'S REVEALING ACCORDING
TO THE DATA

THE DEFINITIONS OF A BELIEVING CHRISTIAN AND A PRACTICING CHRIS-
tian can be put to the test; however, such a test is not trivial. Measuring
belief and practice is not a simple task and thus the caution of Jesus Christ
to "Judge not according to the appearance, but judge righteous judgment"
(John 7:24). The purpose of this chapter is not to judge, but to rather measure how effective various Christian denominations, and denominational
groupings, are performing in inspiring their members to be Believing and
Practicing Christians.

QUANTITATIVE ANALYSIS

To achieve an accurate measurement of effectiveness, we will ana-
lyze data from three robust quantitative studies conducted in the United
States from 2000 to 2008—one from the Barna Group and two from
the National Survey of Youth and Religion (NSYR). All three studies are
highly respected and widely sourced in the public domain for religiosity across a large number of behavioral attributes. The Barna and NSYR
studies are not directly correlated, but they do share common attributes
with respect to religious belief and practice (although stated slightly differently in each study). The following are the common attributes from all

three studies with example biblical references as to their importance in living as a Believing and Practicing Christian:

Attributes Relating to Belief

    a.   Belief in God (Mark 11:22 and John 5:24)

    b.   Belief in the Importance of Faith (Matthew 17:20 and Acts 14:22)

    c.   Belief in the Reality of Evil (1 Peter 5:8 and Luke 10:18)

    d.   Belief in Jesus Christ (John 6:40 and Acts 16:31)

Attributes Relating to Practice

    a.   Praying to God (1 Thessalonians 5:17 and Luke 18:1)

    b.   Reading the Bible/Scriptures (John 5:39 and 2 Timothy 3:16)

    c.   Attending Church (Hebrews 10:25 and 2 Thessalonians 2:1)

    d.   Attending Sunday School (Hebrews 10:25 and John 5:39)

    e.   Attending Small Group Activities (Matthew 18:20 and Acts 2:46)

    f.   Volunteering (Luke 9:24 and Galatians 6:10)

    g.   Sharing the Gospel (Mark 16:15 and 2 Timothy 4:2)

    h.   Paying Tithes and Offerings (Matthew 23:23 and 2 Corinthians 9:7)

One can certainly suggest a number of alternative attributes to measure a Christian's commitment to Christ and to their own Christian faith; however, the above attributes are those that are available in common for examination across the three selected studies. To that end, we are simply using what we have to synthesize and compare. The analysis will examine data for three age categories:

- **Youth**: Ages 13 to 17 using data from the wave 1 NSYR study
- **Young Adults**: Ages 18 to 23 using data from the wave 3 NSYR study

- **Adults**: Ages 18 and older using data from a Barna Group study

The National Survey of Youth and Religion (NSYR) Studies

Wave 1: The NSYR wave 1 study was conducted from July 2002 through April 2003 by researchers at the University of North Carolina at Chapel Hill using a random-digit-dial (RDD) method, employing a nationwide sample of 3,290 teenagers between the ages of thirteen and seventeen in the fifty states.[6] The study reported on the shape and influence of religion and spirituality in the lives of American youth across dozens of denominations, namely Christian, which were then compiled and categorized into denominational groupings according to the RELTRAD method. RELTRAD is a method of classifying religious tradition based on both doctrine and historical changes in religious groups. The RELTRAD categories include Black Protestant, Roman Catholic, Evangelical Protestant (or Conservative Protestant), Jewish, Mainline Protestant, no religion, and "other" religion. The other category can be further broken down into such categories as Eastern religious traditions and LDS/Mormons.[7]

Table 1 summarizes the NSYR wave 1 data across the twelve selected attributes for the Christian denominational groupings only. The NYSR elected to separate LDS/Mormons from the other category and therefore LDS/Mormon data is reported separately. All numbers are in percentages. Note the wave 1 NSYR study unfortunately did not ask any questions relating to belief in Jesus Christ:

	A	B	C	D	E	F	G	H	I	J	K	L
All Christian Youth	90	57	44	NA	71	29	47	29	30	25	48	40
Conservative Protestant	94	67	58	NA	78	27	55	36	43	28	56	41
Mainline Protestant	86	50	37	NA	66	12	44	25	35	29	51	39
Black Protestant	97	73	48	NA	82	26	41	27	23	15	41	42
Roman Catholic	85	41	28	NA	62	8	40	19	13	22	37	37
LDS/Mormon	84	69	69	NA	75	37	71	62	56	50	72	56

Table 1: NSYR Wave 1 Data (Youth)[8]

Legend of the Actual NSYR Wave 1 Data Attributes:

A=Believes in God

B=Importance of faith shaping major life decisions (extremely or very important)

C=Believes in the existence of demons or evil spirits (definitely)

D=Attribute Not Available in wave 1 NSYR data relating to belief in Christ

E=Frequency of teen praying alone (at least once a week)

F=Frequency of reaeding the scriptures alone (at least once a week)

G= Frequency of attending religious service once a week or more

H=Frequency of attending religious Sunday School (one or more times per week)

I=Frequency of attending youth group (one or more times per week)

J= Frequency of teen volunteerimg (occasionally or more)

K=Shared own religious faith with someone not of faith in the prior year

L=Donates money to a church or charity

Wave 3: The NSYR wave 3 study was conducted using a computer assisted telephone interviewing (CATI) system from September 2007 through April 2008 by researchers at the University of North Carolina at Chapel Hill. Efforts were made to recontact respondents from the NSYR wave 1 study with a resulting sample size of 2,532 young adults between the ages of eighteen and twenty-three in the fifty continental states.[9] Like the wave 1 study, the wave 3 study reported on the shape and influence of religion and spirituality in the lives of American young adults across dozens of denominations, namely Christian, which were then compiled and categorized into denominational groupings according to the REL-TRAD method. Table 2 summarizes the NSYR wave 3 data across the 12 selected attributes for the Christian denominational groupings only. All numbers are in percentages:

	A	B	C	D	E	F	G	H	I	J	K	L
All Christian Young Adults	83	48	51	75	34	7	23	12	17	15	44	35
Conservative Protestant	87	57	63	82	42	10	28	15	22	20	51	37
Mainline Protestant	68	33	32	59	24	5	12	6	15	13	42	35
Black Protestant	97	72	60	90	43	7	25	15	22	13	40	30
Roman Catholic	80	34	38	67	22	2	15	4	8	8	36	30
LDS/Mormon	83	59	73	78	54	23	60	44	37	36	65	53

Table 2: NSYR Wave 3 Data (Young Adults) [10]

Legend of the Actual NSYR Wave 3 Data Attributes:

A=Believes in God

B=Importance of religious faith shaping daily life (very or extremely important)

C=Believes in the existence of demons or evil spirits (definitely)

D=Believes Jesus Christ is the son of God

E=Frequency of young adult praying alone (daily or more)

F=Frequency of scripture reading alone (daily or more)

G=Frequency of attending religious service (once a week or more)

H=Frequency of religious Sunday School attendance (one or more times per week)

I=Is involved in any organized religious groups such as Bible study, prayer group, or religious group, not including regular worship service attendance

J=Volunteers occasionally or more

K=Shared own religious faith with someone not of faith in the prior year

L=Donates money to a church or charity

The Barna Group Study

The Barna Group study was conducted from January 2000 through June 2001 using a telephone interview methodology employing a nationwide random sample of 6,038 adults (ages eighteen and over—average age of forty-four years old) in the forty-eight contiguous states.[11] The distribution of respondents coincided with the geographic dispersion of the US adult population. The study reported the religious activities and behaviors among twelve denominational groupings based upon respondent self-reporting of the church they most often attend. Although the twelve groupings are relevant, there is an understanding that some denominations encompass more than one denomination associated with that label (for example, there are more than two dozen Baptist denominations in the US). Some denominations were excluded due to small sample sizes. Table 3 summarizes the Barna Group data across the twelve available attributes (all numbers are in percentages), with "All Adults" defined as all adults who participated in the study—Christian and non-Christian:

	A	B	C	D	E	F	G	H	I	J	K	L
All Adults	69	68	27	40	82	38	43	16	15	16	32	18
Adventist	76	73	37	45	79	49	47	18	27	16	42	16
Assembly of God	96	86	56	70	93	66	69	35	29	30	61	22
Baptist (any type)	85	81	34	55	92	55	50	30	22	19	51	20
Catholics	70	68	17	33	88	23	48	6	8	12	17	13
Church of Christ	80	81	36	54	92	53	58	37	28	22	51	29
Episcopal	59	60	20	28	85	30	30	11	13	19	12	17
Lutheran (any type)	72	63	21	33	84	32	43	13	13	19	27	21
Methodist (any)	73	74	18	33	90	43	49	18	15	19	28	23
LDS/Mormon	84	90	59	70	95	67	71	62	27	40	55	24

Christian non-denominational	89	86	48	63	94	66	61	21	32	22	59	26
Pentecostal/ Foursquare	90	94	47	73	97	75	66	36	37	25	73	27
Presbyterian (any)	76	71	22	45	89	48	49	17	18	26	33	17

Table 3: Barna Group Data (Adults) [12, 13]

Legend of the Actual Barna Group Data Attributes:

A=Believes that God is the all-powerful, all-knowing perfect creator of the universe who rules the world today

B=Strongly agrees that their religious faith is very important

C=Strongly disagrees that Satan is just a symbol of evil

D=Christ was sinless

E=Prayed to God in past seven days

F=Read from the Bible, other than while at church, in past seven days

G=Attended a church service, other than a special event such as a wedding or funeral, in past seven days

H=Attended a Sunday School class at a church, in past seven days

I=Participate in a small group that meets regularly for Bible study, prayer or Christian fellowship, not including a Sunday School or twelve-step group, in past seven days

J=Volunteer at your church in past seven days

K=Strongly agrees that they have a personal responsibility to tell others about their religious beliefs

L=Donates money

Alignment of Attributes and Denominational Groupings

Before conducting the analysis it was necessary to align the twelve attributes from all three studies and to group the twelve denominations used in the Barna Group study into the RELTRAD method. This alignment was necessary in order to achieve "apples to apples" comparisons across denominational groupings along the three age categories for all three studies.

Alignment of the Twelve Attributes: Table 4 shows the alignment of the twelve attributes across all three studies, describing each attribute as it appeared in the study:

	Barna Study Attribute Descriptions		NSYR Wave 1 Study Attribute Descriptions		NSYR Wave 3 Study Attribute Descriptions
A	Believes that God is the all-powerful, all-knowing perfect creator of the universe who rules the world today	→	Believes in God	→	Believes in God
B	Strongly agrees that their religious faith is very important	→	Importance of religious faith shaping major life decisions (very to extremely important)	→	Importance of religious faith shaping daily life (very or extremely important)
C	Strongly disagrees that Satan is just a symbol of evil	→	Believes in the existence of demons or evil spirits (definitely)	→	Believes in the existence of demons or evil spirits (definitely)
D	Christ was sinless	→	Questions relating to Jesus Christ were not asked during this wave	→	Believe Jesus Christ is the son of God
E	Prayed to God in past 7 days	→	Frequency of teen praying alone (at least once a week)	→	Frequency of young adult praying alone (daily or more)
F	Read from the Bible, other than while at church in past 7 days	→	Frequency of scripture reading alone (at least once a week)	→	Frequency of scripture reading alone (daily or more)

G	Attended a church service, other than a special event such as a wedding or funeral, in past 7 days	→	Attending religious service once a week or more	→	Attending religious service once a week or more
H	Attended a Sunday School class at a church in past 7 days	→	Frequency of religious Sunday School attendance (one or more times per week)	→	Frequency of religious Sunday School attendance (one or more times per week)
I	Participate in a small group that meets regularly for Bible study, prayer, or Christian fellowship, not including a Sunday School or 12-step group, in past 7 days	→	Attribute of Frequency of youth group attendance (one or more times per week)	→	Is involved in any organized religious groups such as Bible study, prayer group, or religious group, not including regular worship service attendance
J	Volunteer at your church in past 7 days	→	Volunteers occasionally or more	→	Volunteers occasionally or more
K	Strongly agrees that they have a personal responsibility to tell others about their religious beliefs	→	Shared own religious faith with someone not of faith in the prior year	→	Shared own religious faith with someone not of faith in the prior year
L	Donates money	→	Donates money to church or charity	→	Donates money to church or charity

Table 4: Alignment of the NSYR and Barna Group Data Attibutes

There are obvious variations in attributes, especially between the Barna Group study and the NSYR studies. Believing Jesus Christ was sinless (Barna) is different than believing Jesus Christ is the Son of God (NYSR wave 3). However, despite such variations, the alignments are sufficient to provide high-level assessments and comparisons of the beliefs and practices of the denominational groupings being examined.

Denominational Alignment: The alignment between the wave 1 and wave 3 NSYR studies is of no consequence since both used the REL-TRAD method of categorization. Table 5 provides a summary of how denominations were grouped in the NSYR studies according to the REL-TRAD method. If you are a Christian, see if you can find the denomination you belong to:

Denominational Grouping	Christian Denominations Included
Conservative Protestant	American Baptist Association, American Baptist Churches in the USA, Assemblies of God, Bible Church/ Bible Believing, Calvary Chapel, Charismatic, Charismatic Baptist, Christian and Missionary Alliance. Christian Reformed Church, Church of Christ, Church of God. Church of God International, Church of God of Anderson, Indiana, Church of God of Cleveland, Tennessee, Free Will Baptist, Full Gospel, Fundamentalist, Fundamentalist Baptist, General Association of Regular Baptists, General Baptist, General Conference, Grace Brethren Church, Holiness, Independent, Independent Baptist, Interdenominational Protestant, Mennonite, Missionary Association, Missionary Baptist, Missouri Synod, Evangelical Free Church, Evangelical Presbyterian Church, Four Square, Free Methodist, Free Will Baptist, Full Gospel, Fundamentalist, Fundamentalist Baptist, General Association of Regular Baptists, General Baptist, General Conference, Grace Brethren Church, Holiness, Independent, Independent Baptist, Interdenominational Protestant, Mennonite, Missionary Association, Missionary Baptist, Missouri Synod, National Missionary Baptist Convention, Nondenominational, North American Baptist Conference, Other Church of God, Pentecostal Holiness Church, Plymouth Brethren, Presbyterian Church in America, Reformed Presbyterian Churches of North America, Seventh-day Adventist, Southern Baptist Convention, Spanish Pentecostal, United Pentecostal Church International, Wesleyan Methodist, Wisconsin Synod, Worldwide Church of God

Mainline Protestant	Congregationalist, Disciples of Christ, Episcopalian, Evangelical Lutheran Church in America, Moravian Northern Baptist, Presbyterian Churches of the USA, Quaker or Friends, Reformed Church in America, United Brethren in Christ, United Church of Christ, United Methodist Church
Black Protestant	African Methodist Episcopal Church, African Methodist Episcopal Zion, American Baptist Churches in the USA, American Baptist Association, Apostolic Pentecostal, Christian Methodist Episcopal, Church of God in Christ, Church of God in the Apostolic Faith, Church of God International, Churches of Christ, Holiness, Independent Baptist, Interdenominational Protestant, Missionary Baptist, National Baptist Convention of America, National Baptist Convention, USA, Inc., National missionary Baptist Convention, Nondenominational, Southern Baptist Convention, United Baptist Church of God
Roman Catholic	Roman Catholic
LDS/Mormon	The Church of Jesus Christ of Latter-day Saints (LDS) or Mormon

Table 5: RELTRAD Categorizations used by the NSYR[14]

The groupings in Table 5 are not exhaustive but rather meant to provide an idea of how individual Christian denominations were categorized into the five denominational groupings according to the RELTRAD method in the NSYR studies. In cases where overlap was possible, there were questions in the NYSR surveys relating to ethnicity in order to clearly classify each respondent.

With respect to the Barna Group data, which was not originally classified according to the RELTRAD method, Table 6 shows the alignment made for the purposes of our exercise. The alignment is consistent with the classification in Table 5 with the exception of Black Protestants, who are disbursed among the Conservative and Mainline Protestant groupings according to the selected denomination (Methodist, Presbyterian, and so on).

Since the Barna Group data did not follow the RELTRAD method of denominational grouping, the segmentation of Black Protestants is not

	Barna Study		NSYR Studies
CP	Adventist Assembly of God Church of Christ Pentecostal/Four Square Baptist Christian non-Denominational	➡	Conservative Protestant
MP	Episcopal Lutheran Methodist Presbyterian	➡	Mainline Protestant
RC	Catholics	➡	Roman Catholic
LDS	LDS/Mormon	➡	LDS/Mormon
BP	No Available Category		Black Protestant

Table 6: RELTRAD Alignment with the Barna Group data

available and thus will be removed from the analysis. In general, Black Protestants have the effect of slightly raising the averages for the believing attributes among Protestants and slightly lowering the averages for the practicing attributes among Protestants. The dispersion of Black Protestants in the Barna Group data does not materially affect the final results for the individual denominational groupings.

Table 7 (see page opposite) shows the Barna Group data recalculated using the RELTRAD method. The "All Adults" portion now represents all Christians surveyed, non-Christians having been removed from the data.

Limitations of the Exercise

Three primary limitations to this data comparison exercise should be well understood before commencing. The first relates to the inconsistency of faith traditions among the denominational groupings. For example, Catholic faith traditions do not include regular personal scripture reading, Sunday School attendance, or small group activities, so the Catholic percentages relating to these attributes are predictably low. Regardless of how appropriate an attribute of belief or practice is from a biblical

	A	B	C	D	E	F	G	H	I	J	K	L
All Adults	78	77	34	49	91	47	55	28	19	23	38	20
Conservative Protestant	86	83	39	58	92	59	54	29	26	21	54	22
Mainline Protestant	72	69	20	35	87	39	45	16	15	20	27	21
Roman Catholic	70	68	17	33	88	23	48	6	8	12	17	13
LDS/Mormon	84	90	59	70	95	67	71	62	27	40	55	24

Table 7: Barna Group data recalculated in RELTRAD[15]

perspective, it does not mean the attribute has become part of the fabric of religious tradition and culture of one or more Christian denominations.

The second limitation relates to the comparability of the attributes. In some cases, the attributes from the three studies are not "one-to-one." For example, relating to volunteering, this exercise compares the Barna Group's survey question of having volunteered in the past seven days with the NSYR's wave 1 and 3 survey questions on having volunteered occasionally or more. Or relating to evil in the world, the exercise compares the Barna Group's survey question on whether or not Satan is real or simply a symbol of evil, with the NSYR's wave 1 and wave 3 survey questions on whether demons or evil spirits exist. In both of these cases, the attributes are similar but not identical.

The third limitation is the accuracy of applying a quantitative measurement to something that is inherently qualitative to a subject matter that is full of interpretational nuances. The wording of questions and the meaning of terms can have a tremendous impact on the way individuals provide their answers. The book *America's Four Gods: What We Say about God—and What That Says about Us* by Paul Froese and Christopher Bader bring this point home, stating, "it is not clear what Americans mean when they talk about God."[16] Knowing their expertise in conducting studies in religiosity, I am satisfied the research teams at Barna and the University of North Carolina at Chapel Hill fully comprehended this dynamic in their study designs in order to minimize this effect.

These three limitations, although meaningful, are certainly acceptable given the high-level nature of this exercise. Keep in mind again that the purpose of this exercise is to examine *leading* indicators of belief and practice among denominational groupings in order to measure their effectiveness in inspiring their members in matters of religiosity. If one grouping scores a 60 on a given attribute and another grouping scores 40 on the same attribute, then we can reasonably conclude the first grouping is doing a better job than the second grouping in inspiring members to live that particular attribute.

ANALYSIS RESULTS

Table 8 provides a data summary for Christian youth (YO), young adults (YA), and adults (AD) across the twelve attributes for the comparable denominational groupings for all three studies combined. Included in the table are composite scores (mean averages) for each of the attributes and age categories within each denominational grouping. The composite scores act as indexes of effectiveness for individual attributes as well as the combined belief (B) and practice (P) attributes. The "Integrated" label is an average of all scores (belief and practice) into one number representing a total religiosity score.

General Legend

A= Belief in God

B= Belief in the importance of religious faith

C= Belief in the existence of evil

D= Belief in Jesus Christ

E= Practice of personal prayer

F= Practice of scripture reading

G= Practice of attending religious services

H= Practice of attending Sunday School

I= Practice of participating in small group religious activities

J= Practice of volunteering

K= Practice of sharing religious faith with others

L= Practice of donating money to church or charity

Universal (Total) Results and Observations

Looking at all age groups combined across all denominational groupings provides an immediate set of observations about the whole of Christianity in the United States. The belief composite is, predictably, significantly higher than the practice composite, indicating more faith (believing) than works (practicing) across all denominations. This is especially true among young adults whose busy lives are conducted at the expense of spending time in spiritual activities.

	A	B	C	D	E	F	G	H	I	J	K	L	Composite
TOTALS													
YO	90	57	44	0	71	29	47	29	30	25	48	40	B = 64, P = 40
YA	83	48	51	75	34	7	23	12	17	15	44	35	B = 64, P = 23
AD	78	77	34	49	91	47	55	28	19	23	38	20	B = 51, P = 33
Composite	81	58	41	58	62	25	38	19	21	19	41	31	
Integrated	Belief (B) = 59			Practice (P) = 32									Total = 39
CONSERVATIVE PROTESTANT													
YO	94	67	58	0	78	27	55	36	43	28	56	41	B = 73, P = 46
YA	87	57	63	82	42	10	28	15	22	20	51	37	B = 72, P = 28
AD	86	83	39	58	92	59	54	29	26	21	54	22	B = 66, P = 45
Composite	89	69	53	70	71	32	46	27	30	23	54	33	
Integrated	Belief (B) = 70			Practice (P) = 39									Total = 48
MAINLINE PROTESTANT													
YO	86	50	37	0	66	12	44	25	35	29	51	39	B = 58, P = 38
YA	68	33	32	59	24	5	12	6	15	13	42	35	B = 48, P = 19

AD	72	69	20	35	87	39	45	16	15	20	27	21	B = 49, P = 34
Composite	75	51	30	47	59	19	34	16	22	21	40	32	
Integrated	Belief (B) = 51				Practice (P) = 30								Total = 36
CATHOLIC													
YO	85	41	28	0	62	8	40	19	13	22	37	37	B = 51, P = 30
YA	80	34	38	67	22	2	15	4	8	8	36	30	B = 55, P = 16
AD	70	68	17	33	88	23	48	6	8	12	17	13	B = 47, P = 27
Composite	78	48	28	50	57	11	34	10	10	14	30	27	
Integrated	Belief (B) = 51				Practice (P) = 24								Total = 32
LDS/MORMON													
YO	84	69	69	0	75	37	71	62	56	50	72	56	B = 74, P = 60
YA	83	59	73	78	54	23	60	44	37	36	65	53	B = 73, P = 47
AD	84	90	59	70	95	67	71	62	27	40	55	24	B = 76, P = 55
Composite	84	73	67	74	75	42	67	56	40	42	64	44	
Integrated	Belief (B) = 74				Practice (P) = 54								Total = 59

Table 8: Consolidated Scores Across all Studies [17]

Another observation is the relative decrease in belief and practice over time. With the exception of the LDS/Mormon grouping, where faith increased with age, for all denominational groupings, belief and practice appear to become weaker with age. Notice, however, that practice is strong among youth, decreases significantly during the young adult years, and then increases during adulthood.

Graph 1 provides a pictorial summary of the composite scores for the three age categories across all twelve attributes for all denominational groupings mapped against the total population (All). The graph is followed by brief summaries for each of the denominational groupings.

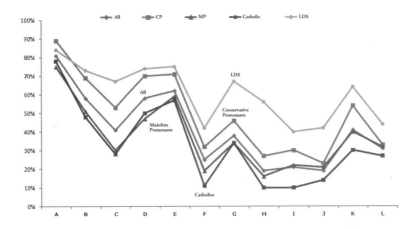

Graph 1: Composite Scores for all Denominational Groupings

Conservative Protestants: Conservative Protestants (CP) outperform the total population across all attributes, signifying a strong system of Christian belief and practice among its denominations. Particular strength is demonstrated in the belief attributes of the existence of evil (C), belief in Jesus Christ (D), and personal prayer (E). Conservative Protestant separation from the total population is weakest for the attributes of volunteering (J) and the practice of donating money to a church or charity (L).

Mainline Protestants: Mainline Protestants (MP) map closely to the total population, being slightly weaker than the total population across the belief attributes (A through D). Despite the large volume of Catholics in the United States, the mirrored mapping of the Mainline Protestant scores to that of the total Christian population suggest the average Christian in America believes and practices much like a Mainline Protestant.

Catholics: Catholics scored lower than the total populations across all twelve attributes, signifying a weak system of Christian belief and practice among its congregations. Because the faith traditions of Catholicism do not include several of the attributes relating to practice, the lower scores were predictable; however, the weaker scores for belief in the importance of religious faith (B) and belief in Jesus Christ (D) suggest a less committed and less knowledgeable Christian population than the total population. Given the tremendous volume of Catholics in the United States, it is clear the weaknesses in belief and practice among Catholicism dramatically lower the scores for the entire Christian population of the country.

LDS/Mormons: Latter-day Saints outperform the total population across all twelve attributes combined with particular strengths demonstrated in the belief of the existence of evil (C), belief in Jesus Christ (D), attending religious services (G) and Sunday School (H), participation in small group activities (I), volunteering (J), and sharing religious beliefs (K). With the exception of belief in God (A) where Conservative Protestants scored the highest, LDS/Mormons outperformed all denominational groupings across the remaining eleven attributes for belief and practice.

In trying to explain the high scores of LDS/Mormons across all attributes, one might turn to the historical emphasis of full member participation. Joseph Smith, the founder of the LDS/Mormon Church, once said, "a religion that does not require the sacrifice of all things never has the power sufficient to produce the faith necessary unto life and salvation."[18] Culture is another aspect worth considering. In her book *Almost Christian: What the Faith of Our Teenagers Is Telling the American Church*, Kenda Creasy Dean includes a chapter titled "Mormon Envy," attributing the disproportionately high scores among LDS/Mormon teenagers in the NSYR wave 1 study to a strong culture of religiosity and devotion within The Church of Jesus Christ of Latter-day Saints.[19] This brief exercise suggests the LDS/Mormon Church is doing the most effective job in inspiring its members to live the twelve selected attributes of belief and practice, followed by Conservative Protestants.

As a final note, analysis of the scores reveals a generality that the older the denominational grouping the lower its scores—following somewhat the organizational life cycle mentioned in section one. Catholicism is the oldest of all of the denominational groupings and records the lowest scores across all attributes and age groups. Mainline Protestantism includes older denominations such as Presbyterian, Methodist, and Lutheran, in some cases formed shortly after the reformation, with scores only slightly above that of Catholicism. Conservative Protestantism includes denominations formed during and after the Great Awakenings, followed closely by Mormonism, which is less than 200 years old (one-tenth the age of the Roman Catholic Church). One might hypothesize the older the denomination, the more complacent its institutions have become.

Age Effect on the Numbers

Breaking up the composite scores into age groups reveals interesting insights among the denominational groupings. Graph 2 provides a pictorial view of the composite scores for **1) core beliefs** (belief in God and Jesus Christ—attributes A and D); **2) all beliefs** combined (attributes A through D), and **3) all practices** (attributes E through L) among youth, young adults, and adults, respectively. Because Black Protestant data was available for the youth and young adult populations, it has been added to this particular analysis regarding age.

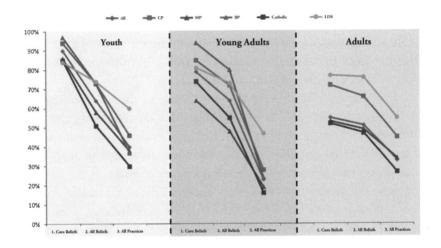

Graph 2: Composite Scores by Age for all Denominational Groupings

Graph 2 highlights how Black Protestants among youth and young adults excel in the belief-related attributes for youth and young adults; however, Black Protestant youth and young adult scores drop sharply for the practice-related attributes. We are unable to understand how those dynamics carry over into adulthood due to the unavailability of Black Protestant data for adults. And while LDS/Mormons enjoy the highest scores for all three categories among adults, LDS/Mormon youth and young adults—despite scoring the highest among all denominations for practices—score lower on the belief-related categories.

Catholics are weak across all three categories among all age groups, with Mainline Protestants scoring the lowest in the belief categories for young adults. Conservative Protestants are consistently strong in all three categories across all ages but record the most dramatic gaps between beliefs and practices, suggesting a strong emphasis on faith and less emphasis on works. LDS/Mormons on the other hand record the lowest differentials between beliefs and practices, suggesting a more balanced emphasis on both faith and works.

MAKING SENSE OF THE DATA

Several articles and books have been written, analyzing and explaining the data outlined in this chapter for all three studies. As a professional researcher, it took all the self-control I could muster to keep the analysis of the data simple and to the point, maintaining the focus of identifying how denominational groupings are performing in inspiring their members to live a Christian life in belief and practice.

If you are a Christian, you belong to one of these denominational groupings and can likely testify of yourself or others who fit the mold illustrated in these numbers or buck the trend by being weaker or stronger than the data suggests. One of the object lessons here is to apply these studies to yourself and conduct a self-inventory of how you are performing personally across these twelve attributes of belief and practice. Anyone can develop a clever definition of a Christian that fits a set of carefully selected biblical passages and claim to be a disciple of Christ; however, walking the walk of a Christian is an entirely different story which is why Jesus Christ taught, "by their fruits ye shall know them" (Matthew 7:20).

Indeed, defining a Christian is *revealing* according to the data. Perhaps instead of asking someone "Are you Christian?" the more relevant question might be "How strong of a Christian are you?"

Chapter 8

IT'S COMPLICATED ACCORDING TO THE CRITICS

THE EXISTENCE OF MODERN-DAY PHARISEES—THE "CRITICS" AMONG the Christian community—complicates matters in sustainably defining a Christian. Modern-day Pharisees are not Jews or other non-Christians, but rather Christian detractors who dubiously criticize other Christians or entire Christian denominations just as the Pharisees of old criticized Jesus Christ and his ministry. The existence of such critics is nothing new. Jesus Christ during his public ministry was often confronted by the Pharisees who challenged his authority and spiritual legitimacy. The word "Pharisee" comes from the Latin word *pharisæus*, meaning "set apart."[1] As a movement that began around the time of the Hasmonean Dynasty (140–37 BC),[2] the Pharisees viewed themselves as defenders of the Mosaic Law and the oral Torah as part of a renewal movement that was devout, political, cultural, social, religious, and educational.

PARALLELS OF ANCIENT AND MODERN-DAY PHARISEES

To understand how Pharisees can exist today, one must consider the parallels between these and ancient religious cynics. For example, Modern-day Pharisees believe they are the keepers and defenders of Christian doctrine as they interpret it from the Bible, just as the ancient Pharisees believed they were the keepers and defenders of the true spiritual law of God as they interpreted it from the Torah. Modern-day Pharisees are prideful and closed-minded to Christian beliefs they perceive to be in contrast to their own; just as the ancient Pharisees were prideful and closed-minded to the teachings of Christ, which they perceived to be in contrast to the Mosaic law. A review of the pharisaical pattern and how that pattern is repeated by Modern-day Pharisees provides a glimpse into how these contemporary Christian critics are alive and well in the present.

THE PHARISAICAL PATTERN

A study of the New Testament reveals a specific pattern of behaviors and attitudes among the Pharisees of Jesus's time—a pattern that will be referred to as the *pharisaical pattern*. This pattern can still be observed today among the Pharisees of our time:

- **Pride and Hypocrisy**: The Pharisees were prideful, believing they were the chosen people through privilege, being already saved and not in need of any counsel or direction from those they considered to be inferior. The pride of the Pharisees evolved into hypocrisy. The became blind to the truth, thinking they were right when in actuality they were wrong, often leading to the teaching of false doctrine.

- **Panic and Paranoia**: Panic and paranoia took hold of the Pharisees, who found fault with teachings they had not studied or experienced. They believed evil of that which was good, and focused on the letter of the law and not the spirit of the law. A lack of faith led them to discount miracles, rejecting the influence of the spirit of God.

- **Contention and Destruction**: Being afraid of the truth and the threat of that truth to their personal and professional disposition, the Pharisees became jealous, contentious, accusatory, demanding, deceptive, and frustrated when exposed in their stratagem. When all else failed, the Pharisees sought to destroy according to the tradition of their fathers.

Even after the death of Christ, the scriptures suggest the Pharisees continued their pharisaical pattern, originating in pride and ending with the persecution—even the death in some cases—of the Christians. Although one might find relief that this pattern of bigotry fizzled away with time, the fact is that it has not. Although the Pharisees as a movement came to a historical end, the world has endured pharisaical behaviors and attitudes ever since, keeping the pattern alive. Just as the Pharisees of old, Modern-day Pharisees are oblivious to their attitudes and actions, believing they are the defenders of the true gospel. In actuality, they leave a wake of division and contention behind them.

PRIDE AND HYPOCRISY OF MODERN-DAY PHARISEES

Modern-day Pharisees Are Prideful

Jesus described the Pharisees as loving the "uppermost rooms at feasts," enlarging "the borders of their garments," and being "called of men, Rabbi, Rabbi" (Matthew 23:2–7). John described the Pharisees as loving "the praise of men more than the praise of God" (John 12:43). The Savior told the parable of a Pharisee in the temple who exalted himself above the publican in prayer (Luke 18:10–11), revealing the pride of the Pharisees who felt they were the chosen people of Abraham (Matthew 3:9).

Today some Modern-day Pharisees harbor the same prideful disposition and lack the type of humility that should characterize a disciple of Christ. Such individuals might include ministers who relish in the spotlight of attention among their congregation, or individuals who presume their belief system to be superior to that of others, openly criticizing people or religions not of their faith. Such pharisaical attitudes inhibit personal growth and breed division among the children of God, especially among Christians.

Modern-day Pharisees are Hypocritical and Blind

The Bible suggests Jesus spent a considerable amount of time engaging with the Pharisees. On multiple occasions Jesus proclaimed the Pharisees to be hypocrites (or full of hypocrisy)—eight times in one continuous sermon as recorded in Matthew chapter 23 (verses 13–15 and 23–29). Hypocrisy among the Pharisees generally came in the form of attempting to appear holy and righteous on the outside while on the inside being despicable and heartless. In describing the Pharisees, Jesus quoted Esaias, saying, "This people honoureth me with their lips, but their heart is far from me" (Mark 7:6; see also Matthew 15:7–9), accusing them of teaching "the commandments of men." Not only did the Savior consider the Pharisees to be unrighteous (Matthew 5:20), but he also warned the people of "the leaven of the Pharisees, which is hypocrisy" (Luke 12:1) and their teaching of false doctrine (Matthew 16:12 and Mark 8:15). The Pharisees were considered to be spiritually blind (Matthew 23:16–22) in their twisting of doctrines and principles, even as they believed themselves to be teaching the correct doctrines and principles (John 9:39–41).

Today, Modern-day Pharisees exhibit the same hypocritical behaviors. Some of the more well-known cases might include TV evangelist Jimmy Swaggart, who for many years openly preached the gospel of Jesus Christ only to be caught with a prostitute in 1988 and again in 1991.[3] Or TV evangelist Jim Bakker, who became entangled in a sex scandal that led to his imprisonment on accounting fraud.[4] More recently was Ted Haggard, leader of the National Association of Evangelicals (NAE) from 2003 until 2006, who preached against homosexuality and publicly mocked Catholics, Mormons, Muslims, and Jews[5] and then later admitted to sexual immorality and purchasing illegal drugs.[6] in 2006.

More common may be less-known ministers who preach biblical interpretations that rationalize certain lifestyles relating to money, sex and other forms of immorality. Even more typical are individuals who give the public impression of living a holy and Christian life while behind closed doors live a repeated pattern of purposeful sin and indulgence. Such pharisaical practices discourage and frustrate the impressionable seeker of truth and turn away the spiritually hungry from the word of God. As humans, we all sin, but when we conceal sin from others behind a cloak of imaginary righteousness as a spiritual leader or influencer, the work of the Modern-day Pharisee is in full bloom.

THE PANIC AND PARANOIA OF
MODERN-DAY PHARISEES

Modern-day Pharisees Find Fault and Focus on the Letter of the Law

The Pharisees found fault with Jesus and his doctrine, although few ever took the time to listen and learn as a disciple. When certain Pharisees took the time to listen to Jesus, they were moved (John 7:32–48). The Pharisees were obsessively focused on the Mosaic law, accusing Jesus and his disciples of not keeping the Sabbath (Matthew 12:2, Mark 2:24, John 9:13–16, Luke 6:1–10, and Luke 14:1–6), making company with sinners (Mark 2:16, Matthew 9:11, and Luke 5:30–33), and not keeping the Jewish traditions (Matthew 15:1–6 and Luke 11:37–42). The Pharisees ignored the spirit of the law, which includes love and compassion (Luke 7:36–50). In desperation, the Pharisees proclaimed the good works being performed by the Savior was the work of evil (Matthew 9:34 and 12:24). They were unable to realize that the scriptures they used to defend the law and reject Jesus were the same scriptures that testified of Jesus and his ministry.

Modern-day Pharisees, much like the ones of old, criticize other Christian religions—often based upon superficial study and ignorance. They arrogantly focus exclusively on their own biblical interpretations and refuse others the right to do the same, even going as far as to ascribe the good fruit of certain sects of Christianity they disagree with as the work of evil. Before Paul's conversion, he was exceptionally well versed in the scriptures as a Pharisee and believed wholeheartedly that Christianity was wrong (having the supposed scriptural knowledge to prove it). Upon his conversion the scriptures did not change; only Paul's perception and interpretation of the very same scriptures changed, allowing him to see the truth. Before his conversion Paul suffered from "Saul's Syndrome"—a well-intentioned religious belief that was in actuality incorrect.

Modern-day Pharisees Lack Faith and Minimize
the Influence of the Spirit

Jesus told the Apostle Thomas, "blessed are they that have not seen, and yet have believed" (John 20:29), meaning there are some things that are not empirical and can only be realized in faith. The Pharisees demanded a sign from Jesus (Matthew 12:38–39, Matthew 16:1–4 and Mark 8:10–13), while discounting and explaining away the miracles wrought by the Savior (John 9:17–34) and rejecting God's counsel (Luke 7:30).

The Pharisees of our time replace the seeking of signs with the need for empirical biblical proof, debating theology as if it were a game of tennis. They look for signs despite Paul's teaching that "Eye hath not seen, nor ear heard, neither have entered into the heart of man, the things which God hath prepared for them that love him. But God hath revealed them unto us by his Spirit" (1 Corinthians 2:9–10); the Modern-day Pharisee is quick to bask in the warmth of the Spirit but is slow to rely on the inspiration of the Spirit.

THE CONTENTION AND DESTRUCTION OF MODERN-DAY PHARISEES

Modern-day Pharisees are Afraid, Contentious, Accusatory, Demanding and Deceptive

The ministry of the Savior threatened the Pharisees: they became afraid of the truth (Matthew 27:62–64 and Luke 19:37–40) and how that truth might impact their influence. The fear of the Pharisees was preceded and proceeded by contention (John 8:13), accusations of blasphemy (Luke 5:21, Matthew 26:65, Mark 2:7, Mark 14:64, and John 10:33), jealousy (Luke 16:14 and John 12:19), demands for answers (Luke 17:20), deception (Luke 11:53–54, Matthew 22:15–22, 34–40, John 8:3–9, Matthew 19:3–9, Mark 10:2–9, and Mark 12:13–17), and anger (Matthew 21:45–46).

The pattern of the Jesus-era Pharisee is repeated in the present day as ministers and individuals create strife and discord among Christians in a quest to prove who's right. For those in the ministry, fear could come the form of loss of income. For the individual, fear potentially comes in the form of loss of social status or self-esteem. Contention today can easily be seen in religious online forums, social media and websites, with accusations of blasphemy in rich abundance toward those in disagreement. Jealousy comes when Christlike attitudes clash with anger-filled viewpoints, leading to demands for historical biblical and archeological evidence. The pattern completes itself with cleverly worded questions and deceptive content that spawn anger and frustration. Christians are called to defend the gospel (Philemon 1:7, 17); however, when defense becomes a plan of contention (Philemon 1:16), the line of foolishness is crossed (Titus 3:9), and the Modern-day Pharisee bears the responsibility of division among the saints.

During the Republican primary elections in 2007, Dr. James Dobson of Focus on the Family challenged the Christian credentials of then-candidate Senator Fred Thompson. Despite Thompson's being raised in the Churches of Christ and attending church regularly,[7] Dobson said of Thompson, "Everyone knows he's conservative and has come out strongly for the things that the pro-family movement stands for . . . [but] I don't think he's a Christian; at least that's my impression."[8] Richard Land, the head of the Ethics and Religious Liberty Commission at the Southern Baptist Convention, said in 2011 of Mormonism, "It's just not Christianity. It's another religion, like Islam."[9] Dobson and Land likely see themselves as defenders of the faith, making statements such as these that add nothing to a positive and productive public discourse on Christianity. Are Dobson and Land defenders of the faith or Modern-day Pharisees? I will allow the reader to decide.

On a grander scale was the 2012 presidential election, during which the airwaves were full of politically conservative Christians calling to express their dismay with a Mormon-Catholic ticket in Mitt Romney and Paul Ryan. The two men were billed as the first ticket without a Protestant since Abraham Lincoln, and discontent was fueled by religious bloggers such as CNN's Stephen Prothero, who proclaimed, "Billy Graham and Ralph Reed are putting politics before God" in their support of the Romney-Ryan ticket,[0] Many conservative Christians vowed never to vote for a Mormon or a Catholic despite the fact that the Romney-Ryan partnership was more in line with their philosophical views (prolife, pro–traditional marriage, and so forth) than was Barack Obama. Post-election analysis suggests the absence of this traditionally strong Republican voting base may have cost Romney-Ryan the election given their overwhelming victory among independents. If any conservative Christian either refrained from voting or voted for Barack Obama solely based on the religious affiliation of Mitt Romney or Paul Ryan, such a person clearly harbors pharisaical tendencies.

Modern-day Pharisees Turn to Destruction When All Else Fails

In the centuries before Christ, it was common for the ancestors of the Pharisees to kill those prophets with whom they disagreed (Matthew 23:31). After repeatedly failing to curtail the success of the Savior's ministry, the Pharisees began tracking him (John 11:57), conspiring against him (Matthew 12:14, Luke 6:11 and John 11:47–53), and working to take him (John 18:3) with the intention of putting him to death at the hands of Pontius Pilate.

Although Modern-day Pharisees are less likely to turn to physical violence against those they spiritually disagree with, in today's media-driven world there are other ways of destroying or seriously harming a person or an entire religion. Local and national movements among individuals and entire Christian denominations have in the past attacked other Christian denominations using pamphlets, books, and flyers. Today, the attack vehicles have evolved into websites, blogs, and forums. In many cases, these materials go beyond contentious debate and accusations against a particular Christian denomination and into vicious attacks that seek to destroy religious credibility and leave the denomination for dead in a virtual sense. In a word, the creators of such materials seek to *crucify* the Christian denomination they are in disagreement with—much like the Pharisees of old. One need only search the Internet using terms such as "anti-[insert denomination]" to gain access to a plethora of crucifying content and materials against that particular denomination. This is especially true for Catholicism, Evangelicalism, and Mormonism.

THE MODERN-DAY PHARISEE EXERCISE

Are you or someone you know a Modern-day Pharisee? Although the short answer may be no, the qualified answer may surprise you. In table 9 on page 139 is a set of questions that help rate the degree of pharisaical attitude of the person completing the exercise. To obtain a rating, the individual must answer each question on a scale of 1 to 5 according to the likelihood of exhibiting that particular attitude or behavior per the following:

1 = not likely at all

2 = not likely

3 = somewhat likely

4 = likely

5 = very likely

Honesty is the key to an accurate score. The exercise examines attitude more than action in measuring the likelihood of acting upon each one of these scenarios, which correspond directly to the very actions taken by the Pharisees toward Jesus. After completing the exercise, a total score can be derived at the bottom of the grid by adding up the numbers selected for each of the questions.

	1	2	3	4	5
1. How likely are you to believe you are more privileged or blessed, as a result of your religious beliefs, than those of one or more Christian denominations that are not your own?					
2. How likely are you to reject the notion that you can be educated on spiritual matters from those who do not adhere to the same Christian beliefs as you?					
3. How likely are you to lead people to believe that you live a strong Christian life when in reality you do not?					
4. How likely are you to believe the scriptural interpretations you embrace are the only true interpretations and leave no room for others to have their own scriptural interpretation?					
5. How likely are you to provide spiritual guidance to others on matters you know little or nothing about?					
6. How likely are you to privately criticize or mock other Christian religions or individuals whose beliefs are contrary to your own?					
7. How likely are you to call the beliefs of another self-proclaimed Christian evil?					
8. How likely are you to challenge the Christian credentials of a self-described Christian solely based upon their religion?					
9. How likely are you to place a higher value on maintaining scriptural purity than on respecting basic Christian values?					

10. How likely are you to reject believing a doctrine, practice, principle, or event that has no scriptural evidence to support it but does not contradict the scriptures either?					
11. How likely are you to reject the hand of God being credited for miracles that happen in Christian denominations that are not your own?					
12. How likely are you to reject the influence of the Holy Ghost (i.e., the Spirit) in your life if it is directing you in a path that is contrary to the beliefs of the Christian denomination you belong to?					
13. How likely are you to feel spiritually threatened by the influence of Christian denominations that are not your own?					
14. How likely are you to become jealous of the happiness or success of individuals who belong to Christian denominations that are not your own?					
15. How likely are you to proactively contend in public (or in public forums) with a self-described Christian not of your denomination for the sake of either proving them to be wrong or proving yourself to be right?					
16. How likely are you to accuse an individual of blasphemy or some form of heresy for believing in doctrines they believe to be Christian that are in contrast to your own Christian beliefs?					
17. How likely are you to demand an answer to a theological question from someone belonging to a Christian denomination that is not your own?					
18. How likely are you to attempt to use the words of an individual belonging to a Christian denomination that is not your own to prove they are theologically wrong?					
19. How likely are you to publicly belittle, mock or otherwise claim the beliefs of a self-described Christian, or entire Christian denomination that is not your own, to be false?					
TOTAL Score (add up the numbers selected above)					

Table 9: Modern-day Pharisee Test

- A score of less than 40 indicates the person taking the test has low pharisaical tendencies and is not likely a Modern-day Pharisee.

- A score of 40 to 59 indicates the person taking the test has moderate pharisaical tendencies and could develop into a Modern-day Pharisee if those tendencies are not reversed

- A score of 60 to 79 indicates the person taking the test has high pharisaical tendencies and is a Modern-day Pharisee

- A score of 80 or more indicates the person taking the test is not only a Modern-day Pharisee but is also an individual whose misdirected passion for Christianity causes division among Christians on a regular basis.

NOTE: This exercise has been automated and can be taken online at www.findyourchristianity.com.

So how does one know when strong personal convictions on spiritual matters cross over into pharisaical territory? Answering this question requires prayer and objective self-assessment. In general, when convictions become a platform for contention, then a pharisaical pattern exists.

THE MISDIRECTED PASSION OF THE MODERN-DAY PHARISEE

The world has always had people who unite and people who divide. Jesus proclaimed, "Think not that I am come to send peace on earth: I came not to send peace, but a sword. For I am come to set a man at variance against his father, and the daughter against her mother, and the daughter in law against her mother in law . . . And he that taketh not his cross, and followeth after me, is not worthy of me" (Matthew 10:34–35, 38). The sword Jesus was referring to is the truth, meaning those who sacrifice truth for the sake of peace are not worthy of the kingdom. One can easily distort this proclamation into a ticket to attack others who practice Christianity differently in the name of upholding interpreted truth. Some see themselves as crusaders defending the gospel regardless of the consequences.

The pharisaical pattern of pride and hypocrisy, followed by panic and paranoia, leading to contention and destruction is a good personal litmus test to whether one has crossed the line into becoming a Modern-day

Pharisee. Of course, this can only be understood if considered in an honest, self-reflective way. For all his passion Paul used the words "meekness," "temperance," "kindness," "longsuffering," "patience," "love," "gentleness," and "forbearing" in his letters to the Galatians, Colossians, Ephesians, Timothy, and Titus in relation to how one is to treat fellow Christians and others. In one letter Paul urges Titus "to speak evil of no man, to be no brawlers, but gentle, shewing all meekness unto *all men*" (Titus 3:2, emphasis added).

The Modern-day Pharisee is a divider, not a unifier. The Savior said, "Every kingdom divided against itself is brought to desolation; and a house divided against a house falleth" (Luke 11:17). While we "should earnestly contend for the faith" (Jude 1:3), there comes a point where contending evolves into contention, and contention is to be avoided (1 Corinthians 1:11). The final section of this book will revisit the issue of contention and address unity among Christians.

SPIRITUAL PROFILING

American society has debated the benefits and dangers of racial profiling—the act of suspecting or judging someone solely on race. Examples of racial profiling include spotting a person of Middle Eastern origin and concluding that person is a terrorist; concluding all African Americans are untrustworthy; or believing all Caucasians are greedy. Although some may argue the accuracy and value of racial profiling among certain communities of people, the unintended consequences as a result of error can be divisive and in some cases catastrophic.

The same can be said of "spiritual profiling"—the act of suspecting or judging someone solely on their denominational affiliation. For example, identifying those who attend church to be Christians, those of a particular denomination to not to be Christians, or those of a particular denomination to be strong Christians can often lead to erroneous and contentious conclusions.

Because of their strong internal biases, Modern-day Pharisees are not only famous for spiritual profiling, but for being in error a great deal of the time. Niccolo Machiavelli wrote, "Men in general judge more from appearances than from reality. All men have eyes, but few have the gift of penetration." An even higher authority told Samuel the prophet, "the

Lord seeth not as man seeth; for man looketh on the outward appearance, but the Lord looketh on the heart" (1 Samuel 16:7). Although Jesus left open the possibility to judge righteously (John 7:24), the Savior said it was best not to judge at all (Matthew 7:1). Spiritual profiling is typically a hit-and-run form of judgment, a quick assessment based upon a set of predisposed biases leading to a conclusion or accusation.

Consider the following profiles of six individuals: one is a primary Founding Father of the United States of America; one is the most infamous mass murderer of all time; one gunned down two people in cold blood based solely on their profession; and three are major biblical figures. Can you guess who they are?

1. A man raised in a strong Christian environment who believed Christianity needed to be restored, rejected the Trinity and the miracles of Christ, and created his own Bible by deleting books and verses he believed to be in error.

2. A gentle man who saw firsthand the work of God, performing miracles himself, and was eventually responsible for the deaths of forty-two youth who insulted his appearance.

3. A musician and poet who was also a murderer, adulterer, and polygamist, putting the welfare of his unrighteous son above the welfare of righteous God-fearing individuals.

4. A highly educated man, brilliantly literate in the scriptures, who became responsible for the killing of Christians in large numbers, even participating firsthand in one such death by aiding an accomplice to the deed.

5. A passionate leader raised by a devout Christian mother, who sponsored a Christian movement, and started a famous public speech with the words, "My feeling as a Christian points me to my Lord and Savior as a fighter."

6. An educated minister affiliated with the Presbyterian Church, father of three, who became one of the most passionate voices against abortion in the history of the United States.

What do the outward characteristics of these individuals suggest to you when it comes to determining if they are Christian—or even some sort of godly person? Although more information can always be gathered, is there enough information provided from the above descriptions to judge which people are Believing Christians, which ones are Practicing Christians, and which ones are not Christian at all? The answers to who these individuals will be given at the end of this chapter.

To illustrate the point of how difficult it is to determine a Christian from outward appearances, consideration will be given to the Founding Fathers of the United States, famous individuals from history and the modern era, and prominent biblical figures. What you are about to read will likely surprise you.

SPIRITUALLY PROFILING AMERICA'S FOUNDING FATHERS

Much has been written about the great men referred to as America's Founding Fathers, with a predominance of literature describing the Founders as strong Christians expounding fierce Christian values. But was that the case? An examination of the religious beliefs and practices of five of the seven men American historian Richard B. Morris calls the "key" Founding Fathers[11] produces a few interesting clues in helping us draw our own conclusions.

George Washington

There is no shortage of stories about George Washington and his devotion to God, especially from writers such as Episcopal Minster Parson Weems. However, other authors and historians have questioned such depictions of Washington, including Paul Boller and David Holmes. Baptized into the Church of England, Washington was casual in his church activity attending church only fifteen times in 1768 according to his diary,[12] often visiting various denominations, according to historical records.[13] Unlike most Anglicans, Washington was never confirmed[14] and rarely took communion when offered.[15]

An examination of the speeches, letters, and public communications of Washington finds him using such words as "Providence," "Heaven," "the Deity," "the Supreme Being," "the Grand Architect," and "the Author of all Good" in place of "Father," "Lord," "Redeemer," and "Savior"—language more indicative of a Deist than a Christian. A Deist is one who relies on reason and observation as a religious philosophy pointing to the existence of a supreme being without the need for supernatural miracles, the infallibility of the scriptures, the atoning sacrifice of Christ, or Trinitarian-type beliefs.[16] Even in a 1793 letter to the Philadelphia Protestant Clergy, an organization to which he could freely express his religious views, Washington never mentions Jesus Christ and instead refers to "the Divine Author of life and felicity."[17]

Those closest to Washington describe him as a God-fearing man who ordered chaplains for military forces, discouraged cursing, and insisted on attendance to Sunday services among his troops. Despite his spiritual character, to call Washington a strong Christian would be erroneous. On his deathbed Washington never asked for clergy to attend to him and was buried with both Episcopal and Masonic funeral services.[18] Of Washington a biographer of James Madison in 1830 wrote: "Mr. Madison does not suppose that Washington had ever attended to the arguments for Christianity, and for the different systems of religion, or in fact that he had formed definite opinions on the subject."[19] Although he appears to have lived some of the traits consistent with a Practicing Christian, Washington's profile is more consistent with that of a Deist than that of a Believing or Practicing Christian.

Ben Franklin

Like Washington, Ben Franklin appears to have been a Deist. Raised in the Calvinist-Puritan tradition, Franklin rejected the ambiguity of theology and instead focused on the logic and truth offered by math and science. A biographer commented, "Franklin adopted much from Deism that would have alienated him from Puritanism,"[20] including absence from church services and publishing content consistent with Deistic beliefs.[21] Despite moving away from traditional Calvinist beliefs, Franklin maintained many of the values associated with Calvinism, joined a Presbyterian Church in Philadelphia, contributed financially to the building of religious structures, "remained open to the possibility of divine intervention," and believed organized religion offered potential benefits for society.[22]

In response to an inquiry from a Congregationalist minister and president of Yale College regarding his religious beliefs, Franklin gave the following response shortly before his death:

> I believe in one God, Creator of the Universe: that he governs the World by his Providence. That he ought to be worshiped. That the most acceptable Service we can render to him, is doing good to his other Children. That the Soul of Man is immortal, and will be treated with Justice in another life, respecting its Conduct in this.[23]

In the same response from Franklin, regarding Jesus Christ, he wrote: "I have with most of the present Dissenters in England, some Doubts as to his Divinity: tho' it is a Question I do not dogmatise upon, having never studied it, and think it needless to busy myself with it now, when I expect soon an Opportunity of knowing the Truth with less Trouble."[24] Despite questioning such Christian teachings as the Trinity, the resurrection and other supernatural precepts, Franklin was not one to discuss or write about such matters in public.[25] Although one might question the degree to which Franklin was a Believing or Practicing Christian, many of his actions and characteristics suggest a godly soul who looked out for the welfare of others.

John Adams

John Adams was a Congregationalist who held strong Unitarian beliefs.[26] In contrast to Trinitarianism, Unitarianism ascribes to the belief that God is a single person, not three, maintaining Jesus Christ was a prophet of God, subordinate to the Father, but not God himself.[27] Adams was known as a regular churchgoing individual who married the daughter of a Congregationalist minister and was unafraid to use outwardly Christian language in his public discourse.[28] Of Christianity, Adams declared:

> [It] is the brightness of the glory and the express portrait of the character of the eternal, self-existent, independent, benevolent, all powerful and all merciful creator, preserver, and father of the universe, the first good, first perfect, and first fair. It will last as long as the world. Neither savage nor civilized man, without a revelation, could ever have discovered or invented it.[29]

Adams's embracing Unitarian beliefs, yet marrying into a staunchly Christian family and demonstrating Christian characteristics in public, paints a complex portrait of Adams with respect to being a Christian.

With such statements by Adams as "[God] has given us Reason, to find out the Truth, and the real Design and true End of our Existence," and "This would be the best of all possible Worlds, if there were no Religion in it,"[30] one might conclude Adams was more of a "Christian Deist."

Thomas Jefferson

Baptized into the Church of England, Jefferson was raised in a strong religious environment and blessed with a Christian education in his younger years. Upon attending William and Mary College, Jefferson discovered the Enlightenment movement and became enamored with the works of Bacon, Locke, and Newton, and enjoyed the influences of the Scots, English, and French of the eighteenth-century Age of Reason.[31] This mixture of experiences gave Jefferson a unique outlook and caused one author to write that religion "mesmerized him, enraged him, tantalized him, alarmed him, and sometimes inspired him."[32] This philosophical struggle can be witnessed in Jefferson, having maintained a strong Anglican and Episcopalian membership throughout his life while scolding Christianity and its negative impact on the lives of innocent men, women, and children throughout history.[33]

Jefferson was said to be a restorationist, believing Christianity to have fallen away from its original truths. To Benjamin Rush Jefferson wrote:

> To the corruptions of Christianity I am indeed opposed; but not to the genuine precepts of Jesus himself. I am a Christian, in the only sense he wished any one to be; sincerely attached to his doctrines, in preference to all others; ascribing to himself every human excellence; & believing he never claimed any other.[34]

Restorationist views were a prime condition for the adoption of Deism.[35] Jefferson admired and revered the teachings of Jesus Christ but rejected the miracles attributed to him and did not consider him to be the Savior.[36] Jefferson referred to the doctrine of the Trinity as "incomprehensible jargon of Trinitarian arithmetic,"[37] while adhering to more Unitarian views of rejecting the virgin birth and the Resurrection. Jefferson went as far as to remove from the Bible those passages he believed to be in error, including the letters of Paul, Peter, John, and Jude, as well as the book of Revelation. Jefferson's censored version of the Bible was later published as *The Life and Morals of Jesus*. Jefferson helped replace divinity professorships at William and Mary with professorships of science and law and eventually established the University of Virginia as an alternative to the more Anglican-Episcopalian influenced university.[38]

Like many of the Founding Fathers, Jefferson emerges as a complex religious figure difficult to pinpoint. Although having demonstrated Christian practices and beliefs in his lifetime, Jefferson did not believe "all the way" with respect to Jesus Christ; therefore, one cannot with confidence consider Jefferson a Believing Christian.

James Madison

James Madison was born into a devout Christian family, baptized into the Anglican faith, and attended the College of New Jersey—a college known for its training of Presbyterian clergy.[39] Madison studied under John Witherspoon, the only clergyman to sign the Declaration of Independence, where he learned to read the Bible in Greek and Hebrew.[40] Madison later fought passionately for religious freedom, believed in separation of church and state, and maintained an interest in religious matters.

Madison had ample exposure to the Enlightenment and was said to have had high regard for Unitarian principles.[41] It is rare to find documents providing insight into Madison's views on religion. One such document is an exchange with an Episcopal clergyman in 1825, where Madison used the phrase "Nature's God" and omits any references to Jesus and the Bible, leading one to believe Madison was in some respects a Deist.[42]

James Madison proposed the plan to divide the central government into three branches. He discovered this model of government from Isaiah 33:22: "For the Lord is our judge, the Lord is our lawgiver, the Lord is our king."

Those close to Madison suggest that by the end of his life he returned to more traditional and orthodox Christian beliefs. Although not one to freely express his religious views, Madison can be reasonably thought of as a Believing Christian with characteristics consistent with that of a Practicing Christian.

Christianity and the Founding Fathers

Many believe the Founding Fathers were not only Christians, but also strong Christians who helped build a Christian nation. And while folklore and oral tradition paints these five Founding Fathers as described, the actual facts regarding their lives and beliefs suggest a much different story.

Among all of America's Founders, many could be considered Believing and Practicing Christians, such as Alexander Hamilton, John Hancock, James McHenry, and Benjamin Rush. Other Founders such as Thomas Paine and Ethan Allen were Deists.

Records suggest the following religious affiliations among the Founding Fathers,[43] keeping in mind that many considered themselves to be affiliated with more than one church denomination:

- Episcopalian/Anglican   88
- Presbyterian   30
- Congregationalist   27
- Quaker   7
- Dutch Reformed/German Reformed   6
- Lutheran   5
- Catholic   3
- Huguenot   3
- Unitarian   3
- Methodist   2
- Calvinist   1

The five key Founders examined in this chapter were God-fearing men with godly characteristics, who were truly inspired of God. However, according to the definitions we developed earlier, one would be hard pressed to categorize them as Believing or Practicing Christians—despite the fact so many have profiled them to be that and more. Can you begin to understand the dangers of spiritual profiling?

SPIRITUALLY PROFILING HISTORICAL AND MODERN INDIVIDUALS

History provides us with a number of individuals who seemed to be one thing and turned out to be another, illustrating the challenges of spiritual profiling.

Adolf Hitler

Adolf Hitler is one of the most notorious figures in history, responsible for the deaths of millions of innocent people. The early spiritual profile of Hitler could easily lead one to conclude he was a Believing Christian and perhaps even a Practicing Christian. Hitler's mother "was a devout Catholic, . . . raising her children in the tenets of the Church."[44] Despite Hitler's later views that despised Christianity, he once promoted a movement called "positive Christianity," likely for the sake of political expediency.[45] Hitler went as far as to testify in public the following in a speech given in April of 1922 in Munich:

> My feelings as a Christian points me to my Lord and Savior as a fighter. It points me to the man who once in loneliness, surrounded only by a few followers, recognized these Jews for what they were and summoned men to fight against them and who, God's truth! was greatest not as a sufferer but as a fighter. In boundless love as a Christian and as a man I read through the passage which tells us how the Lord at last rose in His might and seized the scourge to drive out of the Temple the brood of vipers and adders. How terrific was His fight for the world against the Jewish poison. To-day, after two thousand years, with deepest emotion I recognize more profoundly than ever before in the fact that it was for this that He had to shed His blood upon the Cross. As a Christian I have no duty to allow myself to be cheated, but I have the duty to be a fighter for truth and justice.[46]

Although historians often disagree as to the religious views of Hitler, some evidence supports a characterization that he at one time may have been a Believing Christian.

Reverend Jim Jones

Reverend Jim Jones, the founder and leader of the People's Temple, was responsible for the mass suicide of over 900 people and the murder of five others in Jonestown, Guyana, in 1978. Before that disastrous event, the charismatic leader had great interest in religion as a child,[47] when a Methodist superintendent took him under his wing despite his sympathetic views on communism.[48] In 1965 Jones became a Disciples of Christ minister focused on ministering to the African American community.[49] Under Jones the Peoples Temple grew into an international ministry with nearly one thousand followers settling into Guyana in 1977 ahead of the devastating tragedy of 1978.

Reverend Paul Jennings Hill

Reverend Hill was a fierce antiabortion activist who was convicted of murdering a doctor and clinic escort outside of an abortion clinic in 1994—a crime for which he earned the death penalty and was executed in 2003. Before the murders, Reverend Hill had a wife and three children, graduated from Belhaven College and Reformed Theological Seminary, and was ordained in 1984 as a minister affiliated with the Orthodox Presbyterian Church and the Presbyterian Church in America.[50] Although Reverend Hill was later excommunicated for his radical views on abortion,[51] some Christians today still laud his actions in taking a stand against what many believe to be the single greatest abomination in the sight of God.

Timothy McVeigh

Timothy McVeigh is the poster child for homegrown domestic terrorism, having bombed the Alfred P. Murrah Federal Building in Oklahoma City in 1995, killing 168 people and injuring over 800 more.[52] The religious profile of McVeigh includes being raised and confirmed a Roman Catholic,[53] attending mass regularly with his father.[54] Before his execution, McVeigh requested and was given the sacrament of anointing of the sick by a Catholic priest.[55] Although statements made by McVeigh and writings gathered suggest he was more of an agnostic, his personal history suggests he lived a Christian life.

Pastor Fred Waldron Phelps Sr.

As of 2012, Fred Phelps is the pastor of an independent Baptist Church, the Westboro Baptist Church (WBC), in Topeka, Kansas. Phelps was inspired after attending a Methodist revival meeting and left his commission at West Point to become a minister, attending Bob Jones University, the Prairie Bible Institute, and John Muir College.[56] Phelps preached against promiscuity, profanity, dishonesty, vulgarity, and sins of the flesh.[57] By all accounts Pastor Phelps appeared to be a decent Christian man. However, Phelps began directing WBC members to picket funerals of fallen soldiers to protest homosexuality in the military. The actions of WBC led President George W. Bush to sign into law the Respect for America's Fallen Heroes Act in 2006.[58] The work of Phelps and his followers became so offensive among not only gays and military families, but also people of all religions, that the Southern Poverty Law Center labeled Phelps and the WBC a hate group in its 2006 intelligence report.[59]

Christianity and Figures from History and the Modern Era

Each of the individuals studied in this section start off with what seems to be a strong Christian background and upbringing, only to end in shame and disgrace uncharacteristic of a follower of Jesus Christ. Each of these men appear on the surface to be (or to have been) Believing Christians but certainly not Practicing Christians at the time of their crimes.

For men such as Hitler, Jones, and Hill, society typically sees only the end result and makes a judgment based upon their most recent transgressions. The final verdict almost always includes the accusation that the individual was not a Christian, when in fact they apparently were at one time or another. Oddly enough, often those who are close to such individuals before their crimes (friends, family, acquaintances, and so on) will describe them as being strong Christians with a passion to change the world for good.

These examples remind us of the challenges of spiritual profiling in the reverse: judging an individual to be a Christian, even a strong Christian, only to find out what was lurking in their heart was nothing short of evil. Remember that the Lord told Samuel that man looks on the outward appearance but that God looks upon the heart (1 Samuel 16:7). Which do you suspect is a more accurate assessment of spiritual character? Once again we see the pitfalls of spiritual profiling.

SPIRITUALLY PROFILING BIBLICAL FIGURES

Just for fun, we will take this profiling exercise to the extreme and consider a number of biblical figures. While we might consider a prophet or "the Lord's chosen" to be godly and worthy of our veneration, that might all depend on which point in time we profile them.

The Prophet Elisha

The Prophet Elisha witnessed Elijah being taken up into heaven (2 Kings 2:11), performed the miracle of the oil for a widow (2 Kings 4:1–7), blessed a barren woman to have a child (2 Kings 4:8–17), brought a child back from the dead (2 Kings 4:18–37), cleansed a leper (2 Kings 5:1–14), and caused an ax to float on top of the water (2 Kings 6:1–7). After becoming a prophet in Israel, and before he performed these great works, Elisha was responsible for the deaths of forty-two children (or youth) after cursing them for calling him bald (2 Kings 2:23–24). Elisha was indeed a prophet, but how would the parents of the forty-two children describe Elisha following their deaths?

King David

King David was a man after God's own heart (Acts 13:22). David slew Goliath (1 Samuel 17:51), conquered Jerusalem (2 Samuel 5:1–12), brought the ark of the covenant into the holy city (2 Samuel 6:17), defeated all enemies he went to battle with, was blessed to be a progenitor of Jesus Christ (Matthew 1:1), and is the object of attribution to many of the psalms in the Old Testament. Despite these great triumphs, David was a murderer, sending Uriah the Hittite to his death, an adulterer in lying with the married Bathsheba (2 Samuel 11:4, 15 and 27), and loving his enemies more than his friends (2 Samuel 19:5–6). The spiritual profile of David could turn up something good or bad depending on when it was done. As the Lord later spoke to David's son Solomon, he praised David and made no mention of his grievous sins of the past (2 Chronicles 7:12–18 and 1 Kings 15:4–5), signifying the mercy and forgiveness of the Lord.

Solomon

David's son Solomon was blessed by the Lord to be the wisest man to ever live (1 Kings 3:12). Solomon built the temple envisioned by his father David (1 Kings 6:38), created a great nation, and was permitted to author a portion of the Old Testament. However, Solomon took unto himself 700 wives, 300 concubines, and became an idol worshiper in his later years (1 Kings 11:3–6). Once again, an accurate spiritual profile of Solomon would depend on the time when it was taken.

Paul

Paul is known as one of the greatest Christian missionaries that ever lived, having been directly visited of the Lord on two occasions (Acts 9:5–6 and Acts 23:11), and whose writings dominate the New Testament. Before becoming Paul, as Saul he persecuted the Christians sending many men and women to their death (Acts 22:4, 20, Acts 26:10–11, and Galatians 1:13–14). It was the conversion of Paul that created the change in his understanding of the scriptures and his attitude toward the gospel of Jesus Christ, but before that time a profile of Saul would have certainly yielded one of pure evil toward Christianity.

Christianity and Figures from the Bible

No one is perfect, not even these revered individuals from the Bible, including prophets, kings, and apostles. The moral agency of man provides the freedom to choose in mortality, and that means we as the children of God will make good choices and bad choices. When observers attempt to spiritually profile an individual as being a Christian or not, or God-fearing or not—including these venerated biblical figures—it is often without the benefit of knowing their past and certainly not their future. Without such knowledge the judgment, made may be seriously flawed.

AVOIDING DRIVE-BY SPIRITUAL PROFILING

Many strong self-described Christians of the modern era put their trust and faith in those they consider to be Christians by their own definition. Likewise, these same Christians may tune out and write off those whom they believe are not Christians and therefore consider them to be untrustworthy or undeserving of their respect. Although this strategy may hold intermittent value in extreme cases, such a strategy will at times fail, and in some cases fail spectacularly.

The Error of Profiling a Christian Who May or
May Not Be a Christian in Waiting

Individuals like Hitler, Jones, Hill, McVeigh and Phelps appear at one time to be strong and passionate Christians with solid Christian credentials; however, time revealed a different person in each case, calling into question their commitment to Christianity as believers and practitioners. Spiritual profiling is often conducted at a moment in time without the benefit of the full picture. The Apostle Paul was once evil, but after his conversion he became as fierce a Christian as the world will ever know. King David and his son Solomon were at one time godly and fully converted; however, their sinful actions demonstrate the human fragility that is in need of constant repentance to reconcile the Christian to God.

The Error of Profiling a Non-Christian Who May Be a Christian

Spiritually profiling an entire group of people or even a single individual is fraught with error. An earlier chapter discussed how Ted Haggard mocked the Catholic religion; how Richard Land declared Mormonism isn't Christianity; and how James Dobson questioned the Christian credentials of Senator Fred Thompson—each conducting a spiritual profile to a questionable end. Such spiritual profiling makes the accusers look like a Modern-day Pharisees creating division and inhibiting the unity of the faith.

The Error of Circular Profiling of Christians and Non-Christians

Based solely on hearsay and the murmurings of public discourse, some Americans today readily profile America's Founding Fathers as Christians. Then upon learning most of the key Founders were Deists they may re-profile the Founding Fathers as non-Christians and become skeptical of their character, thus completing a bogus 360-degree spiritual profile. This, of course, is nonsensical.

To a great number of Christians who venture into spiritual profiling, an individual who believes as a Unitarian or a Deist is not capable of making godly contributions to society and thus discounts their every word (the action of a Modern-day Pharisee). In the case of the Founding Fathers, such an attitude would have been a huge mistake. The Founding Fathers were certainly not atheists, and to consider a portion of this distinguished group to be agnostic would be equally incorrect. God was important to the Founders but not necessarily Christianity in general nor a denomination of Christianity specifically. For this reason the Founders avoided outwardly religious language in the founding documents and supported separation of church and state. History suggests that many of the Founders were men of prayer with a profound belief in God, even in Jesus Christ and the Church; they simply did not adhere to a common set of Christian theological beliefs and did not let that create friction nor impede their greater mission.

In order for Christians to come "in the unity of faith" (Ephesians 4:13), there must be an acceptance that great things can come from those who believe in and practice Christianity different from what "we" do ("we" meaning you personally or whatever your denomination of Christianity may be). Such individuals may live Christian values and practice principles in a way that fosters goodness and harmony. To this end people of faith must avoid spiritual profiling leading to the denial of anyone who professes to be Christian, or to discount the perspectives and contributions of those who love and honor God the Father but hold unconventional beliefs relating to Jesus Christ. And if for whatever reason you still can't accept as a Christian a particular individual who considers themselves to be a Christian, or even an entire denomination who considers themselves to be Christian, then let not that feeling keep you from associating with them positively and serving with them in the community in which you live.

ANSWERS TO THE OPENING PROFILES

By now you probably know the answers to the profiling questions presented at the beginning of this chapter:

1. A man raised in a strong Christian environment who believed Christianity needed to be restored, rejected the Trinity and the miracles of Christ, and created his own Bible by deleting books and verses he believed to be in error. THOMAS JEFFERSON

2. A gentle man who saw firsthand the work of God, performing miracles himself, and was eventually responsible for the deaths of forty-two youth who insulted his appearance. THE PROPHET ELISHA

3. A musician and poet who was also a murderer, adulterer, and polygamist, putting the welfare of his unrighteous son above the welfare of righteous God-fearing individuals. KING DAVID

4. A highly educated man, brilliantly literate in the scriptures, who became responsible for the killing of Christians in large numbers, even participating firsthand in one such death by aiding an accomplice to the deed. THE APOSTLE PAUL

5. A passionate leader raised by a devout Christian mother, who sponsored a Christian movement, and started a famous public speech with the words "My feeling as a Christian points me to my Lord and Savior as a fighter." ADOLF HITLER

6. An educated minister affiliated with the Presbyterian Church, father of three, who became one of the most passionate voices against abortion in the history of the United States. REVEREND PAUL HILL

Section 3

WHERE ARE THE CHRISTIANS?

A Categorization

"Christianity, if false, is of no importance, and if true, of infinite importance. The only thing it cannot be is moderately important."

—C. S. Lewis

NOW THAT WE UNDERSTAND WHO THE CHRISTIANS ARE AND WHAT A Christian is from the first two sections, it is time to tackle the question of "Where are the Christians?" One might answer the question with "I'm right here," or "They're at my church," or "They're all around me." Such answers are fair and likely correct. However, one needs to think about the question in an entirely different manner.

There are an estimated two billion Christians in the world today, comprising approximately 33 percent of the world's population.[1] As of 2008, an estimated 173.4 million people in the United States identified themselves as Christians (76% of the population) according to the American Religious Identification Survey (ARIS). A report by Pew Research in 2011 places the number as high as 246.7 million Christians in the United States.[2] America has a Christian population that is over double that of the entire world on a per capita basis. And in fact, the United States has one of the largest Christian populations on a per capita basis of any country in the world.

The heavy concentration of Christians in the United States should result in a more principled and moral society . . . right? Some may say yes; others may say no. The factual answer is unfortunately a resounding no depending on one's perspective.

While people around the globe believe the world is becoming more corrupt,[3] the perception of the United States in particular is one of increasing corruption. In a study conducted by Transparency International in 2010, America's corruption perceptions index (CPI) fell out of the top twenty for the first time in the index's fifteen-year history—an index among 178 nations based upon independent surveys on corruption.[4] Beyond perceptions are the hard facts such as the United States has the highest incarceration rate in the world (730 adults per 100,000).[5] Americans need only consider the events of the last decade to understand corruption and dishonesty has deeply permeated the social, commercial, and political fabric of the United States.

The 2006 financial crisis in the United States, fueled by the subprime mortgage debacle, revealed spectacular greed in the American financial markets. Cronyism in American federal and local governments along with congressional insider trading, government bailouts, a continuous flow of congressional scandals, and questionable practices among the mainstream media have revealed a culture of corruption at the highest levels of American politics and journalism. In a speech to the American Bar Association, FBI Director Robert Mueller said, "Anyone who follows the news these days and sees repeated references to corporate fraud and public corruption might think the nation is in the midst of a moral crisis." Mueller asked the defense attorneys, "Have we as a society become more corrupt? Or have we in the FBI simply become more adept at rooting out fraud and corruption?"[6]

Wait a minute! Increasing dishonesty, corruption and crime in a country that is 76 percent Christian? Aren't dishonesty, corruption, and crime exactly the opposite of what Jesus Christ taught his disciples to be? With three of four Americans identifying themselves as being Christian, one of the highest concentrations of Christianity in the world, shouldn't this trend of evil practices be going in the opposite direction, or at least remain stable or decrease? While one might shoot holes in my logic here, a case can be made that the stronger the Christian the less likely they are to be dishonest, to be corrupt, and/or to commit crime. So what then is going on here?

Perhaps the crime and corruption in America is being performed by the 24 percent of the population who are not Christian. Unfortunately not! A study conducted in 1997 by Denise Golumbaski, a research analyst for the Federal Bureau of Prisons,[7] suggests approximately 65 percent of those incarcerated in the United States affiliated themselves with a particular Christian faith, with 20 percent claiming to have no religion or be atheist, the remainder being other non-Christian religions. It appears Christians make up the vast majority of those incarcerated, suggesting the 24 percent are not the only ones to blame.

Christians are not perfect and make mistakes, and in a predominantly Christian society, the majority of criminals and those not living lives of discipleship are bound to be Christian; however, much more is going on here to consider as you will soon see.

Edmund Burke once said, "All that is necessary for the triumph of evil is that good men do nothing," echoing what Paul wrote that a Christian is called to overcome evil with good (Romans 12:21). Christians are supposed to be a light unto the world (Matthew 5:14–16), helping the light to overcome darkness (John 1:5, Matthew 4:16, and Ephesians 5:8), acting as a guide to those who are lost in the darkness (Romans 2:19). Those who believe in Christ and practice the teachings of Christianity are to bring goodness to a society not evil and wrongdoing.

So I ask again: in such a great country where Christianity abounds in vast numbers but where its moral fabric is becoming increasingly corrupt and unholy . . . *where are the Christians?* In the next four chapters the reader will understand there are four primary answers to this question with a great deal of supporting data behind each one:

- Some are leaving: these are the **Departing Christians**
- Some are hiding: these are the **Adequate Christians**
- Some are vacillating: these are the **Hesitant Christians**
- Some are endeavoring: these are the **Laboring Christians**

Each of these Christian types is in varying degrees Believing and Practicing Christians. You will soon have an opportunity to understand exactly what type of Christian you are and why America is operating so far under its Christian potential. In this section, our expedition shifts into high gear.

Chapter 9

THEY'RE LEAVING–LOSING
THEIR BELIEF AS
DEPARTING CHRISTIANS

PART OF THE PROBLEM IS, OF THE 76 PERCENT OF THOSE WHO CALL themselves Christians in the United States, a portion of those are literally or psychologically losing their faith (that is, "the lights are on but nobody's spiritually home"). These are Christians that don't believe as they once did (or perhaps never did), who are living watered-down doctrines of Christianity and losing their testimony of the Savior through inactivity and prolonged sin without repentance. Simply put, some Christians are leaving the faith—consciously and subconsciously.

LOSING FAITH IN THE SCRIPTURES

An estimated six billion Bibles have been sold since its first publication,[1] making it the single bestselling book of all time. Many can recall the proverbial "Family Bible"; however, it appears the family Bible doesn't have the impact it once had. A study conducted by the American Bible Society (ABS) found 82 percent of Americans consider the Bible as sacred scripture, down four percentage points from the previous year, while only 69 percent believe the Bible to contain "everything a person needs to know to live a meaningful life," down six percentage points from the previous year.

Lamar Vest, president and CEO of the ABS explains, "There are probably five Bibles on every shelf in American homes. Americans buy the Bible, they debate the Bible, they love the Bible . . . they just don't read the Bible."[2] The survey results support Vest's claim in that over half of the respondents could not identify the first five books of the Bible, with 46 percent saying they read the bible no more than once or twice a year.[3] Statistics from the earlier studies referenced in chapter 7 are consistent with the ABS study results. Barna reported only 38 percent of adults had read from the Bible in the last seven days, while the NYSR data reported 17 percent of youth and six percent of young adults read the scriptures at least once a week. Jesus Christ told his disciples to "search the scriptures" (John 5:39), an admonition that is apparently falling on deaf ears among most Christians according to these studies conducted over the last decade.

But why? Why aren't more Christians taking the time to read the scriptures in order to better understand God, his Son Jesus Christ, and their own spirituality? In my own experiences, four reasons come to mind:

Value: The most obvious answer to the question is that Christians do not see a value in reading the scriptures. In a society driven by tangible results, extrinsic rewards, and return on investment, many Christians may not fully comprehend the value being delivered to them intrinsically by studying the scriptures asking, "What's in it for me?"

Doubt: The Bible has come under intense secular scrutiny over the last several decades, even centuries, giving fence-sitting Christians new reasons to forgo study of the scriptures. Agenda-driven scholars and atheists point to a number of perceived inconsistencies with the Bible such as Jesus saying, "Blessed are the poor in spirit" in Matthew 5:3, versus Jesus saying, "Blessed be ye poor" in Luke 6:20. Or 1 John 1:7, stating, "the blood of Jesus Christ his Son cleanseth us from all sin," versus Matthew 12:32, which states: "And whosoever speaketh a word against the Son of man, it shall be forgiven him: but whosoever speaketh against the Holy Ghost, it shall not be forgiven him, neither in this world, neither in the world to come." Add to that the many variations in the original New Testament manuscripts pointed out by biblical scholars and authors such as Dr. Bart D. Ehrman,[4] and a Christian with a vulnerable testimony may question the legitimacy of the scriptures.

Confusion: Adding to the scriptural dilemma for Christians is biblical translation. The dozens of English Bible translations, many of which offer substantially different meanings, can leave the susceptible Christian bewildered and confused. As recently as mid-2011, yet another translation was being released by the Members of the Committee on Bible Translation specifically to address inequality of women in society. This latest New International Version brings back terms like "mankind," which it changed to "human beings" in its 2005 revision, but still keeps a gender neutral position in voiding terms like "he" and "him."[5]

Some of the changes include new scholarship coming forth from the Dead Sea Scrolls—a source of biblical controversy relating to inclusion and canonization. To the lukewarm Christian desiring to begin a personal scripture studying regiment, the myriad English biblical translations can easily confuse and thwart that desire.

Lethargy: During the weekly Catholic liturgy, carefully selected passages from the Bible are read from the pulpit for all in the congregation to hear. In mega-church services pastors passionately read verses in the Bible as a means to motivate and excite those in the congregation. In these examples, it is not the intention of the Church to discourage personal Bible study, but rather to inspire it. In these examples, church members may feel they are receiving adequate Bible exposure and therefore feel no promptings to study the scriptures on their own.

Overlooking issues relating to literacy and rejecting the notion of "not having time to study," these four reasons are why more Christians are not regularly studying the scriptures on their own. The word of God is likened to a lamp illuminating the way (Psalm 119:105), providing the believer a multitude of benefits including a knowledge of the Lord Jesus Christ (2 Timothy 3:15–16). The alarmingly low amount of reading from the scriptures is a credible leading indicator of Christians straying from, or even losing, their faith and testimony in the Lord, in his gospel, and in his church.

THE SHRINKING CHRISTIAN POPULATION IN AMERICA

The seventy-ninth annual edition of the *Yearbook of American & Canadian Churches* from 2012 recorded declining membership among five of the ten largest denominations. The only three to report gains were the Assemblies of God (up 3.99 percent), the National Baptist Convention

U.S.A. (up 3.95 percent), and The Church of Jesus Christ of Latter-day Saints (up 1.63 percent). The following summarizes the numbers by denominational ranking in the United States:

1. The Catholic Church: **down** 0.44 percent

2. The Southern Baptist Convention: **down** 0.15 percent

3. The United Methodist Church: **down** 0.22 percent

4. The Church of Jesus Christ of Latter-day Saints: **up** 1.62 percent

5. The Church of God in Christ: **no update** reported

6. National Baptist Convention, USA, Inc.: **up** 3.95 percent

7. Evangelical Lutheran Church in America: **down** 5.90 percent

8. National Baptist Convention of America, Inc.: **no update** reported

9. Assemblies of God: **up** 3.99 percent

10. Presbyterian Church (USA): **down** 3.42 percent

In an attempt to explain the decline, Eileen Linder, the yearbook's editor, states, "For the age cohorts known as Gen X'ers and Millennials (people now in their 30s and 20s respectively), formal membership may lie outside of their hopes and expectations for their church relationships."[6]

The 10-percent decline in Christian self-identification since 1990 as reported by the American Religious Identification Survey (ARIS) prompted William Donohue, president of the Catholic League, to tell Lou Dobbs of CNN, "The three most dreaded words are thou shalt not. . . . Notice they are not atheists—they are saying I don't want to be told what to do with my life."[7] The ARIS study of 54,461 respondents sees the issue differently: "Americans are slowly becoming less Christian and that in recent decades the challenge to Christianity in American society does not come from other world religions or new religious movements (NRMs) but rather from a rejection of all organized religions."[8] The abandonment of organized religion means a less predictable, less directed and organized Body of Christ where individuals may still pray to and believe in God, but choose to worship outside of a structured congregation.[9]

A *Newsweek* poll conducted with over 1,000 adults in 2009 found Americans to be deeply religious, but that only 48 percent believed faith could help answer all or most of the country's current problems.[10] The poll also found that 68 percent of respondents believed that religion is losing its influence on American life (an increase of ten points from a similar poll in 2000) while those claiming to have "old-fashioned values about family and marriage" decreasing thirteen points from a 1987 poll conducted by *Newsweek*. Although 48 percent described themselves as "religious and spiritual," 30 percent considered themselves to be spiritual but not religious (SBNR). Demonstrating the impact of politics on religion, the poll found that more Evangelicals consider themselves to be Democrats (35 percent) than Republicans (34 percent) with the divide being even larger among Roman Catholics (50 percent to 17 percent, respectively).

Gallup conducted its own survey in 2009 reporting 13 percent of Americans claiming no religion at all with 78 percent describing themselves as Christian—a number that has been declining for decades according to Gallup's analysts from a peak of 91 percent in 1948.[11] Remaining steady over the last few decades, but still relatively low, is just over half of Americans (56 percent) believe religion to be "very important" in their lives.

Considered by many to be the most passionate Christians in America, Evangelicals are alarmed at the dwindling belief among many of its members. With the National Association of Evangelicals claiming thirty million adherents and mega-churches on the rise,[12] Evangelical leaders are still concerned by the growing number of those considered to be SBNRs and the impact they may be having on congregations and society on the whole. The SBNR tends to not be theologically conservative and tends to live by a more general mantra of "love your God (whomever or whatever it may be) and love your neighbor," according to Sven Erlandson, a pastor and author.[13]

Although the data sourced in this section focuses on the United States, similar patterns are emerging around the globe. The *World Christian Encyclopedia* reported an explosion of those who consider themselves to be nonreligious or atheist from 3.2 million in 1900 to 918 million in 2000.[14] Agnosticism and atheism combined are growing at 8.5 million converts a year worldwide.[15] So while there are massive gains for Christianity in places like Africa and the Third World, losses in the Western World overcome such gains.[16]

A Post Christian America?

These startling statistics of Christians leaving the fold have prompted some to begin using the term "Post-Christian America." Even the staunchest of Christian conservatives, R. Albert Mohler Jr., president of the Southern Baptist Theological Seminary, commented on the trends outlined in the ARIS, saying, "This pattern has now changed, and the Northeast emerged in 2008 as the new stronghold of the religiously unidentified."[17] For Mohler, the pattern revealed a culture-shift for American religion in what he referred to as "a post-modern, post-Christian, post-Western cultural crisis, which threatens the very heart of our culture."

Is Mohler's outlook too pessimistic? Perhaps not.

Mohler is not only considering the most recent statistics, but he is also indirectly affirming the works of German philosopher Hermann Keyserling, who introduced the phrase "Post-Christian" in his 1929 book titled *America Set Free*. Keyserling's work grew legs into the 1960s with the "death of God" movement leveraging the phrase used by Nietzche in the nineteenth century. The movement was expanded upon in Harold Bloom's 1992 work, *The American Religion: The Emergence of the Post-Christian Nation*, providing additional fuel to the notion of a Post-Christian America.[18] Mohler continues, "Once Christianity is abandoned by a significant portion of the population, the moral landscape necessarily changes."[19] So while America is still predominantly Christian, the slow and steady exodus of many of its adherents is helping to produce a moral breakdown that is bound to negatively impact its society.

THE CHRISTIAN SMORGASBORD

Given that nearly 34,000 Christian denominations exist in the world today, with America playing host to a massive variety of such denominations, it is not surprising that exposure to a smorgasbord of faiths can produce hybrid theological points of view. These hybrid belief systems produce watered-down versions of the originals causing confusion and eventually a departure from the faith (that is, apostasy).

The documenting of this uneasy trend of diluting theological principles starts with the 2002 Barna study of 630 US-based adults that found Christians adopting beliefs that conflict with biblical teachings and those of their own church. A whopping 76 percent of adults surveyed rejected the notion that "the Bible can only be correctly interpreted by people who have years of intense training in theology," opening the door to personal scriptural interpretation.[20] More alarming perhaps was the fact that 51 percent of respondents believed "praying to deceased saints can have a positive effect in a person's life"—not just Catholics, but a good portion of Protestant, Evangelicals, and non-Evangelical born-again Christians. The same study found that 50 percent of adults believe it to be possible to earn one's way to heaven and that 74 percent reject the biblical concept of original sin. Of startling concern to conservative Christians was the fact that 44 percent of respondents believe "the Bible, the Koran and the Book of Mormon are all different expressions of the same truths" and another 54 percent believe "truth can be discovered only through logic, human reasoning and personal experience." These statistics reveal a movement toward syncretism—the process of combining different, and often contradictory, belief systems.[21]

A study conducted seven years later with over 2,000 respondents in 2009 by the Pew Forum on Religion and Public Life echoed the Barna results, finding 65 percent of adults in the United States have widely adopted elements of Eastern faiths and New Age thinking.[22] The same study revealed 28 percent of those who regularly attend church often visit multiple churches outside of their own tradition; 25 percent believe in astrology; 24 percent believe in reincarnation; and 26 percent find "spiritual energy" in physical things.[23]

Even the mecca of Mormonism in the state of Utah is facing the threat of syncretism with the percentage of Latter-day Saints dipping below 63 percent in a recent census with projections of an LDS-minority by 2030.[24]

As a belief system becomes diluted, and a loss of conviction and loyalty takes place in a church home as being the center of teaching, worship, and fellowship, the Christian is more likely to drift and eventually fall away. The dynamic is reminiscent of Paul's letter to the Ephesians when he wrote, "That we henceforth be no more children, tossed to and fro, and carried about with every wind of doctrine, by the sleight of men, and cunning craftiness, whereby they lie in wait to deceive" (Ephesians 4:14). The stimulation of mixing and matching doctrines and principles gives way to confusion and the inability to reconcile contradictions, leaving the believer in a state of despair and uncertainty. This is especially destructive when children are involved, leading to a future generation of mixers and matchers that are likely to meet the same fate.

FED UP, DISILLUSIONED, AND DISMAYED

The final reason why Christians are leaving has to do with experiences that cause them to be disillusioned, fed up, or otherwise dismayed to the point of apostasy. Such experiences are never justification for a departure from one's faith; rather, such negative experiences are catalysts to accelerating an already established personal trend as the proverbial "straw that broke the camel's back."

Negative experiences might include adversity such as the death of a loved one, a natural disaster, or other events outside of a person's control, where faith is challenged and hope gives way to the inability to explain why God would let such a thing happen. Apostasy can happen through excessive focus on empirical proof, leading the Christian away from faith into a wasteland of doubt. Being offended by another in church, lack of spiritual experiences, or the insistence on a more tangible God can all lead to the same treacherous doom. Because God's thoughts are not our thoughts (Isaiah 55:8) the vulnerable Christian may allow his or her self to be overcome by a chosen profession that is incompatible with faith and Christian principles, allow a worldly view to distort established doctrine, or decide it is more important to accept logic and reasoning than the inspiration of the Holy Ghost.

The young adult version of the falling away process has its own unique set of dynamics after leaving a parent's home to go to college or to venture out on their own. Christian Smith in his book, *Lost in Transition,* examines the spiritual plight of young adults using the wave 3 NSYR data cited in chapter 7. Smith identifies five conditions that fuel the spiritual crisis: "confused moral reasoning, routine intoxication, materialistic life goals, regrettable sexual experiences, and disengagement from civic and political life."[25] From a 2011 study, the Barna Group categorizes three types of young adults including *prodigals* (those who were once Christian and leave the faith); *nomads* (those who wander away from the church and are therefore less active); and *exiles* (those conflicted between the culture of church and the world they live in).[26] In addition to formulating these segments, the Barna Group questions the traditional notion of young adults naturally falling out of church activity and attributes college experiences and the lack of Bible knowledge as catalysts to apostasy, suggesting young adults will eventually return to the church in which they were raised.[27]

MEET THE DEPARTING CHRISTIAN

This brings us to the first part of answering the question "Where are the Christians?" A portion of the Christian population is departing—either permanently or for an extended time. This book defines such an individual as a **Departing Christian**. The word "departing" is used because their decision is always in flux and not always permanent, thus the "-ing" instead of the "-ed." The Departing Christian is no longer converted (Matthew 18:3), is more out than in (Acts 7:51), and has become hard-hearted (Ephesians 4:18).

The Departing Christian can change his or her wayward direction by asking for the help of God who will be quick to answer (Matthew 7:7); however, when the Departing Christian resists conversion, then a transformation to counteract the darkness that is pulling him or her away can be difficult. The counsel in ministering to these departing brothers and sisters is to "leave the light on," giving hope to those who stay and illumination to those who will someday desire to find their way back. Most will return after learning the answers they sought were already there, and have always been, in Christianity. For others, a return to the Church may be prompted by a significant emotional experience in their life such as marriage and the birth of one or more children.

Chapter 10

THEY'RE HIDING—NOT PRACTICING THEIR FAITH AS ADEQUATE CHRISTIANS

THE SECOND PLACE CHRISTIANS CAN BE FOUND IS "IN HIDING." THESE are Christians that are not leaving but are instead concealing themselves in the shadows unseen, ducking any and all spiritual responsibility in a desire to be left alone. These are Christians who Paul describes as those who profess, "they know God, but in works they deny him" (Titus 1:16). These are Christians who don't know their religion, who live a form of "Christian-atheism," avoid practicing their faith, and are content with their level of believing without the works that come from that belief in Christ. This group is the largest contingent of Christians in the United States today, whose potential is enormous when it comes to building and realizing the kingdom of God on earth—a potential that is being sorely unrealized today.

IGNORANT OF THEIR OWN RELIGION

The tenets of virtually all Christian denominations today include love, service, and sacrifice—each powered by faith in Jesus Christ, giving hope to the Practicing Christian. The words "love," "service," "sacrifice," "faith," and "hope" are all verbs (although some mistakenly consider faith a noun). Verbs are action-oriented. If every Christian lived the tenets of the denomination to which they belong, the world would be a fantastic place. Unfortunately many are ignorant of their religion and therefore unable to fully live by its precepts.

A survey by the Pew Research Center's Forum on Religion and Public Life among adults found a sizable number of Christians don't know their religion, and are in fact lacking basic intelligence relating to Christianity in general. The study of over 3,400 individuals in the United States conducted in 2010 included a large number of self-described Christians who were asked thirty-two questions regarding religious knowledge and twenty-seven questions on Christianity, world religions, and religion in public life. Table 10 provides a summary by Christian denomination of the average number of questions answered correctly:

	Religious Knowledge	Christianity, World Religions, and Religion in Public Life			Total
	(out of 32)	Bible and Christianity (out of 12)	World Religions (out of 11)	Religion in Public Life (out of 4)	Out of a possible 59 questions
White Evangelical Protestant	17.6	7.3	4.8	2.3	32.0
White Mainline Protestant	15.8	5.8	4.9	2.2	28.7
Black Protestant	13.4	5.9	3.9	1.7	24.9
Catholics	14.8	5.4	4.7	2.1	27.0
LDS/Mormon	20.3	7.9	5.6	2.3	36.1
Total	16.0	6.0	5.0	2.2	29.2

Table 10: Pew U.S. Religious Knowledge Survey[1]

Interestingly, the Pew survey scores map directly to the belief, practice, and integrated composites of the adult data from chapter 7 in terms of ranking. Among Christian denominations, The Church of Jesus Christ of Latter-day Saints (LDS/Mormon) scored highest in all categories, followed by white Evangelical Protestants and white Mainline Protestants. The case can therefore be made that the more an individual knows about their religion, the Bible, Christianity, and religion in general, the more likely they are to live the faith tradition they belong to—the opposite case being equally true. Table 11 provides the data for comparison, turning the Pew scores into percentages and composites based upon the number of questions answered correctly from the survey (out of fifty-nine questions) and comparing that to three composite scores from chapter 7. Table 11 is followed by graph 3, which pictorially illustrates the data.

Denomination	Belief Composite	Practice Composite	Integrated Composite	Pew Study Composite
Conservative Protestant	70	39	48	54
Mainline Protestant	51	30	36	49
Catholic	51	24	32	46
LDS/Mormon	74	54	59	61
Total	59	32	39	49

Table 11: Belief and Practice Composite Comparison
with the Pew Study

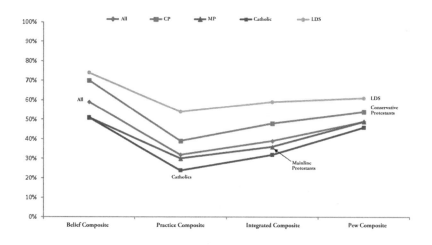

Graph 3: Belief and Practice Composite Comparison
with the Pew Study

This direct correlation is striking, especially given the Pew, Barna, and NSYR studies were conducted separately without any thought of integration.

A lack of knowledge of one's religion can manifest itself into disregarding core precepts and allowing the encroachment of false doctrines. A 2009 Barna study examined specific beliefs among 1,871 self-described Christians and found validation to its earlier 2002 study that shockingly low percentages of Christians believe in the reality of Satan, that Christ was sinless while on the earth, that the Bible is accurate, and that the Holy Spirit is a living force as opposed to a symbol of God's power.[2]

In 2006, America's Roman Catholic bishops held a conference to discuss among other things the misunderstandings, and in some cases total disregard, for church teachings—especially those surrounding homosexuality, marriage, contraception, and Holy Communion.[3] Referencing the earlier Pew study and the fact that Evangelical church attendees increasingly believe many religions can lead to eternal life, R. Albert Mohler said, "They (survey results) represent at best a misunderstanding of the Gospel and at worst a repudiation of the Gospel."[4] Doctrinal misunderstandings are not isolated to one or two churches but rather across the board in Christianity.

When Christians are ignorant of their own religion they will wander, be hesitant to share their faith, be reluctant to attend church services, and generally miss out on the opportunity to reach a greater potential in Jesus Christ. Consistency in the gospel is critical to becoming "stedfast, umoveable, always abounding in the work of the Lord" (1 Corinthians 15:58). Because Christians cannot serve two masters (Luke 16:13), nor mingle evil with that which is holy (1 Corinthians 10:21), it is important to know one's religion and to live that religion to the best of one's ability.

LUKEWARM CHRISTIANITY

The Christian in hiding is a lukewarm Christian. To be lukewarm means to not be a passionate disciple of Jesus Christ, but to also refrain from serious sin, demonstrating a mediocre commitment to the gospel. The lukewarm Christian has some faith but fails to act on that faith. The words that come to mind are "indifferent," "irresolute," "undecided," "apathetic," and "uninterested." Of the lukewarm Christian, John the Revelator wrote, "I know thy works, that thou art neither cold nor hot: I would thou wert cold or hot. So then because thou art lukewarm, and neither cold nor hot, I will spue thee out of my mouth" (Revelation 3:15–16). If that isn't a warning to the lethargic disciple of Christ, then what is?

The Christian Atheist

Pastor and author Craig Groeschel describes himself as a recovering Christian Atheist: "a person who believes in God but lives as if he doesn't exist."[5] Groeschel penned a brilliant treatise on the subject, describing the many reasons a person can slip into Christian atheism including not knowing God, being ashamed of one's past, being unsure of God's love, not practicing prayer, not believing in God's church and a number of other characteristics that lead to unbelief.[6] The imagery of a Christian Atheist is priceless, envisioning a well-meaning individual with a crucifix around their neck, living a life that does not exemplify the symbol to which they bear.

The *Christian Atheist*, as Groeschel describes it, has been called by other names in years past. The term "cultural Christian" came about in the 1970s and was made popular in the 1980s and 1990s. Several of the Founding Fathers examined in chapter 8 might be thought of as cultural Christians. The term "nominal Christian" has been used by the Lausanne Committee for World Evangelization as "a person who has not responded in repentance and faith to Jesus Christ as his personal Savior and Lord."[7] The Barna Group coined the term *Casual Christian* to describe the indecisive disciple of Christ. As one of the seven tribes resulting from a 2009 study of 30,000 respondents in the United States, Casual Christians are described as being ambivalent about their faith representing 66 percent of the adult population.[8] The Barna Group describes casual Christians as being "comprised of significant proportions of minimally active born again Christians and moderately active but theologically nominal Christians."[9] Another of the seven tribes identified by the Barna Group, *Captive Christians* (making up 16 percent of the United States adult population) do not consider Casual Christians to be genuine followers of Christ, putting them at risk to becoming Modern-day Pharisees or overly judgmental at the very least. Evangelical leadership is concerned with an upcoming generation of Casual Christians who they perceive to be more interested in environmental issues and acceptance of homosexuality than they are in abortion and gay marriage.[10]

MEET THE ADEQUATE CHRISTIAN

Each of these terms—Christian Atheist, Cultural Christian, Nominal Christian, and Casual Christian—arrive at the same destination of describing a Christian who believes in Jesus Christ but fails to practice what they profess to believe. Each of these terms is an excellent descriptor of the Christian in hiding—the Christian who believes but does not act. As good as each of these terms are, they still all lack a key element of what this book is trying to make clear with respect to describing an under-performing disciple of Christ. For this reason, the term the *Adequate Christian* is used.

The Adequate Christian believes what he or she is doing as a Christian is "good enough" and has no reason to exercise additional faith. The Adequate Christian is lukewarm and nonchalant in his or her approach to works, and nominal in his or her attitude toward Christ. The Adequate Christian relishes in biblical passages relating to being saved by grace, feeling justified in their conscious, lackadaisical approach to practicing Christianity as an active servant of God. In a twisted way, the Adequate Christian rationalizes himself or herself not as a goat but a sheep in praising God but not having served him (Matthew 25:31–46). The Adequate Christian believes the building of the kingdom of God on earth is the responsibility of others and *plans* to wait until the eleventh hour to labor while receiving the same wage as those who will have labored since the beginning of the day (Matthew 20:1–16)—if he or she plans to labor at all!

Adequate Christians are Believing Christians who lack the conviction of faith to become a Practicing Christian and are stuck somewhere in the middle in the realm of "sufficient." Adequate Christians don't comprehend the wisdom of the adage "use it or lose it" and its relationship to the servant who buried his talent and was cast out (Matthew 25:14–30). The Adequate Christian proclaims he or she would be the Good Samaritan in the parable from the Bible (Luke 10:30–37) but acts more like the priest and Levite in regularly passing over the poor and needy in the community. The Adequate Christian glosses over the writings of James, not realizing he wrote his epistle to those who were already saved (that is, using the term "my brethren" continually), urging them to claim their reward in heaven by exercising faith in doing good works. While the spirit is willing but the flesh is weak (Matthew 26:41), the Adequate Christian over time becomes so out of spiritual shape and so out of touch with the Holy Ghost that they are unable to distinguish between a weak spirit and the weak flesh.

The Adequate Christian is well known to the Christian Community. Rick Warren, an author and one of America's best-known pastors, shares that God's love and concern for the poor is mentioned in over 2,000 verses of scripture, yet so many simply miss it. Warren shares that these verses from scripture are not metaphoric or mysterious in their meaning but rather at the core of discipleship in the gospel of Christ. Richard Sterns and Lamar Vest encapsulate this teaching in a 2009 article titled "Christians Losing Their Way":

> How did Christianity drift so far from Jesus' mandate to care for the widows and orphans? How did "whatever you do for the least of these you do for me" get skewed—intentionally or not—to "what is the minimum required of me?"[11]

Where are the Christians? Unfortunately many of them, perhaps 66 percent as Barna suggests, are hiding behind distorted interpretations of scripture and thoughtless rationalization in a "good enough" world, hoping the work gets done with as little effort from them as possible. So much potential can be unleashed from this drowsy chosen generation of disciples if they would simply live the admonition of Paul, who wrote, "now it is high time to awake out of sleep: for now is our salvation nearer than when we believed" (Romans 13:11).

Departing | Adequate | Hesitant | Laboring

Chapter 11

THEY'RE VACILLATING–LIVING UNDER THEIR POTENTIAL AS *HESITANT CHRISTIANS*

MANY OF THE CHRISTIANS, WHO AREN'T DEPARTING OR HIDING BECAUSE of their unbelief, are instead dithering and vacillating with great faith waiting to be cut loose! A large group of Christians out there has enormous potential who are sitting on the sidelines indecisive about entering the game. Christianity is not a journey that requires us to do the most; Christianity is a journey that requires us to do what we are able. Composer Gian Carlo Menotti passionately stated, "Hell begins on the day when God grants us a clear vision of all that we might have achieved, of all the gifts we wasted, of all that we might have done which we did not do."[1] Olympic gold medal swimmer Geoffrey Gaberino puts it a different way, saying, "The real contest is always between what you've done and what you're capable of doing."[2]

The question of all Christians then becomes "What is your personal potential in Christ?" Paul wrote, "I can do all things through Christ which strengtheneth me" (Philippians 4:13). Jesus taught, "with God all things are possible" (Matthew 19:26). This counsel translates into our understanding what God's will is for us (our potential) and then to rely on the Lord for the strength to carry it out (reaching that potential). It is God's will that matters and unfortunately many Christians are living far below their potential according to the will of the Lord. Imagine for a moment a world where everyone lives up to the spiritual potential the Lord has endowed us with. The eroding state of current spiritual affairs in the United States could be entirely turned around if every Christian rose up and did just that—live up to his or her full potential in the Savior! But what is that potential? Once again the scriptures provide us the answer.

EACH ACCORDING TO HIS SEVERAL ABILITY

The parable of the talents in Matthew 25 is a well-known and often quoted scriptural passage. It centers around servants who are given talents (a unit of money that can also metaphorically represent gifts given to us by God) and their stewardship of those talents. The parable is understood as an admonition to do the most with what God has given us. Although that is an important lesson, a small phrase in verse 15 that is often overlooked sheds light on another significant message in the parable. In this verse, the master is giving talents to each of the servants—one receives five, another two, and the last one receives one talent: "*to every man according to his several ability*" (Matthew 25:15). In other words, each servant had specific abilities and the number of talents given to him was according to those abilities.

Likening this scripture to ourselves, we are all given talents by our Heavenly Father—each according our "several ability." One person may have an abundance of talents, another only a few. The number of talents and the types of talents are irrelevant; what is most important to comprehend is that whatever talents, gifts, and capabilities God has given us, he has done so fully understanding our potential to manage those gifts. Therefore, our life's potential is that which God has given us, and it is up to us, through Him, to figure that out.

WHERE MUCH IS GIVEN, MUCH IS REQUIRED

The three servants in the parable were given talents by the master but not told specifically what to do with them. Each servant made his own decisions in managing the talents given to him. The servant given five talents earned another five talents and the servant with two talents earned another two talents. It is clear that these two servants were familiar with the principle of "For unto whomsoever much is given, of him shall be much required" (Luke 12:48). In the event the servant who was given five talents, having earned only two more, perhaps he may have not measured up to the potential expected of him. It is equally clear the third servant who buried his talent did not measure up to his potential, succumbing to fear, perhaps even laziness, and was therefore cast out.

Strong Practicing Christians are much like the servants with five and two talents in the parable, putting their faith into action to reach the potential given to them by the Lord. This can be referred to as "magnifying one's talents." There is much to do, so few who are willing to do it (Luke 10:2), and so little time to get it done (John 9:4). Whereas Believing Christians are looking to do as little as possible, Practicing Christians are looking to do as much as the Lord is calling them to do. Those endowed with great potential by the Lord are called to do more than those who may have been endowed with less according to their several ability.

SACRIFICE AND REWARDS

In the parable of the talents, there was a third servant who buried his talent and in doing so was cast out. So what did the first two servants in the parable have that the third ones did not? One might be tempted to say "know-how," but we know that the master took the servant's ability into account when bestowing the talent. One might say the third servant was fearful while the first two were not. Perhaps, but those with faith in the Lord do not fear man (Hebrews 13:6). While we can theorize about the differences between servants, one principle worth focusing on is sacrifice.

The first two servants were willing to sacrifice their time in magnifying the talents given to them, while the third servant was not. In six passages of the New Testament, Jesus Christ is recorded to have taught, "He that findeth his life shall lose it: and he that loseth his life for my sake shall find it" (Matthew 10:39). Those who are willing to sacrifice a portion of their lives to serve in righteousness will be blessed (even saved), while those who are not will not be blessed. Those who make such sacrifices put others first and themselves last (Matthew 20:16) and for doing so will be rewarded (Matthew 16:27 and Ephesians 6:7–8).

To reach our full spiritual potential requires us to make sacrifices. We are in a position to make personal sacrifices everyday for friends, family, our church, our community, and even complete strangers. Sacrifices can also come in the form of self-denial, where we make decisions to forego our own personal pleasure and submit to the will of God.

LIKE REWARDS FOR DIFFERING ABILITIES AND RESPONSIBILITIES

There is another lesson taught in the parable of the talents that teaches the principle of receiving according to one's effort. Verses 20 to 23 of Matthew 25 are an account of the two faithful servants who doubled their talents. Notice that the rewards given to each of them in verses 21 and 23 are the same: "Well done, good and faithful servant; thou hast been faithful over a few things, I will make thee ruler over many things: enter thou into the joy of thy lord" (Matthew 25:23). Despite the fact the first servant was given five talents, and the second servant was given two talents, they both reached their God-given potential and received a like reward.

The same cannot be said of the third servant who buried his talent (Matthew 25:18). This fearful and slothful servant did nothing with the talent given him and returned it to the master offering only excuses (Matthew 25:24–25). As a result, the servant was rebuked (Matthew 25:26–27) and received a just punishment for his laziness (Matthew 25:28–30). No doubt had the third servant, who was given a single talent according to his several ability, exercised even a little faith in nurturing that talent (Matthew 25:27), he would have likewise been rewarded. Instead this servant did not even come close to reaching his potential in magnifying that which he was given and suffered as a result.

The book of Luke, chapter 19, verses 12 to 26, offers a parallel version of this parable with an added lesson associated with having to do with responsibility. In verses 12 to 13, the nobleman gives ten servants one pound each and asks them to "occupy" the money. Starting in verse 15, upon his return, the nobleman calls the servants together for an accounting of their trading. The first servant "gained ten pounds" from the one pound and was given an increase in responsibility to preside over ten cities as a reward (Luke 19:16–17). The second servant "gained five pounds" from the one pound and was given an increase in responsibility to preside over five cities as a reward (Luke 19:18–19). Likening this parable to ourselves, the Lord will reward us with varying levels of increasing responsibilities according to the efforts we exert in using the talents we are blessed with. Like the parable in Matthew 25, one of the servants hid his pound in a napkin, offering only excuses for his fear and inaction and as a result was promptly rebuked (Luke 19:20–23).

Does this seem like a harsh lesson for the Christian? Will this parable and its teaching offend the Departing Christian and discourage the Adequate Christian? Perhaps it will, but only if these Christians fail to recognize the bigger picture. Our Heavenly Father gives each of his children talents and capabilities for their journey on earth, expecting those talents and capabilities to be utilized and magnified. The range of "utilized" is wide. At one end of the utilization spectrum is the servant who buries the talent given him and at the other end the servant demonstrates a full-scale magnification of all that is given him and more. The relative midpoint of the two extremes is illustrated in the first parable as putting the money in the bank to gain interest (Matthew 25:27) and thus showing a little effort. It is those who show no meaningful effort at all that are punished and stripped.

Now one might cry foul that they never asked for these talents and therefore should not be held accountable for them. Such an attitude is akin to saying they wished they had never been born. To those who struggle in mortality due to mental or physical infirmities, the Lord is merciful (Luke 6:36), will lift them up (1 Corinthians 6:14), and will strengthen them (1 Peter 5:10), but only if they turn to him (Acts 3:19). The Lord invites all to:

> Come unto me, all ye that labour and are heavy laden, and I will give you rest. Take my yoke upon you, and learn of me; for I am meek and lowly in heart: and ye shall find rest unto your souls. For my yoke is easy, and my burden is light (Matthew 11:28–30).

Discipleship in the gospel of Jesus Christ is not an invitation to bask in the goodness of salvation only, but rather an invitation to be yoked with and labor alongside the Lord. In so doing, the Practicing Christian will find rest. A yoke is "a crossbar with two U-shaped pieces that encircle the necks of a pair of animals working together."[3] The Lord invites us to be yoked with him as a pair (Matthew 11:30), sharing the load side-by-side, making the challenges of meeting our potential in life a little easier.

Notice that we are not invited to jump on the Savior's back and allow him to take us the entire way (he already fully bore the load of our sins on the cross); rather, he invites us to embark on the journey yoked together because "every man shall bear his own burden" (Galatians 6:5). How blessed we all are to have Jesus Christ by our side—if we only allow him to be there.

Remember the question asked at the beginning of this chapter regarding the potential of a Christian? A Christian's potential is that which he or she has been endowed with by our Heavenly Father, and each person born to this earth is called to use that endowment to its fullest and will be rewarded accordingly.

MEET THE HESITANT CHRISTIAN

The potential of Practicing Christians and their impact on society in building and nurturing the kingdom of God on earth is enormous. Jesus Christ taught his disciples, "Verily, verily, I say unto you, He that believeth on me, the works that I do shall he do also; and greater works than these shall he do" (John 14:12). This means that with faith in Christ, our potential is limitless. However, that potential is thwarted by a lack of faith, which is influenced by hesitation. Hesitation has two definitions of interest to consider: "to doubt concerning two or more possible alternatives or courses of action," or "a certain degree of unwillingness."[4]

Although the Apostle Peter had great faith before the arrest of Jesus Christ, he hesitated and crumbled when faced with the adversity that followed (Matthew 26:69–75) before reasserting his faith and boldly declaring the gospel. In hesitation, the Christians decide whether they will serve in a particular instance or forego the sacrifice in being unwilling to lose their lives at that moment and wait for another day. This happens despite the Savior promising that if we seek first the kingdom all other things will proceed as they should (Matthew 6:33). Christians who routinely operate under their potential will be referred to as *Hesitant Christians*.

Hesitant Christians are blessed with great faith but are routinely operating below their spiritual potential and are therefore not living up to the principle of "where much is given much is required" (Luke 12:48). Hesitant Christians have the gift of the Holy Ghost (1 Corinthians 6:19–20) and know when to lend a hand and make the sacrifices necessary to glorify God in service. The Hesitant Christian is who Paul had in mind when he wrote, "Now unto him that is able to do *exceeding abundantly above all that we ask or think*, according to the power that worketh in us, Unto him be glory in the church by Christ Jesus throughout all ages" (Ephesians 3:20–21, emphasis added). The Hesitant Christian may at times be "weary in well doing" (2 Thessalonians 3:13) and therefore misses service opportunities presented by the Lord despite having the given to you by your Heavenly Father (Matthew 25:15). The Hesitant Christian may not understand the reality of evil and how Satan desires all Christians to hesitate so as to slow the work of righteousness on earth.

Hesitant Christians approach their by exercising the faith they are blessed with and serve the Lord by serving others. The impact of one Christian can be life-changing and society-altering as outlined by Richard Sterns and Lamar Vest:

> Throughout history, Christians have had a strong, if sometimes inconsistent, record of battling social ills. While some used the Black Death as an opportunity for fear mongering, Christians were among the few to remain in disease-ravaged cities to care for the sick. While many Christians acquiesced to slavery, it was a Christian, William Wilberforce, who led the fight to end the British slave trade and the Rev. Dr. Martin Luther King, Jr. and others joining alongside him who championed racial equality in the United States. While some sought to shame those suffering with AIDS, Christians from Franklin Graham to Bono have battled to offer practical help to those affected by the deadly disease.[5]

So where are the Christians? A portion of them are hesitating, and as the old adage goes: "he who hesitates is lost"—defined as "a person who spends too much time deliberating about what to do loses the chance to act altogether."[6]

Chapter 12

THEY'RE ENDEAVORING– LIVING DISCIPLESHIP IN THE GOSPEL OF CHRIST AS *LABORING CHRISTIANS*

IN THE IDEAL CHRISTIAN WORLD, THE DISCIPLES OF CHRIST CONTINU-ally embrace all of the values discussed in chapter 6 and live lives exemplary of the Savior. Shortly after the Ascension of Jesus Christ, the Christian community lived in great harmony where "all that believed were together, and had all things common" (Acts 2:44) and were assembled to be taught as Christians (Acts 11:26). Jesus taught that laboring is part of believing (John 6:27–29), demonstrating himself tireless service and teaching his Apostles "For I have given you an example, that ye should do as I have done to you" (John 13:15). All those who desire to follow Jesus Christ should strive to emulate the Savior's example of laboring in the service of others, to bring relief to those in need, to find joy in service (John 13:17), and to enjoy the rewards of labor (1 Corinthians 3:8)—all motivated by love of Jesus Christ (John 14:15).

Again, this is the ideal Christian scenario.

PURE RELIGION

James wrote, "Pure religion and undefiled before God and the Father is this, To visit the fatherless and widows in their affliction, and to keep himself unspotted from the world" (James 1:27). Notice the two components of what James is teaching: 1) serving God actively by attending to the most vulnerable of his children—the fatherless and widows; and 2) keeping oneself clean from the filth of the world. Both components are related. Serving helps others and keeps the server clean, while being clean gives one the attitude to serve. This is true whether it is serving the fatherless and widows, calling a person who needs an encouraging word, lifting a kind hand to a family member, or sharing the gospel with someone. Strong Practicing Christians, regardless of the denomination of Christianity they belong to, focus on these simple truths and take up their cross (Matthew 16:24) and do what they can to be examples of the believers.

MEET THE LABORING CHRISTIAN

From our earlier discussions we know that Christianity is falling short of living ideally in Christ. If a unity of faith were around basic Christian values, then America would be on a different track than it is now (as would the world). The vast majority of Christians are deserting (Departing), settling for mediocrity (Adequate), or vacillating to reach their full potential (Hesitant); however, a small number are anxiously endeavoring, actively striving to live the admonition of Christ in emulating his example. Such people are identified as *Laboring Christians.*

Laboring Christians have cultivated resilient and solid faith through practicing what they believe, recognize their blessings, and are unafraid to do what is required in building and nurturing the kingdom of God. They are intimately familiar with and regularly follow the promptings of the Holy Ghost—especially promptings that call for sacrifice in the service of others and to build unity through love. Being familiar with the scriptures and having put to the test the admonitions of the Lord, Laboring Christians feel joy in living lives of humility and surrendering to Jesus Christ. They pattern their lives after the Savior's. Although Laboring Christians are rare in today's society, their presence can easily grow if Hesitant Christians become converted and awake from their spiritual slumber. The influence one Laboring Christian can have on a society can be enormous as witnessed from our earlier study of Christian history.

SUSTAINABILITY OF THE LABORING CHRISTIAN

Being a Laboring Christian is not easy to sustain, despite the spiritual rewards and joy that comes from it. Living in the world but not becoming of the world (John 15:19) requires constant attention to activities that may not appear to be service-related. For example, earning a living monetarily is necessary to remaining temporally and spiritually solvent, enabling a life of service. Cars need to be fixed, kitchens need to be cleaned, yards need to be mowed, and that's only the beginning. The Laboring Christian juggles all these things and more and still finds time to lose his or her life in service to family and the community.

The Laboring Christian, and all those who desire to become Laboring Christians, should heed the Lord's caution to "run with patience the race that is set before us" (Hebrew 12:1). LDS/Mormon scripture provides similar counsel in more detail: "And see that all these things are done in wisdom and order; for it is not requisite that a man should run faster than he has strength. And again, it is expedient that he should be diligent, that thereby he might win the prize; therefore, all things must be done in order" (Mosiah 4:27). The Lord urges us to push ourselves but to also pace ourselves and become a bit more like the tortoise than the hare—"slow and steady wins the race."

When it comes to sustainability in spiritual labor, especially in the face of great adversity, the Laboring Christian can look to the example of Mother Teresa of Calcutta. Mother Teresa's own words describe her attitude as a Laboring Christian: "By blood, I am Albanian. By citizenship, an Indian. By faith, I am a Catholic nun. As to my calling, I belong to the world. As to my heart, I belong entirely to the Heart of Jesus."[1] Blessed Theresa of Calcutta, as she is now known, served the poor, sick, orphaned, and dying for nearly five decades as part of the Missionaries of Charity, a Roman Catholic religious congregation she founded. Among the vast recognition bestowed on Blessed Theresa for her tireless service is the Nobel Peace prize in 1979. True to her nature, Blessed Theresa refused the ceremonial banquet and gave the $192,000 in award money to the poor in India.

Few will ever live up to the Laboring Christian standard set by Blessed Theresa, and few will need to because that may not be what they are called to. What makes this selfless woman's service even more remarkable is that she did so without personally feeling the presence of Jesus Christ for much of her life. After her death in 1997, Reverend Brian Kolodiejchuk, the postulator or advocate of Blessed Theresa's cause for sainthood, made public many of her letters in a book titled *Mother Teresa: Come Be My Light*, revealing her struggle in the spirit, including the following passage:

> I am told God lives in me—and yet the reality of darkness and cold-
> ness and emptiness is so great that nothing touches my soul. . . . I want
> God with all the power of my soul—and yet between us there is terrible
> separation. . . . I feel just that terrible pain of loss, of God not wanting
> me, of God not being God, of God not really existing.[2]

Blessed Theresa knew by virtue of her vocation that she would face enormous challenges. Yet despite feeling the absence of God's presence in her life, something even the Savior Jesus Christ felt on the cross (Matthew 27:46), Blessed Theresa continued in faith serving those in need fulfilling her sacred vow to serve as a Laboring Christian all the days of her life. The lesson here for all Christians is that no matter what divine inspiration is felt, or not felt, the call to serve is always there and can always be heeded—even in the darkest of times when it would be much easier to keep to ourselves and shut out the needs of others. Despite his thorn in the flesh and infirmities that could otherwise keep him from serving, Paul wrote "that the power of Christ may rest upon me . . . for when I am weak, then am I strong" (2 Corinthians 12:7–10).

EXAMPLES OF LABORING CHRISTIANS

Providing examples of Laboring Christians is a tricky thing. As we will see in a future chapter, a person might be a Laboring Christian for a time and then fade off to becoming a Hesitant Christian or even an Adequate or Departing Christian. This is precisely why the Savior spoke of the need to "endure to the end" (Matthew 24:13)—not for a time, but to the end. In the parable of the seeds, Jesus spoke of those "sown on stony ground" that do well at first but "have no root in themselves, and so endure but for a time" only to fall away (Mark 4:16–17). This was true of King David, who was valiant in serving God and then committed grievous sins for which he paid dearly. Solomon served the Lord fervently before falling away into idol worship at the end of this life. Or Jonah who served the Lord and then ran away when he was called to do something he didn't want to do.

Laboring Christians have come from all walks of life among a multitude of denominations throughout history. Theologians Thomas Aquinas, Martin Luther, and John Calvin; evangelists Justin Martyr, Francis of Assisi, and Billy Graham; and preachers John Newton, Charles Simeon, and Thomas Chalmers all worked tirelessly to teach the gospel and fight for justice among the lowly and downtrodden. [3]

Musician George Frideric Handel and writers Harriet Beecher Stowe and C. S. Lewis produced enduring works that have brought joy and critical thinking to those seeking truth and understanding in a complex world. [4]

Poets John Milton and T. S. Eliot, along with hymn creator Charles Wesley, all left legacies of rhyme and harmony that have inspired generations of the faithful. [5]

Founders of Christian denominations, including John Wesley, Richard Allen, Joseph Smith, Alexander Campbell, and Aimee Semple McPherson, have touched the lives of millions and left a lasting impression on the spiritual landscape of the globe. [6]

Larger than life figures John Wycliffe, Joan of Arc, Ignatius of Loyola, and Phoebe Palmer gave their lives to serving others in society and on the battlefield. [7]

The courageous Harriet Tubman, the inspiring Pope John Paul II, the translator William Tyndale, the astronomer Galileo Galilei, and the spiritual pioneer Origen Adamantius likely never hesitated or thought for their own lives as they forged ahead in their respective callings, influencing the lives of countless people in the process. [8]

While this modest list of Laboring Christians is impressive and full of inspiring figures, some of the greatest Laboring Christians will never be known to the masses and may be working this very moment in schools, churches, neighborhoods, and cities around the world. A key characteristic of Laboring Christians is the silence in which they execute their craft, heeding the counsel of the Savior, who said: "But when thou doest alms, let not thy left hand know what thy right hand doeth: That thine alms may be in secret: and thy Father which seeth in secret himself shall reward thee openly" (Matthew 6:3–4).

Many movements and organizations employ and inspire Laboring Christians. Founded in 1727 in New Orleans,[9] Catholic Charities is a network of charities throughout the world, the largest of its kind in the United States,[10] providing a variety of services to those in need. Organizations like the Salvation Army, the Trinity Broadcasting System, the American Bible Society, the Billy Graham Evangelistic Association, and Mormon Helping Hands are known for their excellence in charitable operations, impacting the lives of millions of people each day around the globe. These organizations provide service opportunities to all Christians helping to inspire their journey to becoming and living as Laboring Christians.

THE OUTLIER OF CHRISTIANITY–THE RARE LATENT CHRISTIAN

The scriptures suggest there are individuals who have faith without works and those with works without faith. What about those with a little bit of faith and an abundance of works? Those people who appear to be strong Practicing Christians driven to a volume of works disproportionate to the faith they possess. The rare picture is an upside-down pyramid where works at the top will at some point overwhelm the limited faith of the individual and collapse under its own weight—perhaps through resentment, frustration, or despair.

On one side of the spectrum, a person may be trying to work his or her way to everlasting life or laboring to feel better in the wake of an event he or she feels guilty for. On the other side of the spectrum, this person may not understand the element of faith and how faith sustainably fuels the works of the Practicing Christian through conversion in Jesus Christ. Focusing on the latter, the weak-in-faith Christian, whose heart is right in performing the works of the kingdom, is known as a *Latent Christian*. Latent Christians are rare and theoretically possible; however, such persons are also statistical outliers and therefore a minor point of our discussion.

The Latent Christian is a rare breed that falls outside the evolution of the common Christian journey. To become a Latent Christian, the Laboring, Hesitant, Adequate, and Departing Christians would have to evolve unnaturally. For example, the Laboring Christian would have to continue in works while losing his or her faith—not a likely scenario. The Hesitant Christian would have to decrease faith while increasing works—also not a likely scenario. The Adequate Christian would have to remain in the same state of faith while increasing works—possible, but certainly not probable. And finally, the Departing Christian would need to slightly increase faith while dramatically increasing works—a highly unlikely development in the journey of a Christian.

Latent Christians are Laboring Christians-in-waiting. Once the component of faith is understood and applied, Latent Christians will be born again, transformed, and experience the power and purpose of gospel-centered works. The Latent Christian is a good person whose heart is being purified, whose intentions are righteous, and whose attitude is unselfish. The beauty of Latent Christians is that they've already accepted and live the principle of sacrifice, a tenet that keeps many Hesitant Christians from reaching their potential as Laboring Christians. Laboring Christians can most effectively witness and share the message of the gospel of Jesus Christ with Latent Christians, being able to share the common aspect of service.

Chapter 13

WHAT KIND OF CHRISTIAN ARE YOU?

Complete the Exercise

By now you know the answers to the question "Where are the Christians?" The Christians among our test case in the United States are spread out among those who are departing, feeling adequate, hesitating, and laboring—briefly setting aside the unique characteristics of the Latent Christian. These Christians move along a continuum based upon the exercising of faith unto works in an often erratic and volatile way. A Christian might be inactive and disillusioned much like a Departing Christian, only to be inspired by a life-changing event that increases his or her faith toward becoming a more active and vibrant Christian.

Conversely, a Christian might be active and faithful much like a Laboring Christian, only to lose interest in the journey of life toward becoming a more inactive and indolent Christian. Although these fluctuations do happen, and can happen frequently over many years, typically a Christian averages out and settles into a pattern and particular point along the continuum. Diagram 2 below illustrates the Christian Continuum.

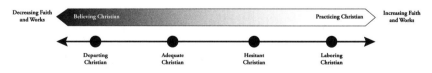

Diagram 2: The Christian Continuum

The question of "Are you a Christian?" now becomes irrelevant and is replaced by the question "What kind of Christian are you?" The Christian community can eliminate the judgmental spirit of deciding who is a Christian and who is not by moving to a more useful and productive dialogue of where people are along the Christian Continuum. Questions such as "Do you have faith?" can turn into "How much faith do you have?" and "Do you believe in works?" can turn into "What kind of works do you do?" Let's take this concept a step further.

IDENTIFYING CURRENT STATUS IN THE CHRISTIAN CONTINUUM

How does one objectively identify where they are along the Christian Continuum? The key word here is "objectively." Chances are, a Christian can come close to pinpointing where they are along the Christian Continuum at any given time. However, to make the exercise more fun and enlightening, this book offers an exercise that can be completed to more accurately identify what kind of Christian a particular individual is, keeping in mind that the exercise identifies location at a given point in time—which can change in future months or years.

The three-part exercise consists of a series of questions based on the Christian profiling outlined in chapter 6, augmented with additional points of belief regarding God the Father. Each of the questions is associated with specific scriptural passages from the Bible, which the individual completing the exercise is invited to review *after* completing the exercise (in order to achieve a more objective score). The questions are answered on a rating scale of 1 to 5 based on the level of agreement the individual has with the particular question across three different parts:

5 = completely agree

4 = agree

3 = somewhat agree

2 = disagree

1 = completely disagree

Part One: Part one evaluates individuals on a primary set of Believing Christian attributes. If the individual completing the exercise is not a Believing Christian, then the remainder of the exercise is a moot point.

Part Two: Part two evaluates individuals on a secondary set of Believing Christian attributes. These eleven attributes measure the depth of belief using tenets that are closely associated with faith in Christ according to the Model of Christian Discipleship (see diagram 5) and the belief system of the Christian.

Part Three: : Part three evaluates your practice (or works) on a set of sixteen Practicing Christian attributes.

After completing the exercise, a person can easily identify what kind of Christian he or she is. It's easy to do. This Christian Profiling Exercise has been automated and is available online at www.findyourchristianity.com. The exercise online is identical to that in this book and provides printouts to streamline the process. You are welcome to use the book or go online. Either way, give it a try so you can generate your own scores and then plot the results. Are you ready? Answer the questions in tables 12, 13 and 14 using the 1 to 5 level of agreement ratings explained earlier:

PART ONE: PRIMARY BELIEVING CHRISTIAN ATTRIBUTES

PART ONE: Believing Christian Attributes—Primary	1	2	3	4	5
1. Jesus Christ is the only true Messiah, the Savior of the world					
2. Jesus Christ is the only begotten Son of God					
3. Jesus Christ is the only way to the forgiveness of sins					
4. Jesus Christ is the only way to everlasting life (salvation)					
5. Jesus Christ is the only way to God the Father					
Primary Believing Score (add up your answers 1 through 5)					

Table 12: Part One of the Christian Profiling Exercise

- NOTE: a score of less than 10 in section one indicates the person taking the test is not a Believing Christian and therefore there is no need to complete the remainder of the exercise.

PART TWO: SECONDARY BELIEVING CHRISTIAN ATTRIBUTES

PART TWO: Believing Christian Attributes—Secondary	1	2	3	4	5
6. God is our Heavenly Father (the Father of our spirits)					
7. God the Father and Jesus Christ are one					
8. God the Father makes all things possible					
9. The Holy Ghost is one in purpose with, and proceeds from, God the Father, being active in the lives of the faithful					
10. The Holy Ghost provides comfort and knowledge from God					
11. All humans suffer from sin, requiring repentance to receive forgiveness					
12. Baptism is a spiritual cleansing and gateway into the Church of Jesus Christ					
13. The Lord's Supper symbolizes a remembrance of Christ's sacrifice if you are a Protestant or a Mormon, or is the literal body and blood of Jesus Christ (Eucharist) if you are a Catholic					
14. The scriptures (for example, Bible) are the inspired word of God					
15. You are able to believe without seeing in spiritual matters as one having faith (that is, you don't need to be given divine evidence)					
16. You consider yourself to be born again, converted, with a new life in Jesus Christ					
Secondary Believing Score (add up your answers 6 through 16)					

Table 13: Part Two of the Christian Profiling Exercise

Primary Believing Score	
Secondary Believing Score	
TOTAL Believing Score	

Table 14: Summation of Parts 1 and 2

Adding the primary believing score from part one (table 12) with the secondary believing score from part two (table 13) determines a total believing score for the individual completing the exercise in table 14. After deriving the total believing score, set this score aside and move on to part three—the exercise on Practicing Christian attributes.

PART THREE: PRACTICING CHRISTIAN ATTRIBUTES

Consideration was given to making the rating scale for this part of the test one of frequency (daily, weekly, and so on); however, various legitimate limitations (handicaps, family circumstances, life situations, and so on) can make it difficult, if not impossible, for some Christians to do certain things according to a particular frequency. Therefore, the part three questions are rated on the same agreement scale used in parts one and two according to the intentions and effort of the individual completing the exercise across the sixteen attributes. Two words need further definition before completing part three of the exercise: *strive* and *regularly*:

- **Strive:** "Strive" means there is an ever-conscious and vigorous effort to live the principle, as opposed to having good intentions that exist in the background of one's life.

- **Regularly:** "Regularly" means it is part of a cultivated discipline of consistent behavior demonstrating a commitment to the principle as opposed to a "when I have time" type of behavior.

PART THREE: Practicing Christian Attributes	1	2	3	4	5
1. You strive to keep all of the commandments of God and the teachings of his Son Jesus Christ					
2. You regularly repent, asking for forgiveness of and turning away from sin					
3. You regularly pray to God the Father—out loud, in secret, and/or even within your heart					
4. You strive to follow the teachings and example of Jesus Christ					
5. You regularly make meaningful personal sacrifices in living the gospel of Jesus Christ					
6. You regularly perform service for others, spending your own personal time to do so					
7. You regularly share the gospel of Jesus Christ with others					
8. You strive to be pure in heart, including earnest attempts to exercise humility, having gratitude in the Lord					
9. You regularly give of your time, talents, and substance to others					
10. You regularly praise God and his Son Jesus Christ in worship					
11. You strive to love others in kindness and charity					
12. You strive to be a good example of Christian values and living					
13. You regularly read and study the scriptures (for example, Bible)					
14. You regularly fellowship with other Christians in worship					
15. You strive to actively forgive and show mercy to others					
16. You strive to be a peacemaker among those with whom you associate					
TOTAL Practicing Score (add up your answers 1 through 16)					

Table 15: Part Three of the Christian Profiling Exercise

IDENTIFYING THE CHRISTIAN TYPE

After completing the three parts of the exercise, the individual plots the total Believing Score and the total Practicing Score on diagram 3 below:

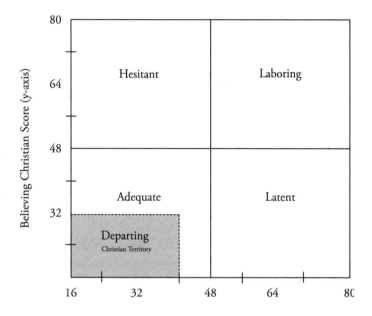

Diagram 3: The Christian Profiling Matrix

The plot begins by locating the Believing Christian score number along the vertical axis (the left portion of the graph, or y-axis, if you remember high school math). The Practicing Christian score is then located along the horizontal axis (x-axis, or the bottom portion of the graph). To identify the type of Christian the individual completing the exercise is at that point in time along the Christian Continuum is to find the intersection of these two points (believing and practicing). The following are a few examples of test takers to help illustrate the process:

- **Bob:** Let's say Bob had scored a 24 in the first part and a 40 in second, giving him a total Believing Christian score of 64. Bob then had a total score of 52 for the Practicing Christian part of the exercise. Using diagram 3 with 64 along the left-side vertical (y-axis) and 52 along the bottom horizontal (x-axis) identifies Bob as being a *Laboring Christian*.

- **Sally:** Sally completed the exercise and came up with a combined score of 50 for the Believing Christian portion (y-axis) and 28 for the Practicing Christian Portion (x-axis), identifying Sally as a *Hesitant Christian*.

- **Roger:** Roger completed the exercise and was surprised to find that he scored 40 for the Believing Christian portion (y-axis) and 22 for the Practicing Christian portion (x-axis), identifying Roger as an *Adequate Christian*.

- **Diane:** Diane reluctantly completed the exercise and learned she was in rare territory with a combined score of 24 for parts one and two and 58 for part three, identifying her as an unlikely *Latent Christian*.

- **Bill:** Bill has struggled with his faith for the last year or two and scored a 20 for the believing attributes and a 30 for the practicing attributes profiling him as a *Departing Christian*; hence, Bill has a lot of work to do on his faith before doing anything else.

The exercise is not perfect, but it can help inquiring (and objective) Christians understand how they are doing with developing faith in the gospel of Jesus Christ and how that faith is motivating them to respond to the calling of practicing discipleship in building and nurturing the kingdom of God on earth. Once again, the Christian Profiling exercise is automated online and can be completed at www.findyourchristianity.com.

INTERPRETING THE TEST RESULTS AND CHARTING A COURSE FOR IMPROVEMENT

So how did you or the person you helped complete the exercise do? Surprised? Satisfied? Uncomfortable? Happy? Upset? The Christian Profiling Exercise is not meant to be definitive, but rather directional. The purpose of the exercise is to help Christians profile themselves as opposed to being profiled by others. The exercise is designed to help Christians ascertain where they are along the Christian Continuum at a particular moment so as to identify the improvements they'd like to make in order to reach their full potential as a disciple of Christ. As a Christian, this exercise should help you conduct a comprehensive spiritual inventory to objectively see where you stand in your journey as a Christian. In short, this exercise should help provide you a critical component in helping to answer the more personal question of "Where's my Christianity?"

For example, Sally identified herself as a Hesitant Christian. If Sally desires to be a stronger Christian and contribute more vibrantly to her community, then evolving to become a more active Practicing Christian may include examining those areas in part three that included lower scores. Roger on the other hand identified himself to be an Adequate Christian. For Roger he would first focus on the elements of faith where he scored low, taking the time to study the scriptures related to those elements and praying for a stronger testimony in Jesus Christ. Once Roger felt an increase of faith taking root, then a gradual focus on more active participation in the attributes of part three will help him move closer to becoming a Laboring Christian.

The journey to Christian improvement will always begin with a desire to become a more committed Christian and by doing so recognizing more fully God's presence in our lives. This is followed by active pursuit of increasing one's faith, resulting in more regular participation in the key elements of a Practicing Christian. Most important, the committed Christian must "Trust in the Lord with all [his] heart; and lean not unto [his] own understanding" (Proverbs 3:5), meaning that reliance on the Lord and the strength He provides is paramount to success. Becoming a more committed Christian is a journey, not a destination, which is why the Savior used the phrase "endure unto the end" (Mark 13:13) and James declared, "Behold, we count them happy which endure" (James 5:11). To endure means to "bear with patience" or "sustain without yielding,"[1] indicating a process and not place where one arrives and exists happily ever after. The focus is on continuous and gradual improvement, sustained over a lifetime. When there are personal setbacks due to sin, bad health or the challenges of life, repentance, healing, and help are available from the Lord to assist one back to the narrow road leading to eternal life.

THE SALT WARNING AND LIGHT ANALOGY

In his Sermon on the Mount as recorded in the fifth chapter of Matthew, the Savior meticulously outlines the kind of people his followers should be, including poor in spirit, meek, thirsting after righteousness, merciful, pure in heart, and peacemakers. Jesus calls on the faithful to live a higher law in keeping the commandments, refraining from anger, seeking reconciliation, abstaining from lust, shunning divorce, avoiding swearing, communicating carefully, exercising humility, and loving one's enemies. Living all of these characteristics are a tall order for even the strongest and most committed of Christians, but this is a goal worth pursuing! Jesus encourages his disciples to "Be ye therefore perfect, even as your Father which is in heaven is perfect" (Matthew 5:48).

The expectation is not perfection in this life, but rather the exercising of faith in preparation for eternal perfection, to reach the potential given to each child of God. Within each of us is the prospect to do all of these things and more, to become like Christ (1 John 3:2), and in doing so to have joy in this life and in the eternity.

In the same sermon, Jesus gives his disciples a warning, saying: "Ye are the salt of the earth: but if the salt have lost his savour, wherewith shall it be salted? it is thenceforth good for nothing, but to be cast out, and to be trodden under foot of men" (Matthew 5:13). Our potential is to season the earth with the gospel of Jesus Christ and to live lives that will enhance and flavor the lives of others as part of a magnificent spiritual feast. However, should we decide to live lethargically under our potential and lose that savor, then we are just "taking up space," cursed as a lukewarm Christian (Revelation 3:16), and not worthy of the greater reward. To further illustrate our potential, the Savior continues in the next three verses of the same sermon by saying

> Ye are the light of the world. A city that is set on an hill cannot be hid. Neither do men light a candle, and put it under a bushel, but on a candlestick; and it giveth light unto all that are in the house. Let your light so shine before men, that they may see your good works, and glorify your Father which is in heaven. (Matthew 5:14–16)

So despite the warning of being cast out for loss of savor in building and nurturing the kingdom on earth, the Savior reiterates that we are a light to the world with immense potential to do good works in glorifying God as Laboring Christians.

AVOIDING KID-GLOVE CHRISTIANITY

When used in the context of dealing with people, the idiom "handling with kid gloves" means to give special treatment, using great care, and extreme sensitivity. During his mortal ministry, Jesus Christ aptly demonstrated love, compassion, and understanding to all those he came in contact with. However, as with the salt of the earth analogy, the Savior did not hold back in letting those who desired to follow him know that "He that loveth father or mother more than me is not worthy of me: and he that loveth son or daughter more than me is not worthy of me. And he that taketh not his cross, and followeth after me, is not worthy of me (Matthew 10:37–38). Or "He that is not with me is against me: and he that gathereth not with me scattereth" (Luke 11:23). When the priest Eli feared his sons more than God, the results were disastrous for him and his family (1 Samuel 3:12–14).

These and other scriptures like them suggest that while there is a time and place for extending compassion and understanding to the weak or wayward Christian, there is never a time or place for pity and false enablement. Too many pastors and capable disciples of Christ are telling Departing, Adequate, and Hesitant Christians, "It's okay. I'm sure you're doing what you can and don't need to do anymore. God knows your faith, and grace will be there to lift you up." In many cases, this is not only the wrong thing to tell someone operating under their spiritual potential as a means of motivation, but from a biblical perspective, this is simply encouraging false doctrine.

Those offering spiritual counsel to the weak must understand the primary issue facing these underperforming Christians who are losing their savor and whose light is being hidden by their own self-inflicted bushels. William Law, an eighteenth-century English Cleric and author of the book *A Serious Call to a Devout and Holy Life*, offers his own answer to that question:

> If you will here stop and ask yourselves why you are not as pious as the primitive Christians were, your own heart will tell you that it is neither through ignorance nor inability, but purely because you never thoroughly intended it.[2]

Law suggests the Adequate and Hesitant Christian lacks desire, commitment, and intention. Pastors and fellow Christians might do well to consider the words of Winston Churchill, who said, "It's not enough that we do our best; sometimes we have to do what's required," helping the underachieving Christian understand what is necessary instead of inspiring excuses. The heralded motto "What Would Jesus Do?" introduced by Charles Sheldon,[3] should lead a minister to providing advice commensurate with the doctrine of Christ toward loving admonishment instead of anxious approval. The pastor or fellow Christian desiring to help must focus on helping bring about real conversion instead of enabling false justification. Kid-glove Christianity is well intentioned but poorly utilized and will often do more harm than good. This will be more fully discussed in the next section.

CHRISTIAN TYPES OF TODAY'S DENOMINATIONAL GROUPINGS

Before we move to our final section, you might be wondering what types of Christians the denominational groupings examined in chapter 7 are and where they end up in the Christian Profiling Matrix in diagram 3. Because the Christian Profiling Exercise provided in this chapter is meant to focus on the individual, the relevancy of applying the exercise to a large group of Christians loses its meaning. However, from a directional perspective, the exercise of plotting the denominational groupings does have some merit and is at the very least curiously interesting.

Because this chapter's exercise is based on a maximum score of 80, and the belief and practice data from chapter 7 is based upon a maximum percentage score of 100, the data from chapter 7 needs to be normalized. This is done by simply multiplying the composite belief and practice scores for each of the denominational groupings by .80. Table 16 provides the results of this normalization exercise:

	Belief Composite	Practice Composite	Belief Composite Normalized	Practice Composite Normalized
Conservative Protestant	70	39	56	32
Mainline Protestant	51	30	40	24
Catholics	51	24	41	19
LDS/Mormon	74	54	59	43
Total Population	59	32	47	26

Table 16: Belief and Practice Composites Normalized

Diagram 4 shows the results of the exercise by applying the normalized scores to the Christian Test Matrix among Conservative Protestants (CP), Mainline Protestants (MP), Catholics (CA), LDS/Mormon (MO), and the total Christian population (AL).

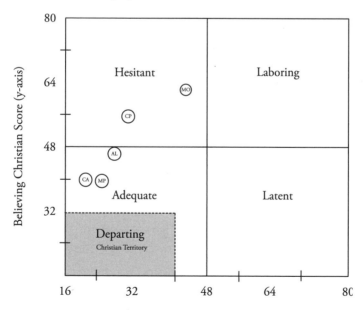

Diagram 4: Denominational Groupings Mapped to the Christian Profiling Matrix

Despite the limitations of this exercise, the results provide a realistic picture of a country with a large number of Adequate and Hesitant Christians who are living far below their spiritual potential. Accounting for the normalcy of distribution, this picture suggests a huge number of Adequate Christians in America explaining much of the "I don't care" attitude that seems to be plaguing our nation. Conservative Protestants and LDS/Mormons demonstrate a clear separation from the rest of the population with distinguishable differentials in belief and practice. Therefore, despite the passionate theological differences that divide the two denominational groupings, Conservative Protestants and LDS/Mormons have more in common than they would likely care to admit.

Section 4

HOW IS CHRISTIANITY TO UNITE?

A Vision

"Of all religions, Christianity is without a doubt the one that should inspire tolerance most, although, up to now, the Christians have been the most intolerant of all men."

—Voltaire

CHRISTIANITY HAS BEEN IN A STATE OF INCREASING DIVISION SINCE ITS inception. Consider the second-century observation of the Greek philosopher Celsus, who wrote that Christians "slander one another with dreadful and unspeakable words of abuse. And they would not make even the least concession to reach agreement; for they utterly detest each other."[1] Although a known opponent of early Christianity, the words of Celsus ring true today. In his treatise titled *Unifying Christians of the East and the West*, the Russian religious and political philosopher Nikolai Berdyaev lamented the division of the Church, writing:

> The separation of Churches or, better said, the schism of Christianity is the greatest failure of the Christendom in history. This failure testifies, how much freedom the Providence of God has given to man, and

how much man has misused this freedom. In the Church there cannot be separation, because the Church is One, and it is homogeneous. Its oneness is determined through the fact that Christ is living in it, that it is mediating the gifts of Grace, and that in it are administered the sacraments. It is not the Church that is divided, but rather Christian humanity.[2]

The full unification of Christianity among the nearly 34,000 denominations in the world today is not likely to happen before the Second Coming of the Savior—at least not on a theological level. However, unity among Christian humanity to reach a greater potential is well within reach and is in fact happening regularly on local levels as disparate denominations band together to fight for common causes. Whereas theology divides deeply the denominations of Christianity, there are common values on which all of Christianity can unite to repel evil and promulgate good. Focusing on values consider the Model of Christian Unity in diagram 5.

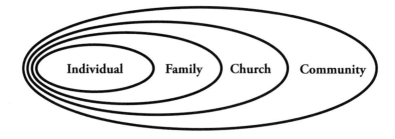

Diagram 5: The Model of Christian Unity

The unification process evolves from the smallest unit of Christianity—the individual—to incrementally larger units of Christianity including the family, church, and community. As each unit is strengthened spiritually, the potential impact on society is not merely cumulative as a result of self-reinforcement, but it is exponential as a result of spiritual synergy. This section explores how to achieve this unity among Christians and why such unity begins with each of us.

THE ANATOMY OF DIVISION AND UNITY

Imagine for a moment the power of a computer. The computer can manage word processing, calculate complex spreadsheets, access unlimited information from the Internet, and process data at blazing speed. Imagine the power of that computer joined together with millions of other computers to form a single massive computing source. This concept is called grid computing and is an "architecture in which CPU resources are shared across a network, and all machines function as one large supercomputer."[3] Grid computing is an example of what can happen when the power of many separate entities comes together to form a single super source.

Now imagine the power of millions of Christians unified in prayer and purpose toward achieving a set of shared common values (not theology) and the super spiritual source that would result from such unification. Whereas a single Christian has the power to change lives within the realm of his or her influence, droves of Christians joined together have the power to change entire communities, even nations and the world. That is the potential of Christianity! The opposite of this power is the unfortunate state of affairs in today's society, where so many Christians sacrifice the strength of spiritual unity for the sake of an interpretive pharisaical Christian purity.

THE BIBLICAL CASE FOR CHRISTIAN UNITY

The Bible does not suggest a plan by which everyone and everything are the same. On the contrary, the Bible teaches there are diversities of gifts, administrations, and operations divided "to every man severally," but each respectively of the same Spirit, Lord, and God (1 Corinthians 12:4–11). Humanity often sees these diversities as competing forces that separate, when in fact they are complementary forces that should unite, all coming from the same divine source (John 15:5). When these diversities are accepted with respect, gratitude, and charity, Christians are joined in the "bond of perfectness" (Colossians 3:14).

The desire of Jesus Christ in the unification of his disciples was the subject of his heartfelt prayer to God the Father, when he pleaded, "that they may be made perfect in one," with Christ dwelling within the disciple and God dwelling within the Savior (John 17:23) forming the perfect union. Paul wrote of "unity of the Spirit" around "one Lord, one faith, one baptism, one God" until "we all come in the unity of faith" (Ephesians 4:3–13), avoiding divisions (1 Corinthians 1:10). The disciples of Christ are urged to "be likeminded" in the "same love, being of one accord, of one mind" (Philippians 2:1–2; see also 2 Corinthians 13:11, Philippians 1:27, and Romans 15:6).

After a mighty spiritual experience in prayer, being filled with the Holy Ghost, the author of Acts records: "And the multitude of them that believed were of one heart and of one soul: neither said any of them that ought of the things which he possessed was his own; but they had all things common" (Acts 4:32)—an incredible demonstration of unity among the believers! Peter implored the faithful to "be ye all of one mind, having compassion one of another, love as brethren, be pitiful, be courteous" (1 Peter 3:8). The book of Acts uses the phrase "one accord" (meaning together) in several passages, signifying unity among the early Christians of the Church (Acts 2:1, 2:46, 4:24, 5:12, and 8:6). Is it any wonder that David proclaimed, "Behold, how good and how pleasant it is for brethren to dwell together in unity" (Psalm 133:1).

THE FORCES THAT UNITE CHRISTIANITY

More powerful than the forces that divide Christianity are the forces that unite Christianity. These forces are inspired and courageous in their efforts to live the gospel of Jesus Christ with the vision of building and nurturing the kingdom of God on earth through a strong and united Body of Christ. Each of these forces leverages the Model of Christian Unity, operating from the inside out.

Inspired and Courageous Individuals: The inspired and courageous individual is a Laboring Christian who strives each day to be a faithful disciple of Christ. This person recognizes the importance of cleansing the inner vessel first (Matthew 23:26), removing the temporal and spiritual obstacles that obstruct their own process of conversion (Matthew 7:5), and strives to live the principles of the gospel outlined in previous chapters. The inspired and courageous individual is far from perfect and may struggle with divorce, wayward children, addictions, disappointments, handicaps, illnesses, lost jobs, transgression, and a host of other spiritual and physical infirmities that are all part of our human existence. These individuals recognize their weaknesses before God, relying on divine guidance and strength to overcome the natural tendencies that lead to the pharisaical attitudes that divide the Body of Christ.

Inspired and courageous individuals are the poor in spirit and those that mourn; they are the meek, those that hunger and those that thirst after righteousness; they are the merciful, the pure in heart, the peacemakers, and often the persecuted (Matthew 5:3–10). An inspired and courageous individual that has already been set free or is waiting to be unleashed exists inside each of us.

Inspired and Courageous Leaders: Being an inspired and courageous individual themselves, the inspired and courageous leader has been given stewardship over others with a commission to shepherd the Church of God (Acts 20:28) with the attitude of a servant (Matthew 20:27). In a type of patriarchal order, the inspired and courageous leader leads by example and fully understands there is strength in numbers (Ecclesiastes 4:9–10), that diversity is a righteous work (James 2) and is representative of God's love of all nations (Acts 17:26–27). The inspired and courageous leader knows the best missionary work is to be "an example of the believers, in word, in conversation, in charity, in spirit, in faith, in purity" (1 Timothy 4:12). By fulfilling his or her commission in ecclesiastical leadership, the inspired and courageous leader unites the Body of Christ across denominational boundaries.

Inspired and Courageous Churches: Inspired and courageous churches are full of inspired and courageous individuals and leaders, all striving to reach their potential as disciples of Christ. These churches call leaders at all levels of the organization who exemplify and live the principles of the gospel of Jesus Christ (1 Corinthians 11:1), are led by the Holy Ghost (Romans 8:14), and possess the characteristics of righteous leaders (1 Timothy 3:1–4), including Jesus Christ (Ephesians 5:23). The inspired and courageous church not only proclaims the gospel (Matthew 28:19) and preserves its truth (1 Timothy 3:15) but also teaches its members to serve (1 Peter 4:10 and Acts 20:35) and make sacrifices (Mark 8:34), reaching out beyond its denominational borders in service.

Inspired and Courageous Communities: Inspired and courageous communities are made up of the individuals, leaders, and churches just described who proactively come together to lift up the greater whole. These communities are aware of the realities of political, denominational, and social limitations, but live in the spirit of the words of the Savior, who said, "Every kingdom divided against itself is brought to desolation; and every city or house divided against itself shall not stand" (Matthew 12:25). The inspired and courageous community focuses on what each component has in common and not on what divides them. With this focus the inspired and courageous community harnesses the power that comes from unity, while respecting and celebrating the differences that make each component of the spiritual society unique (1 Corinthians 12).

It is important to fully understand and appreciate that the unity spoken of here is not an ecumenical compromise where doctrines are watered down and falsely embraced for the sake of short-term cooperation. Rather, the unity spoken of here is one that maximizes humility to leverage the common spiritual values among the children of God, helping Christianity reach its full potential and thus the community. It is a unity that minimizes the pride that magnifies the diverse theological ideals among the denominations of Christianity that create separation and loss of potential. Each of these forces within the Model of Christian Unity—individual, family, church, and community—will be more fully examined in the next four chapters.

Chapter 14

STRENGTHEN THE INDIVIDUAL

THE MOST BASIC UNIT IN THE KINGDOM OF GOD IS THE INDIVIDUAL, comprising the first rung in the Model of Christian Unity. The Savior said, "I am the vine, ye are the branches," and as branches nourished from the same vine we as individuals are to "*bringeth forth much fruit*: for without me [Jesus Christ] ye can do nothing" (John 15:5, emphasis added). The Christian community must begin the unification process by strengthening individuals in Christ so the branches of Christianity can together in harmony bring forth fruit in abundance to feed the lambs and sheep (John 21:15–17) of the Good Shepherd.

THE BIBLICAL CASE FOR STRENGTHENING THE INDIVIDUAL

The cornerstone scripture for strengthening the individual comes from Luke 22:32 with Jesus telling Peter, "when thou art converted, strengthen thy brethren." In this passage, the Savior teaches a profound yet simple lesson that those who are converted are to strengthen those who are not. Because conversion is a continual process, it may be more accurate to say that those who are further along in their conversion to the gospel of Jesus Christ (along the Christian Continuum) should lift up and help those who are not as far along. This is fully reinforced by Paul in his letter to the Romans, where he wrote, "We then that are strong ought to bear the infirmities of the weak" (Romans 15:1). Knowing the truth of this principle the early disciples were urged "to support the weak, and to remember the words of the Lord Jesus, how he said, It is more blessed to give than to receive" (Acts 20:35). In doing so, the stronger disciples of Christ are to receive the "weak in the faith" (Romans 14:1) and to do so without judgment while avoiding "kid-glove Christianity."

The process of strengthening the individual is one that calls for daily encouragement to help guard against the "deceitfulness of sin" (Hebrews 3:13), focusing on language that edifies one another (Ephesians 4:29), and motivating brothers and sisters to good works in the gospel (Hebrews 10:24–25). The route to a stronger individual includes comforting one another (1 Thessalonians 4:18 and 5:11), leading to a glad heart (Proverbs 12:25), and producing hope, joy, and peace "through the power of the Holy Ghost" (Romans 15:13). One of the keys to strengthening others is humility, putting others first (Mark 10:31), and keeping one's pride in check (Romans 12:3).

Our efforts to strengthen others cannot be reserved solely for those with whom we go to church or only those we like and are kind to us (Luke 6:33). Rather, Christian unity comes in strengthening everyone within our realm of influence. This includes our neighbors, our coworkers, strangers, and even our so-called enemies (Matthew 5:43–44). If all Christians followed the simple commandment of loving their neighbors, the impact on individuals, families, churches, and communities would be without bounds.

CONVERSION AND UNITY

Conversion is the key to unity. Pope Benedict XVI, celebrating mass during the Feast of the Epiphany in St. Peter's Basilica on January 6, 2012, said, "[the] unity for which we pray requires inner conversion, both shared and individual," and it cannot be "limited to cordiality and cooperation."[1] The pope went on to say Christians are required to accept "all the elements of unity which God has conserved for us" and that ecumenism is not an option but rather "the responsibility of the entire Church and of all the baptized."[2] The pontiff urged the faithful to make praying for unity an "integral part" of one's prayer life "especially when people from different traditions come together to work for victory in Christ over sin, evil, injustice and the violation of human dignity."[3]

Although some Christians may be in the habit of dismissing the words of the Roman Catholic pope, these words from Benedict regarding unity and conversion are profound and worth pondering. The unity of faith spoken of by Paul in his letter to the Ephesians is achieved only after "the perfecting of the saints" and the edification of "the Body of Christ" (Ephesians 4:12)—all of which requires conversion beginning with spiritually strengthening the individual.

THE SPECIFICS OF STRENGTHENING THE INDIVIDUAL

Moving from the broad to the specific, the details of how to strengthen the individual are found in the exercise questions formulated in chapter 13. The believing and practicing attributes are those that every Christian needs to develop creating an enduring testimony and spiritual foundation on which to live as a disciple of Christ. Living these attributes is not likely to happen in an instant. Some of these attributes are harder to develop than others; however, each has a purpose in strengthening the individual along the axes of faith and works.

Strengthening Faith

The sixteen belief attributes found in chapter 13's exercise (parts one and two) are the basic building blocks of strengthening faith. These attributes flow in logical progression to formulate a pattern of faith, one building upon the other in succession. The recognition and knowledge of each of these attributes opens the spiritual eyes and heart of the willing individual, paving the way for committed discipleship in the gospel of Christ. The following is a review of the sixteen attributes:

Jesus Christ—attributes 1 to 5: The first five attributes focus on Jesus Christ as the Savior of the world, the only begotten Son of God, the single source of forgiveness through the infinite Atonement, the giver of everlasting life, and the only way to God the Father. These beliefs are at the core of Christian faith, helping us understand the divine nature of the Messiah and what he has done for us.

God the Father—attributes 6 to 8: The next three attributes focus on the almighty God, the Father of our spirits, who is one with Jesus

Christ and the primary source of enabling power in our lives, through which all things are possible. The Savior continually referred to and glorified his Father in Heaven, calling him his God (John 17:3 and Matthew 27:46), setting the example of how we should do the same in prayer and thanksgiving, recognizing our divine lineage.

Holy Ghost—attributes 9 and 10: The next two attributes focus on the Holy Ghost, the Spirit of God that resides and moves within us, illuminating truth and providing comfort to the faithful. While God gives us life and Jesus Christ redeems us, the Holy Ghost that manifests these truths to us and acts as a constant spiritual GPS in the life of the disciple of Christ.

Repentance—attribute 11: Repentance is a change of direction, signifying an understanding that one is broken and in need of redemption. The only path to redemption is Jesus Christ, whose atoning sacrifice has the power to deliver us through grace from God the Father.

Baptism—attribute 12: Baptism is a cleansing from sin and a commitment for the Christian to take upon him- or herself the name of Jesus Christ, to keep his commandments, and to follow his teachings. In return, the Lord blesses the individual spiritually. Baptism is the gateway to membership in the Lord's Church and is often followed by receiving the gift of the Holy Ghost.

The Lord's Supper—attribute 13: The Lord's Supper (also referred to as the Eucharist, the sacrament, and other terms) symbolizes the sacrifice made by Jesus Christ and the commandment to partake of his body as the Bread of Life and his blood as the new and everlasting covenant. For Catholics, it is not a symbolism but rather the literal body and blood of Jesus Christ.

The Scriptures—attribute 14: The scriptures are the inspired word of God, which we are urged to search in order to find truth in Jesus Christ. While one can experience all of the aforementioned attributes without the aid of the scriptures, searching the scriptures will accelerate and strengthen the faith-building process.

Pure Faith—attribute 15: Pure faith focuses on one's ability to live by the words of Paul, who described faith as "the substance of things hoped for, the evidence of things not seen" (Hebrews 11:1).

Born Again—attribute 16: Rebirth, or being born again, centers around conversion and the reality that each one of us must be regenerated in Christ to see the kingdom of God (John 3:3), giving up our former lives to God the Father for a new life in his Son Jesus Christ.

Strengthening Works

The pattern for strengthening works runs adjacent to, yet slightly behind, the strengthening of faith (as faith is a prerequisite of works). The sixteen practicing attributes found in part three of the Christian Profiling Exercise are the basic building blocks of strengthening works. These sixteen attributes do not have a logical progression and are often fueled by the spiritual gifts bestowed upon the individual by God the Father. Like those of faith, the recognition and knowledge of each of these attributes opens the spiritual eyes and heart of the willing individual and paves the way for committed discipleship in the gospel of Christ. The following is a review of the sixteen attributes:

Keeping the Commandments—attribute 1: Samuel the prophet wrote, "to obey is better than sacrifice, and to hearken than the fat of rams" (1 Samuel 15:22). Jesus spoke plainly when he told his followers, "If ye love me, keep my commandments" (John 14:15). By keeping the commandments, an individual cultivates obedience and love of the Savior—both valuable characteristics of the disciple of Christ.

Regular Repentance—attribute 2: Repentance is a prerequisite to baptism. Repentance becomes a practicing attribute when regularly performed, helping to develop humility, a contrite spirit, and, most important, a forgiveness of sins following baptism.

Regular Prayer—attribute 3: It is critical that we regularly communicate with our Father in Heaven, offering gratitude for blessings large and small, expressing heartfelt and righteous desires, and receiving personal revelation.

Following Jesus Christ—attribute 4: To be a disciple of Jesus Christ, one must know the teachings of the Savior (Matthew 5:1–16, Matthew 6:5–6, Matthew 7:1–8, Matthew 22:36–40, Matthew 25:41–45, and so on) and the example he left for us to emulate (John 13:15). In following Christ, we become more like him (1 John 2:6).

Regular Sacrifice—attribute 5: In following Christ, denying ourselves and taking up our cross means putting others first and making sacrifices in a variety of forms. When we regularly sacrifice, we become more like the servant Jesus urged us to be (Matthew 23:11).

Serving Others—attribute 6: Perhaps the most meaningful form of sacrifice is found in serving others. When we give our time to lift up, support, and comfort others, we are in reality serving the Lord (Matthew 25:40).

Sharing the Gospel—attribute 7: Although Christ commissions us all to share the gospel with everyone, there is more to it than that. Both the preparation to share (1 Peter 3:15) and the actual act of sharing the gospel strengthen personal testimony, brings joy and happiness to others, and expresses our love for God and our neighbors in a unique and sacred way.

Pure in Heart—attribute 8: The pure in heart are blessed, have an attitude of gratitude to the Lord (Colossians 3:17), and exercise humility and good works for the glory of God. Striving to become pure in heart will aid us in our quest to perfect the other fifteen attributes.

Giving of Oneself—attribute 9: Associated with but not the same as attribute six (serving others) relates to giving. Everyone has something to give in the effort to build and nurturing the kingdom of God. For some, it is money; for others, it may be one or more talents; and for still others, it may be their time in large or small quantities. Sharing our means with others, especially anonymously (Matthew 6:4), brings abundant blessings to both the giver and the receiver.

Praise and Worship—attribute 10: There are hundreds of instances of the words "praise" and "worship" in the Bible, referring to God and his Son Jesus Christ. Regular praise and worship cultivate meekness through our acknowledgement of our nothingness and by the expression of our gratitude and love for God the Father and his Son Jesus Christ

Loving Others—attribute 11: One might think that many of the aforementioned attributes are directly correlated with loving one's neighbor—and they would be right. However, overlapping lessons were a hallmark of the public ministry of Christ, demonstrating the need for constant reinforcement of key gospel principles. One of the most important principles, second only to loving God, is to love one's neighbor.

Being a Good Example—attribute 12: The most effective way to share the gospel is to be a good example of living the gospel. Vigilance in being a good example will purify our thoughts and actions, strengthening us as Christians.

Reading the Scriptures—attribute 13: Having faith that the scriptures are the inspired word of God is important, but even more important is regularly study of the scriptures to know and understand God and his Son Jesus Christ and how to apply the gospel to one's life.

Fellowshipping—attribute 14: When a coal is in a fire, it gives off heat and transfers heat to and from the other coals in the fire. When that same coal is removed from the fire, it will burn hot for a short period and then go cold until it is put back into the fire. Fellowshipping allows disciples to give spiritual and tangible support to, while obtaining spiritual support from, other Christians with whom they worship and socialize. It's essential that a Christian both give and receive spiritual strength through fellowship.

Forgiving Others—attribute 15: We all will, at one point or another, be offended by the words or actions of another. The offense may come from family, friends, strangers, and even church leaders. Jesus taught we are required to forgive them all—regardless of the severity of their transgression against us and regardless of the number of times they offend (Matthew 18:22). Extending forgiveness to others brings spiritual growth, peace of mind, humility, and, most important, mercy from our Heavenly Father for our own transgressions.

Being a Peacemaker—attribute 16: Peacemakers promote peace; however, they can also be defined as those who share the good news (that is, gospel) with others, bringing them peace. Being a peacemaker requires patience, love, understanding, compassion, and a desire for peace, all of which are characteristics of the Savior, who said, "Blessed are the peacemakers: for they shall be called the children of God" (Matthew 5:9).

These thirty-two attributes—sixteen relating to faith (believing) and sixteen relating to love and works (practicing)—can easily overwhelm even the strongest of Christians. Thirty-two ways of strengthening a Christian can appear to be mountain of infinite proportions to those who are young in the gospel and trying to understand where to get started. Just remember, spiritual growth is a journey in which we travel a little bit each day. The prophet Isaiah taught "precept upon precept . . . line upon line; here a little, and there a little" (Isaiah 28:10).

We are all a work in progress on earth, continually laboring on these things continuous improvement, not overnight perfection, as our goal. We may improve only a little day to day, but that is all that is required to make a difference in the community and to arrive safely in the mansions of the Lord in the life hereafter (the eternity). It takes desire and commitment to stay on the narrow path, and the road map and markers provided here are meant to help is meant to help strengthen us on the journey.

Chapter 15

STRENGTHEN THE FAMILY

THE SECOND RUNG IN THE MODEL OF CHRISTIAN UNITY IS THE FAMILY. Every individual born on earth is part of a family. Ideally that family consists of a mother, father, siblings, and extended members (aunts, uncles, cousins, and so on). Far too often, however, families fall short of that ideal, resulting in single-parent families, families where there is no parent present at all, families with two mothers or fathers, and every other variety.

Family reaches far beyond genetics or the physical home. It is not uncommon to hear about persons in the military referring to their family in the service or close friends calling one another brother and sister. My wife and I have adopted two children and are in the midst of raising others who are not biologically our own and have come to embrace the fact that family is not about blood, skin, or last names, but rather about bonds, loyalty, and devotion to one another. Whatever the family configuration, strengthening the family is critically important in the spiritual unification process on the road to Christian unity.

THE BIBLICAL CASE FOR STRENGTHENING THE FAMILY

The Bible provides stories of close-knit blood-related families such as Mary, Martha, and Lazarus (John 11); close in-laws such as Ruth and Naomi (Ruth 1:16); dysfunctional families like that of King David (2 Samuel 11–13) and Jacob with his twelve sons (Genesis 34–37); and even families where one brother murders another like Cain and Abel (Genesis 4:8). It is comforting to know that the families of the Bible were not perfect!

The establishment of the family in the Bible begins shortly after the creation of Adam. "The Lord God said, It is not good that the man should be alone; I will make him an help meet for him" (Genesis 2:18), marking the beginning of marriage between a man and a woman as "one flesh" (Matthew 19:4–6). In this sacred relationship, husbands are urged to "love your wives, even as Christ also loved the church, and gave himself for it" (Ephesians 5:25). This bond between husband and wife is so central to the gospel that Paul wrote, "neither is the man without the woman, neither the woman without the man, in the Lord" (1 Corinthians 11:11).

From the marriage between a man and a woman comes children, which "are an heritage of the Lord" (Psalm 127:3). Those children are called upon to "honour thy father and thy mother" (Exodus 20:12) and to "obey your parents in the Lord" (Ephesians 6:1; see also Colossians 3:20). Children are counseled to "hear the instruction of thy father, and forsake not the law of thy mother" (Proverbs 1:8; see also Proverbs 6:20), calling a son (or daughter) wise in making his father glad or a son foolish in despising his mother (Proverbs 15:20).

Parents in turn are counseled to "provoke not your children to wrath: but bring them up in the nurture and admonition of the Lord" (Ephesians 6:4), and that if a parent will "Train up a child in the way he should go . . . when he is old, he will not depart from it" (Proverbs 22:6). Parents are called upon to provide for the temporal needs "of his own house" and even those relatives that are not of the household (1 Timothy 5:8).

These scriptural passages reveal the design of the family and the manner in which the family operates and interacts with one another. A number of scriptures can be applied as to how the family is called upon to treat one another, although such scriptures are not reserved solely for the family. Family should "be kindly affectioned one to another with brotherly love; in honour preferring one another" (Romans 12:10). Family should "be of the same mind one toward another" (Romans 12:16) living "peaceably" (Romans 12:18) together. Family should treat one another "with all lowliness and meekness, with longsuffering, forbearing one another in love" (Ephesians 4:2), "wherewith one may edify another" (Romans 14:19).

The importance of the family to the greater whole of Christianity is unmistakable. Strong families translate into strong churches and strong communities—all requiring strong individuals as outlined in the previous chapters. And although the Bible does not provide many scriptural passages on family and its importance to the gospel plan, there is enough content to help the inspired Christian understand the role of the family in bringing about the plan of our Heavenly Father for the unity of faith.

THREATENING THE FAMILY WITH DISINTEGRATION

Believe it or not, an entire history and science of the family spans the works of Darwin's evolution of family systems, Morgan's three stages of human progress, and Friedrich Engels's writing on the origin of the family. Whether one considers family as the driver of reproduction, the labor force of a farm, or the basic societal unit by which God's children are raised, the family has evolved as civilization has evolved.

In the last two centuries, the increased emphasis on the family from a spiritual perspective has been distinctive. The formation of The Church of Jesus Christ of Latter-day Saints (LDS/Mormon) in 1830 included a strong emphasis on the family with its founder, Joseph Smith, teaching that families are a central part of God's plan for mankind with the potential to be together in the afterlife. The emphasis on family from the LDS/Mormon Church continued into the twentieth century with such programs as "Family Home Evening" in 1915, and later in 1995 with the introduction of *The Family: A Proclamation to the World*. This one-page, widely distributed proclamation states, among other things, that "the family is central to the Creator's plan for the eternal destiny of His children"; "the family is ordained of God"; and "the disintegration of the family will bring upon individuals, communities, and nations the calamities foretold by ancient and modern prophets."[1]

Although at times an outspoken and controversial Christian figure, Dr. James Dobson founded in 1977 Focus on the Family (FOTF), "a global Christian ministry dedicated to helping families thrive . . . [providing] help and resources for couples to build healthy marriages that reflect God's design, and for parents to raise their children according to morals and values grounded in biblical principles."[2] FOTF is active in defending family values and shares a similar outlook to that of the LDS/Mormon

Church relating to the future of the family. In a July 2001 newsletter titled "The State of the Family," Dr. Dobson writes:

> The demise of families will produce a chaotic world that will be devastating to children. But here is the most important implication of family disintegration. It will represent a virtual end of evangelism, as has occurred in Western Europe. . . . The family is absolutely critical to the propagation of the faith. If it falls apart in nations around the world, we will, perhaps in our lifetime, see another moral collapse as it was in the days of Noah.[3]

In 1981, Pope John Paul II published *The Apostolic Exhortation Familiaris Consortio (The Christian Family in the Modern World)* following the 1980 Synod on the Family. The comprehensive document addresses issues affecting families in the modern era including the spiritual, physical, and social aspects of life. The document is 34,138 words, constituting approximately sixty-four pages.[4] Speaking in Croatia in 2011, Pope Benedict warned Europeans that the traditional family was "disintegrating" due to "the spread of a secularization which leads to the exclusion of God from life,"[5] a similar warning to that of LDS/Mormon Church and James Dobson of Focus on the Family.

These words of caution on what will happen in the wake of a weakened family structure were not just mere threats issued to motivate Christians around the world to refocus their efforts. They were followed by studies years later that revealed in part the consequences outlined by these prophetic spiritual leaders.

For example, within the last two decades, the breakdown of the family has been linked by social scientists and criminologists to increases in violent crime.[6] Beyond crime, the disintegration of the family has been empirically linked to an increase of child abuse in the United States and incidents of "children born out of wedlock and abandoned by their fathers, as well as . . . the number of children affected by divorce."[7] This is precisely why in 1986 Pope John Paul II said, "As the family goes, so goes the nation and so goes the whole world in which we live,"[8] or Jerry Falwell, who said, "God created the family to provide the maximum love and support and morality and example that one can imagine."[9] Blessed Teresa, who witnessed firsthand the impact of family in the lives of children, once said, "What can you do to promote world peace? Go home and love your family."[10]

At the core of the disintegration of the family is divorce. The absence of both parents in the home and the associated economic stress has not only been linked to an increase in child abuse, but a new phenomenon of technology as a form of babysitting. A study released by the Kaiser Family Foundation in 2010 revealed eight- to eighteen-year-olds in the United States devote an average of just over 7.5 hours per day to entertainment media including TV, video games, computers, iPods, and cell phones.[11] The impact of such tremendous exposure to media has a devastating effect on children and youth including lower academic performance, less time reading, and a host of other negatives depending on the media being absorbed.

Winston Churchill wrote, "There is no doubt that it is around the family and the home that all the greatest virtues, the most dominating virtues of human society, are created, strengthened and maintained."[12] With TVs and computers in bedrooms, cell phones attached to the hands of texting teenagers, and video games replacing leisure time reading and playing board games, how is a child to be taught and nurtured in the virtues spoken of by Churchill?

Instead of heeding the admonition of spiritual leaders to concentrate on the family as a means to stop societal chaos, the United States government decades ago decided to throw money at it. An estimated five trillion dollars has been spent on social programs in the United States since 1965, when the War on Poverty was declared under Lyndon Johnson, including passage of the Violent Crime Control and Law Enforcement Act of 1994.[13] Senator Phil Gramm (R-Texas) once said, "If social spending stopped crime, America would be the safest country in the world."[14] It is important to respect the doctrine of separation of church and state; however, that doesn't mean the state needs to ignore the council of Christian leaders as far back as 1830, who have said society must strengthen the family or suffer the consequences. Is there any doubt that as a result of this neglect that we as a society are now suffering the outcome of the disintegration of the family?

THE DIVINE TRIANGLE

How then is the family to be strengthened and how does a stronger family contribute to a stronger and more unified church and community? A place to start is the recognition of what is referred to as the "Divine Triangle." It is known by other names, including the "marriage triangle."

I was informally introduced to this idea many years ago and have seen it pop up in various forms ever since. An extensive search to locate the origin of the triangle was unsuccessful; therefore, it is important to note that I am not the originator of this concept, just a recipient of its benefits.

The object lesson of the Divine Triangle is that the closer individuals in a family come to Jesus Christ, the closer they become to one another. Nowhere is this truer than with the husband and wife, who are the matriarch and patriarch of the family and the glue that holds a righteous family together. Consider diagram 6 below:

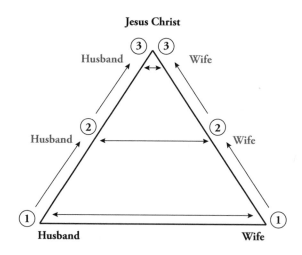

Diagram 6: The Divine Triangle

The husband and wife begin at opposites sides of the base (the circles with the number 1 in them) with Jesus Christ at the apex. As the husband and wife individually move closer to Jesus Christ along the legs of the triangle toward the apex (points 1, 2, and 3), the distance between them becomes smaller and smaller. The closer they become to Jesus Christ as individuals (according to the attributes discussed in the previous chapter—especially love), the closer they become as man and wife in unity with the Savior.

The Divine Triangle can be adapted to put any two individuals or groups at the base, such as a brother and a sister, a son and the rest of the family, a daughter and a mother, and so forth. The result is the same in any case. As the individuals or groups strive to be more devoted to the

Savior, they will become more unified with one another as well. Conceptually, the Divine Triangle can be turned ninety degrees one way or the other, putting Jesus Christ and another individual or group at the base, with a particular individual or group at the top. This can be done to represent *symbolically* the those at the base supporting and strengthening the individual or group at the top. Sometimes one person in the family, or even the entire family itself, needs a little more reinforcement, and in those instances Jesus Christ and one or more family members can be at the base of the Divine Triangle to hold them up. In this case, the Divine Triangle becomes an inspired pillar of support for the individual or group at the apex.

Joshua boldly declared to all of Israel, "And if it seem evil unto you to serve the Lord, choose you this day whom ye will serve . . . as for me and my house, we will serve the Lord" (Joshua 24:15). Strengthening the family begins with a commitment to serving the Lord as individuals. There may be times when only one person in the family makes the commitment and charts a course to inspire the rest of the family. Conversely there may be a period when everyone in the family is able to make the commitment except a wayward child who in rebellion resists the pledge. In the framework of the Divine Triangle, everyone who draws closer to Christ draws closer together, while those who need a little more support can obtain that support from Jesus Christ and those in the family who are able to do so.

PRACTICING HEALTHY FAMILY DYNAMICS

Focusing on spiritual aspects to strengthen the family is important, but it is not the only lesson to be learned. Even the most spiritual of families can find themselves mired in the quicksand of dysfunction and ineffectiveness by losing the balance that maintains a healthy family. There are countless seminars and books on raising strong families, each one invariably including principles such as the art of listening, spending time together, righteous discipline, consistency, and so on. The LDS/Mormon Family Proclamation referenced earlier reads:

> Happiness in family life is most likely to be achieved when founded upon the teachings of the Lord Jesus Christ. Successful marriages and families are established and maintained on principles of faith, prayer,

repentance, forgiveness, respect, love, compassion, work, and *wholesome recreational activities.*[15]

Stephen R. Covey, the author of the mega-bestseller *The 7 Habits of Highly Effective People* wrote a less-known book titled *The 7 Habits of Highly Effective Families.*[16] As the title suggests, this masterpiece provides seven principles for families to live by including the following from the book's table of contents:

1. **Be Proactive**—Becoming an Agent of Change in Your Family

2. **Begin with the End in Mind**—Developing a Family Mission Statement

3. **Put First Things First**—Making Family a Priority in a Turbulent World

4. **Think "Win-Win"**—Moving from "Me" to "We"

5. **Seek First to Understand . . . Then to Be Understood**—Solving Family Problems through Empathic Communications

6. **Synergize**—Building Family Unity through Celebrating Differences

7. **Sharpen the Saw**—Renewing the Family Spirit through Traditions

Covey emphasizes the challenges that exist in raising a family and how being an effective family is not about perfection but rather about planning, readjusting, never giving up, and always hoping. At the start of the book, Covey writes, "I firmly believe that family is the building block of society and that our greatest fulfillment lies there. I also believe the most important work we will ever do is at home."[17] Covey goes on to quote Barbara Bush, who said to the graduating students of Wellesley College, "Our success as a society depends not on what happens in the White House but on what happens inside your house."[18]

WebMD offers its own list of principles to consider from an article titled "Experts Reveal the Key Ingredients to a Happy Family Life," written by Denise Mann and reviewed by Charlotte E. Grayson Mathis, MD. The article outlines[19] what it calls 15 Secrets of Happy Families:

1. Enjoy Each Other

2. Swap Stories

3. Put the Marriage First

4. Break Bread Together

5. Play Together

6. Put Family Before Friends

7. Limit Children's After-School Activities

8. Build and Honor Rituals

9. Keep Your Voices Down

10. Never Fight in Front of the Kids

11. Don't Work Too Much

12. Encourage Sibling Harmony

13. Have Private Jokes

14. Be Flexible

15. Communicate

Dr. Laura Markham, a clinical psychologist and former newspaper executive, trained at Columbia University, offers a similar yet slightly different list of family principles [20] to follow in a web article titled "Raising a Happy Family":

1. Dinner: 30 Minutes to a More Connected Family

2. Surviving Arsenic Hour

3. Getting Your Family Out the Door in the Morning

4. Why Kids Need Routines & Structure

5. The Family That Plays Together

6. Family Meetings

7. Protective Parenting

8. Sanctuary: Making Your Home a Haven

9. Family Culture: Shared identity & belonging

10. Nature: Why Children—and Parents—Need the Great Outdoors

Between Covey's seven habits, WebMD's fifteen Secrets, and Markham's ten principles, one can begin to see overlap between the three. No matter what formula the family decides to use, the formation of a strong family not only begins and ends with a commitment to the gospel of Jesus Christ but also involves the consistent application of tried-and-true principles that allow families to experience the joys associated with being unified in the Savior.

Chapter 16

STRENGTHEN THE CHURCH

THE THIRD RUNG OF THE MODEL OF CHRISTIAN UNITY, FOLLOWING THE individual and family, is the church. Strong individuals and strong families should make for a strong church; however, that is not always the case. Bringing together two or more strong families full of righteous individuals does not guarantee a unified congregation where the whole is greater than the sum of its parts. The lesson behind this unfortunate reality can be illustrated with food. A thick, juicy steak is a favorite of many, as is a good bowl of ice cream; however, steak à la mode is not likely to be a winning menu item.

Taking the analogy a bit further, it is common to use bleach to clean tile grout, purify water, and whiten clothes. Ammonia is likewise useful for cleaning and even has some clever uses in the garden. However, mix bleach and ammonia together and the result is toxic, even deadly.

Ideally one plus one equals three in the synergistic realm, and at a minimum one plus one should equal two in the compatibility realm. However, one plus one can equal one, or even a negative number, when the items being combined are toxic when joined. Such is the potential when bringing people together in church to form a congregation. This is why strengthening the church is a critical and challenging aspect on the journey to unifying disparate Christians toward a stronger society.

THE BIBLICAL CASE FOR
STRENGTHENING THE CHURCH

The "church" being referred to here is the denominational church that the individual or family belongs to, not the greater Christian multi-denominational church. Review for a moment the definition of a Practicing Christian from chapter 6:

> A Practicing Christian is a Believing Christian who commits to *living the precepts of the Church they belong to* including repentance, baptism, receiving the gift of the Holy Ghost and partaking of the Lord's supper—motivating them to keep the commandments, follow the example of Jesus Christ, make sacrifices in building and nurturing the kingdom of God, perform good works, and live a life embodying Christian values.

The individual or family may be strong vibrant members of the church, members that attend only occasionally, or any combination in between. Although the goal is for everyone to be strong vibrant members of the church they belong to, the starting point for some may be something less than that. No matter what the activity level of the Christian may be, the point is they are part of the body, or assembly, of that given church and the objective is to strengthen that church as much as possible so it can help strengthen the greater community.

In the twelfth chapter of his first letter to the Corinthians, Paul addresses the diversity of spiritual gifts and the various positions within the church. In verses 12 to 27, Paul provides a long analogy of different parts of a body and how they work together as one. To fully appreciate the importance and power of this counsel from Paul we will break the passage down verse by verse with brief interpretations:

Verse 12: *"For as the body is one, and hath many members, and all the members of that one body, being many, are one body: so also is Christ."* The church operates like a single body that has many parts, each working together, and together that church is one in Christ.

Verse 13: *"For by one Spirit are we all baptized into one body, whether we be Jews or Gentiles, whether we be bond or free; and have been all made to drink into one Spirit."* The members of a church may come from different backgrounds but have all been inspired by the same spirit to baptism and all partake of the same spirit together.

Verse 14: "*For the body is not one member, but many.*" The church is not just one but many persons.

Verse 15: "*If the foot shall say, Because I am not the hand, I am not of the body; is it therefore not of the body?*" If a member of the church believes they are different from another member (or members)—in activity, talents, contribution, or whatever—and that because of such differences they are not an important part of the church, they are mistaken.

Verse 16: "*And if the ear shall say, Because I am not the eye, I am not of the body; is it therefore not of the body?*" For example, if a member who helps with music believes that because they are not a pastor he or she is therefore not a contributing member of the church, he or she is mistaken.

Verse 17: "*If the whole body were an eye, where were the hearing? If the whole were hearing, where were the smelling?*" For example, if everyone were a pastor, then what would the church listen to on Sunday? If everyone were involved in music, then who would teach Sunday School?

Verse 18: "*But now hath God set the members every one of them in the body, as it hath pleased him.*" God calls everyone to be a contributing member of the church according to his will.

Verse 19: "*And if they were all one member, where were the body?*" If everyone in the church performed the same function, then what would happen to the church?

Verse 20: "*But now are they many members, yet but one body.*" But that is not the case; many are members doing different things that make up a unified church.

Verse 21: "*And the eye cannot say unto the hand, I have no need of thee: nor again the head to the feet, I have no need of you.*" For example, the pastor cannot act like he is more important than, and therefore has no need for, the youth minister or those who clean the chapel for services. Nor can those who teach young children dismiss the value being rendered by those who lead the music.

Verse 22: "*Nay, much more those members of the body, which seem to be more feeble, are necessary.*" This is not the case; those members of the church serving in positions that may seem less important are necessary for the church to serve all of its members effectively.

Verse 23: "*And those members of the body, which we think to be less honourable, upon these we bestow more abundant honour; and our uncomely parts have more abundant comeliness.*" Those members of the church who are serving in positions that appear to be less important should receive more respect and honor, while members of the church that are less endowed with talents and spiritual gifts we should pay more attention to.

Verse 24: "*For our comely parts have no need: but God hath tempered the body together, having given more abundant honour to that part which lacked.*" Those who are spiritually strong and well established have less need of attention. God has brought together the strong and the weak into one church and desires more attention be given to those who require it.

Verse 25: "*That there should be no schism in the body; but that the members should have the same care one for another.*" This is done so that there will be no divisions in the church, but that everyone will treat each member with the same respect and love according to their needs.

Verse 26: "*And whether one member suffer, all the members suffer with it; or one member be honoured, all the members rejoice with it.*" And because the church is united as one, when one of its members is experiencing adversity and pain, all of the other members should have compassion and bear that burden together. Or when one of its members is honored, all of the other members should celebrate and rejoice with that member. The members of the church in unity share pain and joy together as one.

Verse 27: "*Now ye are the Body of Christ, and members in particular.*" Together you and all other members are a united church in Jesus Christ, with each of you being a valuable member of the church.

Paul went through this highly detailed and painstaking analogy to reinforce that every member of the church is valuable and necessary to create a strong and edifying church among all of its members that has Christ at its head. Diagram 7 helps illustrate how the members spoken of in Paul's analogy with almost a limitless number of members in various positions that could be shown here, each one linked directly to Christ at from a spiritual perspective.

Paul doesn't just use this analogy in his letter to the Corinthians; he also employs it in his letter to the Ephesians (Ephesians 1:22–23) and to the Romans (Romans 12:4). As individuals and families are strengthened, and brought into the fold of the church to work in harmony with other members, the church is strengthened.

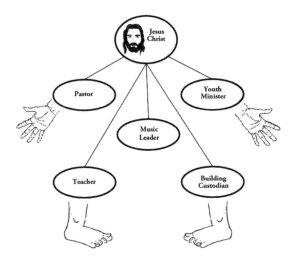

Diagram 7: The Church as the Body of Christ

THE THINGS THAT WEAKEN
AND DIVIDE THE CHURCH

Before discussing how to strengthen church members, it is important to review those things that often divide members. As discussed in earlier chapters, theology is often the primary stumbling block to members of one denomination in uniting with those of another denomination. This is not typically an issue with members within the same denomination— although historically it has happened causing schisms and the dividing of congregations (for example, the many denominations of the Baptist church). With a particular church there are often nontheological issues that divide the congregation and weaken the body including, but not limited to the following:

Politics: There are few things that stir up passionate emotion and immediate response as much as the words "conservative" and "liberal." In the modern era, there are real and perceived connections and ideals attributed to these explosive labels as they relate to spiritual matters. Politcally speaking, the reality is that Christianity is full of both conservatives and liberals, creating a fanatical division among those who choose to delve into issues that have found their way into the political arena. A 2009 study of 3,000 political activists associated with both progressive (liberal) religious organizations (interfaithAlliance, Sojourners, and so on) and conservative religious organizations (Concerned Women for America, the National Right to Life Committee, and so on) reveals there are considerable differences among Christians on issues such as abortion, homosexuality, poverty, and the environment. This study conducted by the Bliss Institute of Applied Politics at the University of Akron in partnership with Public Religion Research found the following:

- *Abortion*: 95 percent of the conservative religious activists surveyed believe abortion should be illegal in all or most cases while 80 percent of the progressive religious activists believe abortion should be legal in most or all cases.[1]

- *Same Sex Marriage*: 82 percent of the conservative religious activists surveyed oppose same sex marriage while 59 percent of progressive activities are in favor of same sex marriage.[2]

- *Environment*: 13 percent of the conservative activists surveyed support additional environmental protection while 87 percent of progressive activists are in favor of additional environmental protection even at the cost of raised prices and lost jobs.[3]

These extreme differences on both sides were further illuminated in their responses to the level of agreement or disagreement with statements relating to the state of society. Predictably, 92 percent of conservative activists believe moral decay is the cause of America's problems and 67 percent felt conversion to Christ will heal the country's misdirected course. Conversely, only about 25 percent of progressive activists agreed that moral decay was a primary issue and only 13 percent believed conversion to Christ would make a positive impact on American society.[4] Similar disparities were reported regarding the Bible and other religious practices and beliefs. These strongly divergent views among self-described Christians are a catalyst for sharp and profound divisions within a particular church and in American Christianity in general.

As a Christian I am a staunch conservative. I am pro-life, oppose gay marriage, and in favor of helping the environment but not at the cost of jobs or increasing the national debt. I have friends who are liberal, and we speak from time to time, and I have come to respect the argument for and against these lightning-rod issues and admire the passion on both sides. My respect for liberal arguments does not change my conservative views, nor does it cause me to separate myself from those who hold liberal views—especially those who are Christian. These are my brothers and sisters, not my political adversaries.

Those Christians that allow the political ideology of liberalism versus conservatism to divide them from other Christians don't stop to realize the two different approaches are not mutually exclusive. The author of Ecclesiastes wrote, "To every thing there is a season, and a time to every purpose under the heaven" (Ecclesiastes 3:1). Personal responsibility, traditionally a conservative value, is a core virtue of the gospel of Jesus Christ; however, there is a role for government programs, traditionally a liberal value, that promote the well-being of society and care for those who are unable to care for themselves (provided their own family cannot do so—1 Timothy 5:8). Like the role of checks and balances in the structure of the US government, conservative and liberal Christians should pause to listen to one another, spend less time being worked up by secular voices that polarize, and find ways of magnifying common principles and motivating political candidates to support righteous causes.

Conservatives and liberals are people and getting to know one another can help bridge emotional gaps and create improved understanding. I had the occasion to spend time with Mark Udall, the senior United States Senator from Colorado in 2012 during an event in Washington DC. Senator Udall is a Democrat with a long history of passionately supporting liberal causes. From an ideology perspective Senator Udall and I should have little in common. However, I came to learn about Senator Udall's extensive experiences in mountain climbing, zeal for the outdoors, and his devotion to family. In coming to know Senator Udall, I began to see "the person" and not just "the liberal." While I may still disagree with much of Senator Udall's political ideology, I am far less inclined to lash out at him with careless disregard because I took a moment to get to know him as a person, even my brother in the family of God.

Social Issues: The two social issues that divide Christians most deeply are abortion and homosexuality. The division caused by these two topics is passionate and in some cases beyond reason. There isn't room enough in a hundred books to resolve the chasms caused by these issues; however, it comes back to how the Christian world must treat theology: passionate and enduring disagreements are going to happen; therefore, locating common values and building upon those values is the more productive path to unity.

I will briefly venture to say regarding abortion that the freedom to make personal choices is an eternal principle of the gospel; however, it is also incumbent on every Christian to make educated choices. Education on the worth of every soul, and the joys of adoption are compelling solutions to abortion, ensuring every choice that is made fully comprehends what is at stake. I know intimately of the tragedies that can come from unwanted children, the joys of adoption, and the impact of education on critical decision making and welcome an open dialogue with those who emphatically support abortion.

With respect to homosexuality, it is worth pointing out that same-sex attraction without lust or action is not in and of itself a sin and that all forms of sexual transgression carry the same weight. Those engaged in heterosexual sex outside of marriage are equally yoked in sin as those engaged in homosexual sex outside of marriage—there is no difference in the eyes of the Lord, despite the fact that society has come to accept heterosexual sin outside of marriage as the norm. Adultery is adultery no matter what gender it is being committed with. Taking it one step further, those engaged in viewing pornography and self-gratification are guilty of the same sin of adultery according to Christ, who was clear and unambiguous when he said, "Whosoever looketh on a woman to lust after her hath committed adultery with her already in his heart" (Matthew 5:28).

With respect to the Church, unless a person has experienced one or more good Christian friends or family who are struggling with homosexuality; those friends who long for and have prayed to rid themselves of the affliction of same-sex attraction for years without achieving success—they have little room to accurately ascertain. The physiological study of the root causes of homosexuality is ongoing and inconclusive and therefore to judge a gay man or woman (or an entire gay community) without applying the understanding, mercy, and love exemplified by the Savior is unrighteous and not becoming of a disciple of Christ. Conversely, passionate activism to promote and encourage homosexuality as an acceptable alternative to heterosexuality is spiritually reckless and may lead to serious unintended consequences.

It is important for church members to live and exemplify gospel principles of love and forgiveness toward those who have chosen abortion and struggle with homosexuality, making sure they work on their own short-comings first before judging others on their shortcomings (Matthew 7:5). Paul wrote, "For all have sinned, and come short of the glory of God" (Romans 3:23). There is a time to rebuke sinners publicly (1 Timothy 5:20), a time to do so in private (Matthew 18:15), and even a time to strip church membership from transgressors, who need to experience godly sorrow and the full impact of the atoning sacrifice of Jesus Christ (2 Thessalonians 3:14–15).

Sin/Pride: Sin separates man from God (Isaiah 59:2) and divides members from one another. The sin that does so most prevalently is pride. Pride is considered one of the "seven deadly sins" and "is the commencement of all sin" according to Saint Augustine.[5] Pride is toxic, attacking congregational unity and sickening the assembly like swift-moving bacteria in the Body of Christ. Pride is individual in nature, but it can spread to groups, creating cliques within churches that are even more lethal and corrosive.

The anecdote to pride is humility and nothing helps cultivate humility like service. When Jesus washed the feet of his disciples (John 13:14), it was not only a fantastic lesson in the master becoming the servant, but it made an indelible mark of humility upon the disciples who went on to serve the people tirelessly. Giving one or more prideful persons in the congregation a responsibility to serve others in the church is a good start to eradicating the disease of pride and strengthening the Body of Christ.

Racism and Other Forms of Prejudice: One might think racism and prejudice would be the last thing a Christian could be stricken with, but both are alive and well in the hearts of many Christians today. Racism and prejudice divide Christians in a way that is entirely pointless and completely contrary to the gospel. Nonetheless, societal norms have bred racism and prejudice over the centuries, making it a strong element of American culture, and one that has been difficult to eliminate entirely.

To those who are prejudiced, a simple biblical lesson can be taught to show the extreme error of their ways: all men and women are created in the image and likeness of God (Genesis 1:26–27). God sent his Son to atone for the sins of all mankind (John 3:16)—not just a select few. From the beginning, God has not given any regard to persons (Deuteronomy 10:17), and "is no respecter of persons" (Acts 10:34). Thus, we should not think ourselves above any others (Romans 12:3). Although at one time segregation may have existed between Jews and Gentiles, Jesus "made both one, and hath broken down the middle wall of partition between us" (Ephesians 2:14). Anyone who attempts to build walls between God's children harbors "evil thoughts" (James 2:4) and breaks the commandments of loving thy neighbor (James 2:8) and loving one another (John 13:34).[6] End of story!

One of the children my wife and I have adopted is mixed race. We are also raising two other boys who are mixed race—all three are sons of our adopted daughter who is unable to care for them. To look into the eyes of these beautiful children we see only goodness, innocence and the love of God manifest in the souls of His creation. While their skin may be different from ours, their beings are every bit a part of the family of our Heavenly Father richly blessed with the same grace in Jesus Christ that we all are. Race is a convenient method of genetically identifying a group of people but it need not be a method of creating separation between the children of God, especially within the church.

Culture: Cultural differences among people do not appear to be formidable on the surface but—underneath ethnic and social differences—can be significant. For example, a southern conservative Protestant of black African descent accustomed to certain practices of worship, being thrust into a Northeastern Mainline Protestant Church of all white members accustomed to their own method of worship is not likely to feel comfortable. A native Latin American Catholic is probably accustomed to a certain pace and style of church services that is significantly different than those found among Catholic churches in Middle America.

Although the Holy Ghost can break through cultural barriers and languages (Acts 2:6), there is no quick and easy solution to the cultural divide among Christians. Bridging cultural separation in congregations requires the minority culture to integrate itself into the majority culture (language, practices, and so on), while at the same time the majority culture must fully welcome the minority culture into its fold. The experience can be enriching and wonderful for both sides when done successfully. Effective integration requires the virtues of patience, love, understanding, and compassion on both sides.

Ministerial Conflicts: Many Christian churches have a ministry that includes more than one pastor or set of leaders. There are assistant pastors, counselors, youth leaders, and other individuals in the ministry who fill important roles of leadership. When there is a lack of solidarity among church leaders, leading to conflict, members may choose to align themselves along leadership lines, which creates division within the church. There have been countless instances of such division that included a splintering of the assembly, the departure of a leader to start a new church, and a disbursement of the congregation. Pride, and sometimes greed, is usually at the center of these disputes among one or more leaders, causing lasting feelings of spite and discontent long after the split. This dynamic is accelerated when the testimony of church members is focused more on a charismatic leader than it is on the doctrines of the gospel of Jesus Christ.

Generational Differences: Differences have always existed between generations in language, attitudes, and the application of technology. From a spiritual standpoint, these generational differences can be magnified when youth begin to feel that the church no longer speaks to them and they are unable to relate to the doctrines, practices, and principles of the gospel as taught in a particular congregation. Aristotle wrote, "youth is easily deceived, because it is quick to hope."[7] The wandering mind and disobedient tendencies of youth are well known to our Heavenly Father prompting the inclusion of the commandment to honor one's father and mother and a litany of scriptural warnings regarding youth (Proverbs 1:8–9, Proverbs 17:25, and so on).

Gospel teachings are timeless and can never be bent or twisted to accommodate youth; however, a wise church is one that applies and relates the doctrines of the gospel to youth in a way that inspires and encourages them. Teaching true and applicable doctrines of Christianity will do more to inspire youth than pizza and rock bands. It is easy to see which denominations are excelling in that effort from the results of the National Survey of Youth and Religion detailed in chapter 7. Without such efforts, a church will not only leave behind a weakened youth, but an ill-prepared generation of young adults who will search elsewhere for spiritual fulfillment.

Gender Conflicts: An issue easily ignored that can divide spiritual communities is gender. Churches allow gender to divide when one sex exerts unrighteous dominion over another, either individually or as a group. The role of women as ecclesiastical leaders varies among Christian denominations. The United Methodist Church began ordaining women in 1956 and as of 2012 had nearly twelve thousand clergywomen serving in every level of the church from bishops to local pastors.[8] In 2006,

Katharine Jefferts Schori was elected the first female presiding bishop in the history of the Episcopal Church, and in 2010 the Presbyterian USA Church reported one in four of its pastors were women.[9] Conversely, the Roman Catholic Church and LDS/Mormon Church ordain only men to the priesthood as part of sacred tradition and revelation; however, both churches have women serving in a variety of church leadership positions both locally and globally.

Gender is a biological reality of our human existence as part of God's plan that includes both men and women (Genesis 1:27). Men and women are different yet complementary to one another physically and emotionally, being spiritually equal and one in Jesus Christ (Galatians 3:28). Although churches may selectively use biblical passages to minimize the ecclesiastical role of women (1 Corinthians 14:34), some equally powerful Old and New Testament passages tell of women risking their lives (Esther 5) and being given prophetic responsibilities (Luke 2:36).

The book *Women in Ministry: Four Views* illuminates the challenge of gender providing four different evangelical perspectives on women in Christian ministry. A traditional view offered by Robert Culver is that women should not have ecclesiastical authority over men. Susan Foh offers an alternative view that women should be allowed to teach but not hold leadership positions. Walter Liefeld goes one step further and makes the case for women in the clergy. Alvera Mickelsen then provides a compelling defense that men and women should be fully equal in ecclesiastical matters.[10] The debate about women in the ministry is lively with strong differences in opinion among various denominations.

A powerful lesson can be gleaned from applying to men and women of the church the analogy of Paul in his letter to the Ephesians regarding husbands and wives. Women may in some cases assume ecclesiastical leadership and lay roles that correspond with, yet are subject to, the leadership authority of men (Ephesians 5:22–24). In all such cases, men are called to demonstrate the utmost respect and love for these and all women, exemplifying the love that Christ has for the church (Ephesians 5:25), treating women as they themselves wish to be treated (Matthew 7:12). This same pattern should apply in the reverse when men are subject to the leadership authority of women. When positive and healthy relationships exist between men and women within the church community, with gender differences being honored and celebrated, the work of the

Lord is magnified and all are edified (1 Thessalonians 5:11).

Personality Conflicts: Although it may seem trite to some, personality conflicts cannot only be divisive, but explosive. Personality conflicts can arise between two or more people and be as simple as one party being logical and the other being emotional, or as complex as both parties being on opposite sides of the Myers-Briggs spectrum. Without recognition and respect for one another's personality types, and the value each can bring to solving problems and dealing with issues, there can be constant clashes and that lead to negative consequences overall.

A biblical solution to personality conflicts is worth pondering and practicing. Each of us must watch what we say (Psalm 141:3), being careful in our communications (Psalm 19:14), courteous to others (1 Peter 3:8), and full of consideration (Hebrews 10:24). When we speak in love (Ephesians 4:15), we can learn to compromise with others (Romans 12:18), especially those with whom we disagree the most. To accomplish all of this, we must strive to be more Christlike because as the Savior is the greatest example of one who ministered to perhaps the broadest range of personality types possible.[11]

Bigotry: Bigotry is much like racism and other forms of prejudice where intolerance of creeds or beliefs that differ from one's own abound in the heart, impacting outward actions. The principles of dealing with bigotry are nearly the same. Bigotry as a religious discriminatory practice is often less cunning than the strategies used by racists or those with extreme prejudice. Bigotry is laced with ignorance, intolerance, self-centeredness, and a complete absence of the love of God. Sometimes bigotry is hidden and in other instances it is on full display.

In 2011, during a celebration of the cleaning of the Church of the Nativity in Bethlehem, one hundred priests and monks from rival Christian denominations commenced a brawl that required Palestinian riot police to intervene. Shouting insults at one another and using brooms and fists, the clergymen dressed in traditional robes attacked one another after one of the priests accidently placed a broom into a space controlled by a rival group. The encroachment sparked the melee among the Greek Orthodox, Armenian, and Roman Catholic groups, who have been at odds as far back as the second century.[12] If church leaders harbor bigotry toward other churches, how can they expect those they lead to not do the same?

Harsh Evangelism: Jesus Christ urged his disciples to teach everyone everywhere, explaining, "this gospel of the kingdom shall be preached in all the world for a witness unto all nations" (Matthew 24:14). In this work of evangelism, the Savior taught, "The harvest truly is great, but the labourers are few: pray ye therefore the Lord of the harvest, that he would send forth labourers into his harvest" (Luke 10:2), signifying the need for as many as possible to be involved in missionary work. During the ministry of Jesus the gospel was first taught to the Jews, a people who believed they were already saved, and then to the Gentiles who often engaged in heathen practices.

In our modern day, evangelism is alive and well in various forms. For example, LDS/Mormons and Jehovah's Witnesses are known for their door-to-door evangelism. Conservative Protestants often evangelize on various types of mission trips. Roman Catholics appoint missionaries who travel to specific areas to evangelize in a variety of methods. The common thread of these evangelization efforts is the focus on the gospel. The words "evangelization" and "gospel" are joined in translation from the Greek word *evangelion* (*ev* or *eu* meaning "good" and *angelion* meaning "message"). To evangelize is to bring forth good news. Division, however, is perpetuated when Modern-day Pharisees, and some Christian denominations, choose to engage in "harsh evangelism." Harsh evangelism is preaching a message by attacking another denomination under the auspices of spreading the good news.

The problem is that there is nothing good or honest about interpretive accusations, half-truths, and building up one's message by tearing down another. This is analogous to the modern-day political attack ad, in which instead of talking about the strengths of his or her candidacy, a candidate instead focuses his or her message on how bad his or her opponent is. Harsh evangelism can regularly be seen in religious online forums, blogs, social media, thousands of websites, books, pamphlets, and other media. A small but revealing exercise to prove this point is to examine the number of Internet search engine results on particular topics such as "false doctrine." Consider the following statements entered into Google in May of 2012 and the number of results provided:

- Mormon False doctrine: 217,000

- Evangelical, false doctrine, 1,860,000

- Catholic False doctrine: 1,910,000
- Christian, false doctrine: 8,610,000

Although a raw exercise, many of these results are tied to websites that attempt to discredit these respective religions and make accusations relating to doctrinal falsehoods. Many of these websites are created by well-meaning "evangelizers" who rationalize their actions as delivering the "good news" to those who are lost and misguided or the warning of false doctrine to the unsuspecting. I was the recipient of harsh evangelism as a Roman Catholic and am regularly evangelized harshly as a Latter-day Saint. I understand the dynamics of receiving a hollow message laced with spite and malice, mingled with goodwill that was (and is) anything but "good news."

The unintended consequences of harsh evangelism are many. My children have been discriminated against by students, teachers, and coaches who have held strong biases against Mormonism. Our home has been vandalized in the past by youth feeling justified in punishing my family for our religious preference. In these and other extreme cases, the biases that led to these acts of discrimination and vandalism were sown through harsh evangelism in local churches at the hands of pastors who failed to comprehend the potential consequences of their actions.

Many years ago, my wife was approached by a young Baptist gentleman who told her of the existence of tunnels joining convents and seminaries where Roman Catholic priests and nuns would meet to have sex. My wife as a second-year Franciscan novice was thoroughly amused by the ridiculous comic book that accompanied the young man's harsh evangelism attempt. Sadly, this young man fully believed what he was taught by his pastor and the contents of the silly handout. Harsh evangelism relies on the intellectual shortcomings and pharisaical posture of the sender, while hoping for doctrinal ignorance and spiritual vulnerability of the receiver.

It is perfectly fine for people and denominations to truthfully and lovingly evangelize Christians and non-Christians through example and testimony as part of the commission of Jesus Christ. It is equally fine for Christians and non-Christians to politely refuse what is being offered. However, there is no place for harsh evangelism among the true disciples of Christ. Like the political attack ad, which may be effective in swaying short-term perspectives, harsh evangelism eventually leaves deep division and lingering animosity between the sending and receiving parties. No doubt many will read this and justify harsh evangelism with the writings of Jude and the actions of Paul while ignoring the example of the Savior, who taught there are many ways to exercise one's faith (Mark 9:40).

These many catalysts of church division discussed are ever present, each one holding lethal potential to divide and poison congregations. Ben Franklin wisely observed, "an ounce of prevention is worth a pound of cure," and such is the case with a church and the forces that create division. The key is to strengthen members spiritually in a way that helps prevent these toxic elements from infiltrating a congregation.

STRENGTHENING MEMBERS AND THE CHURCH

Implicit in the words of Paul's sermon on the Body of Christ is the role of each member in the operation of the church. Although one might limit such a role to that of using God-given spiritual gifts, it is the application of those gifts that brings to life the words of Paul. Paul was inspired to understand what motivates mankind in its quest for discipleship in the gospel of Christ. Humans are complex beings yet follow basic physiological patterns that, when understood, can help motivate people to reach their full potential as children of God.

Perhaps the most comprehensive model of human psychology was developed by Abraham Maslow in his 1943 paper "A Theory of Human Motivation."[13] Maslow found that humans attempt to satisfy the most basic needs first before moving on to more marginal needs in a serial fashion. The five levels identified by Maslow starting at the most basic are physiological (food, water, sleep, and so on), safety (security, employment, health, and so on), belonging and affection (friendship, family, and so on), esteem (achievement, respect of others, and so on), and self-actualization (morality, creativity, and so on). Often termed "Maslow's Hierarchy of Needs," Maslow's model is most typically illustrated as a pyramid much like the following.

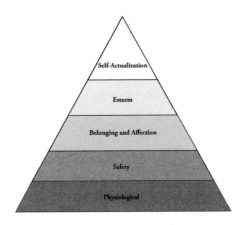

Diagram 8: Maslow's Hierarchy of Needs Model

This model helps describe and predict human behavior, including the members of the Church described by Paul in his first letter to the Corinthians. Those who attend Christian churches are bound by the same human characteristics and therefore churches must understand the model and how it applies to the spiritual realm.

By considering Paul's teaching on the Body of Christ, along with other gospel principles relating to individuals and the Lord's Church, let's reconfigure Maslow's model to reflect a more church-centered model of human dynamics:

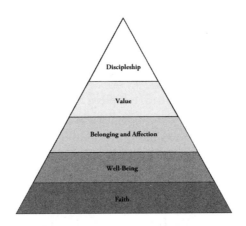

Diagram 9: Spiritual Hierarchy of Needs Model

This "Spiritual Hierarchy of Needs" model closely mirrors Maslow's Hierarchy of Needs in that one level must be soundly satisfied before moving to the next level. In order for the Church to be strengthened, it must create an environment for its members to grow spiritually, thus leading to a synergistic relationship where the whole is more than the sum of the parts (that is, 1 + 1 = 3 or more). Spiritual synergy is achieved when "all things work together for good to them that love God" (Romans 8:28). The levels of the Spiritual Hierarchy of Needs are defined as the following:

- **Faith:** Likened to the physiological level of Maslow's model, faith is the foundation and most basic of all Christian needs leading to rebirth, education, understanding, and the acceptance of gospel truth.

- **Well-being:** Likened to the safety level of Maslow's model, well-being follows faith and is a search for spiritual confidence, meaningful participation in the assembly, and joy in the love of God.

- **Belonging and Affection:** Likened to the level with the same name in Maslow's model, this level finds the Christian yearning for fellowship among members and feeling like a part of a close-knit church family where loyalty and trust abound.

- **Value:** Likened to the Esteem level of Maslow's model, value is the desire to make meaningful contributions to the church family in order to gain the respect of others and feel a righteous sense of pride in being a vibrant member of the Body of Christ.

- **Discipleship:** Likened to the Self-Actualization level of Maslow's model, discipleship is a result of satisfying the previous needs. More important discipleship is a need to make a deeper personal commitment to the gospel, to reach one's spiritual potential, to experience sacrifice in taking up one's cross, and to devote one's life—body and soul—as a follower of Jesus Christ.

As church members move up the pyramid of the spiritual hierarchy, they also move from left to right in the Christian Continuum from diagram 2 in chapter 13. The Laboring Christian is likely one who has effectively realized the four bottom components of the Spiritual Hierarchy of Needs and has entered true discipleship in Jesus Christ. On the other side of the spectrum, Departing Christians are likely struggling with faith and well-being. Adequate Christians are likely struggling with well-being along with belonging and affection. Hesitant Christians are likely struggling with value. Knowing these individuals personally, church leaders are in a position to understand how to most effectively minister to them along their spiritual hierarchy of needs.

The late church leader Gordon B. Hinckley said every convert needs a "friend, a responsibility and a nurturing with the good word of God. . . . It is our duty and opportunity to provide these things."[14] Hinckley's comment addresses the need for belonging and affection (a friend), well-being and value (a responsibility), and faith and discipleship (nurturing with the good word of God).

The Spiritual Hierarchy of Needs integrates the object lesson taught by Paul in the analogy of the Body of Christ regarding the psychology of human nature and the serialization of needs fulfillment. When churches begin focusing more on strengthening individuals and families than on programs and fund-raising, then the Body of Christ will be strengthened and unified. When the Body of Christ is strengthened and unified, it will make sizable and impactful contributions to the community helping to build and nurture the kingdom of God on earth in a multitude of ways.

Chapter 17

STRENGTHEN THE COMMUNITY

THE FOURTH AND FINAL RUNG IN THE MODEL OF CHRISTIAN UNITY FOL-
lowing the individual, family, and church is the community. The ideal
scenario is for a community to be made up of strong individuals, families,
and churches. Unfortunately, because most American Christians are operating under their spiritual potential, most communities in America are
operating under their societal potential. When churches come together—
and there are excellent examples of this happening and the incredible
results that follow—a community is blessed in a multitude of ways.

A community is defined broadly in this sense and can be local to a
neighborhood or encompass an entire nation or even the world. Consider
the following societal lineage and how it maps to the Model of Christian
Unity:

- Individuals make up families
- Families make up neighborhoods
- Neighborhoods make up cities
- Cities make up counties
- Counties make up districts
- Districts make up states

- States make up a nation

- Nations make up the world

This cascade effect of responsibility is sometimes referred to as the doctrine of subsidiarity. With respect to churches, a community can therefore be made up of neighborhood churches, churches around a city, or churches throughout a state or the nation. Scottish town planner and social activist Patrick Geddes is credited with coining the phrase "think global, act local,"[1] a phrase that is applicable to the concept of the church community. An individual's realm of influence, or even a particular church's realm of influence, is largely felt on a local level; however, it is important for the individual or church to have a spiritual vision that reaches far beyond the local boundary to form a global vision (that is, across a city, state, nation, or the world). This vision is not fantasy it is a vision that has become a reality for a number of cities to the benefit of many as will be seen later in this chapter.

THE BIBLICAL CASE FOR STRENGTHENING THE COMMUNITY

The biblical case for strengthening the community is really a culmination of the biblical cases given for strengthening individuals, families, and churches. Strengthening the community is not something most Christians consider or think about—it is simply not a spiritual priority—this despite the fact that a united and strong community is a logical extension of many biblical teachings. Although the Savior taught, "if a house be divided against itself, that house cannot stand" (Mark 3:25), it is common for a community of Christian churches to be perfectly comfortable with being divided and separated from one another.

When Paul learned of the divisions evolving in Corinth among the house of Chloe, he wrote a letter that included the following passage:

> For it hath been declared unto me of you, my brethren, by them which are of the house of Chloe, that there are contentions among you. Now this I say, that every one of you saith, I am of Paul; and I of Apollos; and I of Cephas; and I of Christ. Is Christ divided? was Paul crucified for you? or were ye baptized in the name of Paul? (1 Corinthians 1:11–13)

Let's add and change a few words (italicized) in this passage from Paul to illustrate the point of how one might adapt this scripture to that of a community:

> For it hath been declared unto me of you, my brethren, by them which are of the *local community*, that there are contentions among you. Now this I say, that every one of you saith, I am of *the Conservative Protestant Church*; and I of *the Mainline Protestant Church*; and I of *Catholicism and Mormonism*; and I of Christ. Is Christ divided? was *the Catholic Church* crucified for you? or were ye baptized in the name of *the Conservative Protestant Church, the Mainline Protestant Church, or the Mormon Church?*"

If God calls us to "Bear ye one another's burdens, and so fulfil the law of Christ" (Galatians 6:2), does that pertain only to the people whom we attend church with, or is it for the entire community in which we live? As Christians we are to be "patient toward *all men*" (1 Thessalonians 5:14, emphasis added). If we consider ourselves to be laborers in the vineyard of the Lord, then the reality is there are few of us in number laboring to manage an abundant harvest (Matthew 9:36–38). The harvest includes the entire community around us of those who have yet to come unto Christ. And while each church may evangelize in its own way to bring souls unto Christ, evangelism is only one component of what Christ called his church to do.

Let's adapt the scripture regarding the Body of Christ used in the previous chapter from the first letter of Paul to the Corinthians, chapter 12, to the community. Although Paul's analogy is directed at members of the Church, consider for a moment how this scriptural passage could be applied to the many Christian churches that exist today. Keep in mind that all Christian churches today profess allegiance to Jesus Christ, who "hath put all things under his feet, and gave him to be the *head* over all things to the church, which is his body, the fulness of him that filleth all in all" (Ephesians 1:22–23, emphasis added). Using the denominational breakdown from chapter 6, the picture would look something like the following:

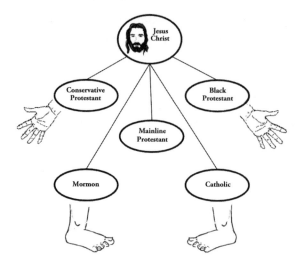

Diagram 10: Christian Denominations as the Body of Christ

Outlining Paul's analogy verse by verse from 12 to 16, replacing members with denominations, yields an interpretation according to the following:

Verse 12: *"For as the body is one, and hath many members, and all the members of that one body, being many, are one body: so also is Christ."* Christianity is one in Christ, but there are many different denominations, and all the denominations are of Christ.

Verse 13: *"For by one Spirit are we all baptized into one body, whether we be Jews or Gentiles, whether we be bond or free; and have been all made to drink into one Spirit."* For by one Spirit, we are all baptized into Christianity. Whether we are Evangelicals, Catholics, or Methodists, we all feel the same Spirit.

Verse 14: *"For the body is not one member, but many."* For the body is not one denomination, but many denominations.

Verse 15: *"If the foot shall say, Because I am not the hand, I am not of the body; is it therefore not of the body?"* If one denomination proclaims that it is not like another denominations, that doesn't make it any less part of the body.

Verse 16: *"And if the ear shall say, Because I am not the eye, I am not of the body; is it therefore not of the body?"* If yet another denomination proclaims that it is not like the other denominations, that doesn't make it any less part of the body.

Limitations with this interpretation start in verse 17 with the phrase "If the whole body were an eye, where were the hearing?" Using this same interpretative direction, there would be an implication that the Body of Christ needs certain denominations to do certain things that cannot be done by other denominations. The interpretation is further limited in verse 18 with the phrase "But now hath God set the members every one of them in the body." A denominational interpretation would suggest God meant there to be many different denominations as part of one body in Christ. These denominational interpretations in verses 17 and 18 would be highly suspect, and thus the interpretation is limited to the reality that we are faced with today: Nearly 34,000 Christian denominations exist, with each one believing to one degree or another that they are the true Church of Christ, the best of all churches, the most biblically accurate, the most devoted, or whatever their reasoning might be as a separate denomination of Christianity.

Surely there will be many that consider this biblical exercise to be full of interpretational error. The point is not to inaccurately interpret scripture but to help us all consider the bigger picture in managing the denominational mess created by man in a world that needs a more unified and capable Christian church and community. If the believers in Jesus Christ are urged to be of one accord, unified in faith and works toward the building and nurturing of the kingdom of God on earth, then why is there so much division among Christians—particularly among the various denominations of Christianity?

Some fundamentalist Christian churches do not consider Catholicism to be a part of true Christianity; even though such churches depend on the Bible compiled and preserved by the very church they disparage. The Roman Catholic Church for hundreds of years has attempted to bring Orthodox Christians into its fold, while Protestant churches have attempted to bring Catholic Christians into its fold. Evangelicals and Baptists accuse LDS/Mormons of not being Christians, while the Baptists have fought and divided among themselves for many decades. Pentecostals criticize believers who don't speak in tongues, while mainstream Christians look down on the unconventional practices of the Jehovah Witnesses and Seventh-day Adventists. The divisive forces within Christianity are doing more damage to the Body of Christ and the faith of its adherents than the ungodly forces of atheism and secularism could ever do.

Theological differences have long been a source of contention among rival Christian denominations, each one providing their own interpretations of the same scriptures. These doctrinal divergences are real, in most cases irreconcilable, and are not likely to be resolved before the Second Coming. That being the case, it is incumbent on all of Christianity to accept this impasse, learn to respect one another's positions, and build upon the substantial commonality that exists among Christian denominations today. In the book *Bridging the Divide: The Continuing Conversation between a Mormon and an Evangelical*, Robert Millet (a Mormon) and Greg Johnson (an Evangelical) discuss the deep differences relating to the theology of their two religions and find meaningful common ground on which to build a productive relationship. There are works such as *Roman Catholics and Evangelicals: Agreements and Differences* (Geisler) and others that create dialogues of understanding and highlight areas of common interests that can be built upon while still respecting sacred theological differences.

Let me be clear: theology is consecrated, meaningful, and important. I do not wish to minimize the significance of theology and how applied theology provides guidance to a church and its members. What I am proposing is that Christianity can hold dear its unique theologies without allowing those divergent theologies to inhibit the work of the Lord in our communities. Once the ocean of theology is drained from the pond of Christian sociology, what is left to be exposed are the true rocks of contention that fuel the ongoing division between Christians. It is easier to manage these nontheological rocks to build bridges of understanding than it is to try and reconcile the theological differences that fuel the ongoing contention between Christians.

THE DIVIDING FORCES THAT WEAKEN THE COMMUNITY

Sir Isaac Newton developed the laws of motion, including the fact that to every action there is always an equal and opposite reaction. Although Newton's laws govern the physical realm, this equal and opposite concept appears to be valid in the spiritual realm. For every force that attempts to unify and strengthen the Body of Christ there is an equal and opposite force that attempts to divide and weaken it.

The dividers of the community today didn't cause the schisms that plaque modern-day Christianity; they simply perpetuate the schisms by resisting unification in fear of validating churches they believe to be heretical. To the divider, the world is black and white and all or nothing. The divider believes the collateral damage that comes as a result of their efforts to spiritually segregate is the price the community must pay to maintain the integrity of true Christianity as they see it.

The divider is much like Saul of Tarsus (Paul), who passionately believed what he was doing was of God and necessary to preserve the true religion, when in fact it was Saul who was persecuting the Lord and kicking "against the pricks" (Acts 9:5). For as much as the divider wants to believe Jesus Christ was an all-or-nothing Lord during his public ministry (Luke 11:23), the fact is the Savior made some compromises for the good of the ministry. Jesus Christ did not free the slaves; he did not proclaim equal rights for women, nor did he end the prejudice against the Samaritans. Sometimes to accomplish the greater purpose righteous and appropriate compromises must be made—compromises that do not include sin or the acceptance of grievous behavior. Rather, these are compromises that are in reality the exercising of humility in welcoming fellow Christians to the table of the Lord.

An example of creating unnecessary division is the National Day of Prayer. Enacted in 1952 by the United States Congress, and observed on the first Thursday of May, the National Day of Prayer is a day set aside whereby Americans—regardless of their religious preference—are encouraged to pray for the United States of America.[2] In 2004, the National Day of Prayer Task Force, headed by Shirley Dobson, whose husband founded the Christian organizational Focus on the Family, announced The Church of Jesus Christ of Latter-day Saints would be excluded from conducting services at events organized by the task force.[3] The reason given by Mark Fried, a task force spokesman, was that the LDS/Mormon faith was in conflict with evangelical principles relating to the Trinity and the inclusion of scripture other than the Bible. The decision caused other Christian churches and organizations to pull out of events and services scheduled by the task force. By the hand of a single group, in the name of supposed doctrinal purity, a day set aside for nationwide prayer to help unify and strengthen the community ended up dividing and weakening the community, and in turn divided and weakened the Body of Christ.

In the early formation of the United States, there was rampant persecution of the Roman Catholic Church by what was eventually termed the "nativist movement," which led to the destruction of Catholic property and the killing of Catholics.[4] The Philadelphia Nativist Riot, Bloody Monday, and the Orange Riots of 1871 and 1872 came as a result of deep anti-Catholic sentiment.[5] In our modern day, dividers carry on the anti-Catholic attitude in an attempt to discredit and exclude the largest Christian faith tradition in the world. As vulnerable as the Roman Catholic Church has been with its legal challenges over the last few decades, what church is not without its own vulnerabilities and weaknesses?

Conventional wisdom suggests the great dividers of the Christian community would come from the atheists and other anti-Christian organizations. However, that is not the case. The primary dividers of the Christian community can be found within the walls of Christianity itself—self-appointed judges and protectors of the faith as they interpret it. In short, these dividers are Modern-day Pharisees. Marcus Tullius Cicero said, "The enemy is within the gates; it is with our own luxury, our own folly, our own criminality that we have to contend."[6] Although dividers are not our enemy, dividers are an enemy to strengthening and unifying the Body of Christ, leaving our communities with lost potential in a multitude of ways.

THE UNIFYING AND STRENGTHENING FORCES OF ECUMENISM

The unifying force that brings together churches in the community and strengthen the sum of the parts are often driven by the spirit of ecumenism. This is a spirit of serving those in need by consolidating the gifts and talents of the community to "minister the same one to another, as good stewards of the manifold grace of God" (1 Peter 4:10). Ecumenism is defined as "a movement promoting worldwide unity among religions through greater cooperation and improved understanding."[7] Ecumenism is often mistakenly interpreted as two or more denominations coming together to water down each other's beliefs to form a compromised treaty of faith. This is not the objective of true ecumenism. Note that two key words in the above definition of ecumenism are "cooperation" and "understanding," not "theological amalgamation."

An example of ecumenism might be three neighborhood churches—a Conservative Protestant, a Catholic, and a Mainline Protestant Church—coming together to help renovate a building used to provide meal services to the poor. Such an ecumenical effort focuses on cooperation and does not require theological alignment. Another example may be local leaders from Conservative Protestant, Catholic, and LDS/Mormon congregations meeting to discuss theological beliefs ahead of the formation of a comparative religion class being held at a local college. Such an ecumenical effort focuses on understanding and does not require doctrinal alliances.

Ecumenism is a bridge-building methodology between churches that would otherwise remain separate, allowing two or more congregations to enjoy expanded fellowship and service with the larger spiritual community. Regarding ecumenism Billy Graham once said, "World travel and getting to know clergy of all denominations has helped mold me into an ecumenical being. We're separated by theology and, in some instances, culture and race, but all that means nothing to me anymore."

Global Ecumenical Efforts

Some ecumenical efforts in the past have been far more grand and global in nature. For example, in 1994 leaders from the Evangelical Protestant Church and the Roman Catholic Church came together to develop and endorse a document titled "Evangelicals & Catholics Together: The Christian Mission in the Third Millennium" (ECT). The comprehensive document outlines common areas of doctrine and future aspirations in an effort to attitudinally unify the two traditionally divergent denominations, concluding:

> We do know that we must affirm and hope and search and contend and witness together, for we belong not to ourselves but to him who has purchased us by the blood of the cross. We do know that this is a time of opportunity—and, if of opportunity, then of responsibility—for Evangelicals and Catholics to be Christians together in a way that helps prepare the world for the coming of him to whom belongs the kingdom, the power, and the glory forever. Amen.[8]

Although the ECT was endorsed by a host of influential Evangelicals and Roman Catholics, the document was also highly criticized by a number of Evangelical theologians (that is, the equal and opposite reaction spoken of earlier) who felt the doctrinal differences between the two denominations are too great to support such a sweeping agreement.[9]

A similar sweeping effort was conducted by the Roman Catholic Church's Pontifical Council for Promoting Christian Unity and the Lutheran World Federation in 1999 with the result being the Joint Declaration on the Doctrine of Justification (JDDJ). The historic effort came as a result of extensive ecumenical dialogue between the two bodies producing the JDDJ, which includes the following statement:

> The present Joint Declaration has this intention: namely, to show that on the basis of their dialogue the subscribing Lutheran churches and the Roman Catholic Church are now able to articulate a common understanding of our justification by God's grace through faith in Christ. It does not cover all that either church teaches about justification; it does encompass a consensus on basic truths of the doctrine of justification and shows that the remaining differences in its explication are no longer the occasion for doctrinal condemnations.[10]

Local Ecumenical Efforts

Some ecumenical efforts in the past have been more focused and local in nature. These efforts act as a unifying and strengthening force to inspire people of different faiths to rally around common values and collectively work together toward righteous solutions. For example, to think Catholics, Evangelicals, and LDS/Mormons could come together and work passionately shoulder to shoulder on anything may have been unimaginable just a decade ago; however, in 2008 Proposition 8 in California changed all that. Proposition 8 was a measure presented to the voters of California that sought to eliminate the rights of same-sex couples to marry. The explosive nature of same-sex marriage generated tens of millions of dollars from proponents and opponents of Proposition 8 polarizing the state and garnering national attention. Because the sanctity of traditional marriage is important to Evangelicals, Catholics, and LDS/Mormons, the three denominations (joined by other Christian denominations as well) organized themselves together statewide and were highly influential in passing Proposition 8.[11] No matter what side of the same-sex issue one might be on, without the ecumenical effort of these diverse Christian Churches, Proposition 8 would have never been passed in California.

THE STRENGTH OF CHRISTIAN
INTRA-FAITH MINISTRY

Nothing brings together and strengthens a community like service, specifically service to the poor. When the Savior gave the world a new commandment to "love one another" (John 13:34) and exclaimed the poor were blessed (Luke 6:20), the door was opened to serving those less fortunate, adding, "For ye have the poor always" (Matthew 26:11). Service not only blesses the lives of the needy (receivers), but even more so service blesses the lives of those performing the service (givers).

There is strength in one Christian serving a single person, a family, a neighborhood, or a community. That strength is multiplied when service is rendered from among a group of Christians from the same church. This strength is exponentially multiplied when service is rendered from among a group of various Christian churches working together to serve a community in need. The act of multidenominational service within the same religion is called intra-faith ministry. For Christianity these ministerial efforts can have a tremendous impact on the individuals who serve and the communities receiving the service. The following are two examples of Christian intra-faith ministry.

Christian Churches Together in the USA

Christian Churches Together in the USA (CCT) is an organization dedicated to Christian unity across its five families of Christian Churches, including Evangelical/Pentecostal, Orthodox, Roman Catholic, historic Protestant, and African American. The purpose of CCT is to facilitate the expansion of "fellowship, unity, and witness among the diverse expressions of Christian faith today," bringing together churches that would otherwise have little contact with one another.[12] CCT was founded in 2001 following a meeting of church leaders in the United States, who addressed what they believed to be a growing need for expanding fellowship, unity, and witness among the diverse faith traditions of Christianity.

An example of how CCT uses the strength of its intra-faith resources is by addressing critical topics during its annual meetings. For example, in January 2008 CCT held its annual meeting in Maryland and included representatives from forty-three different Christian Churches and organizations. Domestic poverty was a key focus of the four-day meeting, which included earnest discussion and prayer on how best to utilize its influence to inspire action on the growing problem in America. Representatives from CCT's five church families led the effort under the topic of "What we have learned in our struggle to eliminate poverty."[13] The results of the meeting led to the creation of an ongoing Domestic Poverty Initiative as one of CCT's primary actions. In addition to bringing attention to and helping organize efforts to eliminate poverty, CCT's charter is focused on inspiring evangelism and promoting racial justice.

Love In the Name of Christ (INC)

Nestled in the Douglas County Lakes Area of Minnesota is the organization Love in the Name of Christ, or Love INC. Love INC networks local Christian church ministries and volunteers, across denominations, to serve the needs of their local community. Love INC mobilizes Christians to work together, with help from community organizations and government resources, to provide coordinated help to the poor—both spiritually and temporally.[14] As of 2012, there were nearly thirty different Love INC member churches across various Christian denominations, including Roman Catholic, Lutheran, Methodist, Presbyterian, and nondenominational.

To understand the strength that a ministerial effort such as Love INC brings to a local community like Douglas County, consider that in June and July 2011 Love INC assisted thirty-eight families through 187 hours of volunteer service.[15] This may seem small, but consider the impact of such an intra-faith Christian ministry over several months, a year, or a decade. These efforts start small and inspire other efforts in local communities as Christians from various faith traditions come together in the work of the Lord.

THE POWER OF INTERFAITH MINISTRY

Serving the poor the responsibility of people of all faith traditions—including those who are not Christian. Ecumenism can reach far beyond Christianity in working together with people of non-Christian faiths to strengthen communities and help those in need. These efforts are often referred to as interfaith ministry.

Although the advantages to the community in having more helping hands is obvious, one might ask how a Christian working with a Jew or a group of Muslims can help unite and strengthen Christianity itself. Good question! Imagine for a moment that a Catholic, Methodist, Evangelical, and an LDS/Mormon were all placed in a room together to discuss religion. These four individuals are likely to focus on the differences in their respective religions and minimize the commonality among their beliefs. Now add to the room a Muslim to join the discussion, and all of a sudden the Christians in the room are likely to feel closer to one another, realizing they have more in common than they originally thought. This example is not about polarizing Christians against non-Christians; on the contrary, it is a win-win situation in that Christians become closer with one another and at the same time learn to work with non-Christians, fostering brotherhood and spiritual understanding.

Multidenominational organizations have access to more resources, a wider reach into neighborhoods, and a greater appreciation for the variation of spiritual cultures. Outside of helping those in need (which is the priority), the by-products of interfaith efforts are increased unity and a strengthening of the Body of Christ. The following are just a few of the multidenominational interfaith efforts that have made a difference in communities across the United States.

Northwest Assistance Ministries of Houston

In 1983, after being overwhelmed with requests for assistance, one social worker and a local clergyman convinced eight other Christian congregations and one Jewish synagogue to lay aside their theological differences to focus on serving the needy of the 242 square mile Northwest Houston area. This effort gave birth to Northwest Assistance Ministries (NAM). From its modest beginnings of ten congregations and a starting budget of less than $50,000, NAM grew into a force of over fifty congregations and a budget approaching $9 million in 2011, serving a staggering 1.5 million residents.[16] The fifty multidenominational congregations of NAM include Anglican, Assembly of God, Baptist, Catholic, Christian Reformed, Church of Christ, Church of Christ Scientist, The Church of Jesus Christ of Latter-day Saints (LDS/Mormon), Episcopal, Evangelical, Evangelical Lutheran, Jewish, Lutheran, Methodist, Nondenominational, Presbyterian, and Seventh-day Adventist.[17]

In a 2012 interview, Anais Watsky, who was an early member and became the NAM director in 1987, explained that although there were minor concerns with the diversity of theological beliefs, there was never enough concern to deny a willing congregation to enter into the NAM fold. Any desire for doctrinal alignment was relinquished in favor of consolidating precious resources to address the growing needs of Houston area families.[18]

Watsky recalled the inclusive nature of the NAM congregational charter was not accepted by all interfaith ministries in the Houston area. After being approached by an eager Christian congregation who did not ascribe to the Triune God belief system, another Houston area interfaith ministry hesitated. After strong objections from a few of its board members who threatened to withdraw funding and support if the divergent congregation were given entrance, the ministry turned away the willing congregation despite its excellent track record of stellar service and volunteerism in other parts of the city. The Modern-day Pharisees strike again!

As mentioned in an earlier chapter, bigotry can be a strong divisive force, even among leaders who should be held to a much higher spiritual standard. In this case, bigotry not only denied an entire congregation the chance to serve, but it reduced the service potential of an entire organization to serve the needy in the city of Houston.

Watsky recounted a period when NAM came under fire from local activists when attempting to open a badly needed medical clinic for the citizens of northwest Houston, Texas. The clinic was consistent with the NAM charter of serving the local community by offering limited health care services for those who could not afford to be treated by local for-profit health care facilities. Respecting the beliefs of a majority of its board members, NAM never intended to provide abortions or birth control as part of its clinic's services; however, because one of NAM's board members was the area president of Planned Parenthood, local activists felt sure NAM would offer such services and picketed NAM headquarters, stirred up the local press, and verbally confronted NAM board members at one of their meetings. To calm the furor, NAM limited the clinic to treating only children with the thought that addressing a portion of the health care need among the area poor was better than nothing at all. The children's health care clinic has become a vibrant component of the services offered by NAM as it continues to look for ways of serving the needy of the northwest Houston area.

As explained in an earlier chapter, politics and social issues always have the potential to divide a unified body and derail the strengthening of the community. Although NAM was righteously endeavoring to serve the poor with badly needed health care services, the misguided passion of a few anti-abortion activists limited NAM's ability to fully realize its service potential for northwest Houston. While the activists felt they scored a victory, the city of Houston lost out on what might have been a great blessing to a large number of people.

Having lived in Northwest Houston as a Latter-day Saint when our congregation joined NAM, I can testify of the incredible blessings that came at the individual, family, church, and community levels. The spirit of service permeated our members strengthening all who embraced the opportunity allowing members to rub shoulders with those of other congregations. It was during this period that my early vision of the Model of Christian Unity was formulated seeing the success that came from multi-denominational service.

Neighborhood Interfaith Movement of Philadelphia

When Bruce Tennyson set out to form a network of Presbyterian churches for collaboration and to serve the northwest Philadelphia area, he had no idea what his efforts would set into motion. Soon after, Tennyson, a Presbyterian minister, began his effort he realized there was more potential in drawing together a multidenominational network of churches than focusing on Presbyterian congregations alone. What then started as ten Protestant congregations, one Roman Catholic parish, and a Jewish synagogue to meet the growing needs of the families of Philly eventually grew into over fifty congregations forty years later, forming the Neighborhood Interfaith Movement (NIM) of Northwest Philadelphia.[19]

NIM includes Protestant, Catholic, Unitarian, Jewish, and Muslim congregations, and other faith-based organizations promoting "vibrant, healthy neighborhoods in Philadelphia by uniting faith, business, civic, and community partners with neighbors to advocate for social justice and to serve people in need."[20] NIM accomplishes its mission by developing programs, hosting events, and inspiring dialogue directed at community needs that focuses on the shared faith-based values of justice, respect, and generosity.

NIM keeps the organization active with fresh ideas and perspectives by seeking out new congregations each year to join the fold. Those who are energetic with a desire to serve are invited to fill board seats (as opposed to a more formal and obligatory process). An annual assembly and other events are held during the year, rotating event locations to ensure all congregations have an opportunity to act as host. During events, great respect is exercised on the part of speakers to recognize the diversity of attendees, keeping subject matters on common spiritual ground.

Reverend Dick Fernandez, who joined NIM ten years into its ministerial journey, commented that NIM has always had the potential to allow theological issues to hamper its efforts to serve the community, but the members simply never permitted such issues to get in the way. "These issues have never bubbled up and perhaps that's because the northwest section of Philadelphia, where NIM is located, has always been a community of rich racial and religious diversity where differences are respected and valued. The length and breadth of this community is unusual in Philadelphia as well as other urban areas across the United States."[21] Reverend Fernandez recounted the neighborhood movements of the late 1950s and 1960s, when neighbors came together to improve their neighborhoods instead of waiting on formalized urban development. These neighborhood movements helped to inspire the development of community ministries in the 1970s, paving the way for the interfaith ministries that thrive in America today.

Fernandez remembers how decades ago it was "causes" that helped to bring together people of diverse belief. "Back then Christians of different faith traditions were drawn together by causes such as civil rights or the Vietnam war; causes that might actually divide a single congregation but had the power to unite a Protestant and a Catholic with like views toward a common purpose," says Fernandez. In the absence of a Vietnam war or civil rights movement, interfaith ministries today bring together people of different faiths to rally around the cause of serving a community in need and the desire for greater understanding.

Interfaith Ministries of Wichita

Those who think interfaith ministries are modern-day phenomena have not considered the history of the Interfaith Ministries of Wichita (IMW). The IMW began in 1885 under the name Wichita Ministerial Alliance when leaders of local Protestant Churches put aside theological differences in favor of serving the needy of local townships. By the 1920s, the ministry had fifty Protestant congregations working together to not only serve the poor but to also address the social injustices of the day. By the 1930s, the Alliance added Jewish, Catholic, and Eastern Orthodox congregations, allowing the ministry to branch out and meet the needs of the war-torn economy in the 1940s. In the 1950s and 1960s, the ministry increased its international relief efforts while advocating domestically for civil rights. In the 1970s, other non-Christian congregations were added, including Buddhist, Hindu, and Muslim, helping to expand the ministry to reach greater numbers of people. Today IMW touches thousands of people in need through seventy different congregations and organizations in the Wichita area.[22]

The rich history of IMW has allowed it to hone a mission that reaches well beyond feeding the hungry and clothing the naked. Decades of relief work and ministry have allowed IMW to consider what it calls "both sides of humanity." One side of that humanity includes purpose, hope, and contentment; and the other side includes alienation, hopelessness, and frustration. IMW believes communities are full of those on both sides, prompting a mission statement that calls "people of all faiths together to build interreligious understanding, promote justice, relieve misery, and reconcile the estranged."[23] Although a far-sweeping mission, IMW has a history of being in the trenches and making a difference through selfless service to the community.

As of 2012 the congregations of IMW contain those of Christianity including Baptist, Catholic, Church of Christ, Church of Christ Scientist, Church of the Nazarene, The Church of Jesus Christ of Latter-day Saints, the Community of Christ, Congregational, Episcopal, Greek Orthodox Lutheran, Mennonite, Methodist, nondenominational, Presbyterian, Unitarian, and United Church of Christ. Other congregations of IMW include Bahá'í Faith, Buddhist, Jewish, and Sangha Soto Zen.

IS INTERFAITH NO FAITH AT ALL?

In her book *A New Religious America*, author Diana Eck describes the United States as the most religiously diverse nation in the world and invites Americans to open their eyes to the changes in religiosity the country is experiencing. Eck points out that the diversity of religions is something the founders of the republic could not have imagined. With such diversity, according to Eck, the challenge in becoming one does not include the blending of religions into a religious "melting pot" but rather "a oneness of commitment to the common covenants of our citizenship out of the manyness of religious ways and worlds."[24]

There exists a dichotomy for the faithful Christian. On one hand, the Christian belief system includes the fact that unless one believes in Jesus Christ and professes faith in him as Lord and Savior they cannot obtain everlasting life. On the other hand, the Christian must live among many who do not believe as he or she does—Christian and non-Christian—with opportunities to serve with such people to strengthen the community and serve those in need. Some will openly embrace the opportunity, while others will openly (and sometimes vocally) reject the opportunity on the grounds of theological conflict. What we have learned here is that many brave Christians are serving shoulder to shoulder with those who do not share the same faith tradition, some who are not even professing Christians, and by doing so are making a difference in their community.

Are those Christians who embrace interfaith efforts exercising loyalty their faith, or are these Christians exercising disloyalty to their faith? While the Modern-day Pharisee would accuse such a person of Christian treason, the practicing disciple of Christ will see things very differently. There is a cynical saying that "Interfaith is no faith at all." I wholeheartedly disagree. One can be entirely true to his or her faith while serving and strengthening their community—the two are not mutually exclusive. Furthermore, when interfaith ministry combines service to the community with religious education, wonderful things take place for all those involved, including a deeper understanding of other faith traditions; a greater appreciation for one's own faith tradition; a strengthening of community bonds; and the synergistic actions that result from the coordination of faith-based resources.

CHRISTIAN UNITY: A PIPE DREAM OR A REALITY WORTH PURSUING?

What has been outlined in this chapter is not just a utopian pipe dream that exists in the same universe as wish-granting fairies, calorie-free ice cream, and world peace. The Model of Christian Unity is already in progress around America and is strengthening communities and unifying Christianity toward reaching a greater measure of its potential. There are hundreds (perhaps thousands) of community building efforts among diverse Christian congregations operating and changing lives around the United States. Therefore, the question of whether it is possible to strengthen and unify the Body of Christ in helping Christianity reach its potential has been answered and is now irrelevant; the more valid and important question is, "Are you going to become a part of the movement of strengthening and unifying the Body of Christ to reach your own spiritual potential, or are you are going to sit on the sidelines or perhaps even fight against it?"

You are an individual who is also a member of a family; a member of the church; and a member of the community. If indeed "God hath not given us the spirit of fear; but of power, and of love, and of a sound mind" (2 Timothy 1:7), then what are you waiting for?

FINAL THOUGHTS ON THE WHO, WHAT, WHERE, AND HOW

OUR EXPEDITION NOW COMES TO AN END, AND WHAT A EXPEDITION IT was! We traveled through two thousand years of history to understand and make sense of the origins of Christianity, how that history has evolved to the present day, and, most important, how that history impacts Christians in the modern era.

We explored the definition of a Christian using the input of the United States's largest and most distinguished Christian churches and organizations augmented by an in-depth study of the bestselling book of all time in the Bible.

We examined powerful data that helped gauge the performance of Christian denominations in how they are inspiring their members to live gospel principles.

We analyzed the Christian population of today to identify and profile its key segments, creating exercises to help individuals identify where they are along the Christian Continuum and their level of pharisaical attitude.

We investigated ways of strengthening and unifying Christianity, covering individuals, families, churches, and communities and the courageous organizations of today who are at the forefront of the effort.

In this expedition, we answered the who, what, where, and how of Christianity in hopes of inspiring the reader to think more critically and constructively of his or her own spirituality and to become one who unites and strengthens from the inside out.

If there were one thought from this book to take with you and keep close, it would be this: most of us as Christians—and Christianity in general—are operating far under our spiritual potential. If we strive to do a little better each day in Jesus Christ, amazing things will happen. Individuals, families, churches, and communities will have more joy, we will get more done, we will serve more people, and the kingdom of God on earth will thrive to the betterment of all mankind.

Much work needs to be done, and it all starts with each one of us.

Christianity is not meant to be a group of exclusive clubs that meet on Sunday to pat each other on the back and bask in the pending glory of everlasting life. Jesus Christ taught to be one of his disciples requires faith to action, not faith to leisure. There is a church hymn written over one hundred years ago whose chorus reads, "Then wake up and do something more, than dream of your mansion above. Doing good is a pleasure, a joy beyond measure, a blessing of duty and love."[1] Every Christian would be wise to heed the advice of this profound lyric:

Wake up and realize who you are and what you are capable of.

Stop dreaming of eternal bliss only and focus on how you live your life each day.

Do something regularly that takes you outside of yourself, something that builds the kingdom of God on earth and exemplifies the ministry of Jesus Christ

And reap the earthly and eternal blessings of living true discipleship in the gospel of Christ.

Where are the Christians? The most meaningful answer to that question will come from you when you ask yourself each day—where am I when it comes to being a disciple of Christ?

NOTES

INTRODUCTION TO SECTION 1:
WHO WERE THE CHRISTIANS?

1. "History," The Lehrman Institute, accessed July 12, 2012, http://lehrmaninstitute.org/history/index.html

2. "Voltaire Quotations," QuotationVault.com, accessed July 12, 2012, http://www.quotationvault.com/author/_Voltaire

3. "Mark Twain Quotes," Notable Quotes, accessed July 12, 2012, http://www.notable-quotes.com/t/twain_mark.html

4. Paul Johnson, *The History of Christianity* (New York: Simon & Schuster, 1976), prologue.

5. Ibid., 22

6. Ibid.

CHAPTER 1: THEY WERE EVANGELIZERS
AND BUILDERS (UP TO AD 299)

1. "Herod the Great," Ingrid Olson, Webchron, accessed July 20, 2012, http://www.thenagain.info/webchron/MiddleEast/HerodGreat.html.

2. Geza Vermes, *The Nativity: History and Legend* (London: Penguin, 2006), 87.

3. Paul Johnson, *The History of Christianity* (New York: Simon & Schuster, 1976), 33.

4. "St. Mark the Apostle, Evangelist," Coptic Orthodox Church Network, accessed July 25, 2012, http://www.copticchurch.net/topics/synexarion/mark.html.

5. "Eusebius Pamphilius: Church History, Life of Constantine, Oration in Praise of Constantine," Christian Classics Ethereal Library, accessed July 25, 2012, http://www.ccel.org/ccel/schaff/npnf201.iii.viii.xxxii.html.

6. Paul Johnson, *The History of Christianity* (New York: Simon & Schuster, 1976), 41.

7. Ibid., 42.

8. Ibid., 44.

9. Ibid., 45.

10. Ibid., 56.

11. "Get to Know Popes of East and West," Amazon, accessed July 13, 2012, http://www.amazon.com/gp/richpub/syltguides/fullview/W4O42BT6T7FQ.

12. "A Brief Summary of Gnosticism," Stephan A. Hoeller, The Gnosis Archive, accessed July 14, 2012, http://www.gnosis.org/gnintro.htm.

13. "The Gnostic Jesus," Douglas Groothuis, Christian Research Institute, accessed July 14, 2012, http://www.equip.org/articles/the-gnostic-jesus.

14. G. R. S. Mead, *Fragments of a Faith Forgotten* (London: Theosophical Publishing Society, 1900).

15. William Tabernee, *Montanist Inscriptions and Testimonia: Epigraphic Sources Illustrating the History of Montanism* (Georgia: Mercer University Press, 1977), 45.

16. John Chapman, "Monarchians," in *The Catholic Encyclopedia* (New York: Robert Appleton Company, 1911), accessed July 25, 2012, http://www.newadvent.org/cathen/10448a.htm.

17. "Benedict XVI, General Audience, St Peter's Square, Wednesday 25 April 2007, Origen of Alexandria: life and work," Vatican, the Holy See, accessed July 21, 2012 http://www.vatican.va/holy_father/benedict_xvi/audiences/2007/documents/hf_ben-xvi_aud_20070425_en.html.

18. Eusebius Pamphilus, *Ecclesiastical History* (London: Bell and Daldy, 1865), 72.

19. Paul Johnson, *The History of Christianity* (New York: Simon & Schuster, 1976), 52.

CHAPTER 2: THEY WERE LEGITIMIZED AND CODIFIED (AD 300–999)

1. *Encyclopedia Britannica Online*, s.v. "Shapur II," accessed July 20, 2012, http://www.britannica.com/EBchecked/topic/538720/Shapur-II.

2. Rowan Williams, *Arius: Heresy and Tradition* (Michigan: William B. Eerdmans Publishing Company, 2002), 97.

3. Norman E. Cantor, *The Civilization of the Middle Ages* (New York: HarperCollins, 1994), 51.

4. Joseph Sollier, "Apollinarianism," *The Catholic Encyclopedia* (New York: Robert Appleton Company, 1907), accessed July 26, 2012, http://www.newadvent.org/cathen/01615b.htm.

5. "Nestorianism," Christian Apologetics and Research Ministry, accessed July 19, 2012, http://carm.org/nestorianism.

6. John Chapman, "Nestorius and Nestorianism," *The Catholic Encyclopedia* (New York: Robert Appleton Company, 1911), accessed July 26, 2012, http://www.newadvent.org/cathen/10755a.htm.

7. John Chapman, "Eutychianism," *The Catholic Encyclopedia* (New York: Robert Appleton Company, 1909), accessed July 26, 2012, http://www.newadvent.org/cathen/05633a.htm.

8. Joseph Pohle, "Pelagius and Pelagianism," *The Catholic Encyclopedia* (New York: Robert Appleton Company, 1911), accessed July 26, 2012, http://www.newadvent.org/cathen/11604a.htm.

9. Paul Johnson, *The History of Christianity* (New York: Simon & Schuster, 1976), 67, 80.

10. Ibid., 69.

11. Ibid.

12. Ibid., 88.

13. Ibid.

14. "The Council of Nicaea," Church History 101, accessed July 26, 2012, http://www.churchhistory101.com/century4-p7.php and "Arianism Versus the Council of Nicaea," John Raymond, Arian Catholic, accessed July 26, 2012, http://www.arian-catholic.org/arian/arianism_v_nicaea.html.

15. *"Babylon the Great Has Fallen!"—God's Kingdom Rules* (New York: Watchtower Bible and Tract Society of New York, Inc., 1963), 477, accessed July 19, 2012, http://www.strictlygenteel.co.uk/babylon/babylon21.html.

16. "Early Trinitarian Quotes," Matt Slick, Christian Apologetics and Research Ministry, accessed July 21, 2012, http://carm.org/early-trinitarian-quotes.

17. "The Catechism of Trent," Nazareth Resource Library, accessed July 26, 2012, http://www.cin.org/users/james/ebooks/master/trent/tpray0.htm.

18. "Bible," Online Etymology Dictionary, accessed July 19, 2012, http://www.etymonline.com/index.php?l=b&p=19&allowed_in_frame=0.

19. Kurt Aland and Barbara Aland, *The Text of the New Testament: An Introduction to the Critical Editions and to the Theory and Practice of Modern Textual Criticism* (Michigan: William B. Eerdmans Publishing Company, 1995), 15.

20. Paul Johnson, *The History of Christianity* (New York: Simon & Schuster, 1976), 53.

21. Ibid., 53–54.

22. Eusebius Pamphilus, *Ecclesiastical History* (London: Bell and Daldy, 1865), 221.

23. "Time Machine: Banned from the Bible in 2003 and Banned from the Bible II in 2007," Share the Files, accessed July 19, 2012, http://sharethefiles .com/forum/viewtopic.php?f=131&t=101420.

24. Bart Ehrman, *Lost Scriptures: Books That Did Not Make It into the New Testament* (New York: Oxford, 2003), 19–20.

25. "Athanasius, Bishop of Alexandria, Theologian, Doctor," Biographical Sketches of Memorable Christians of the Past, accessed July 26, 2012, http:// justus.anglican.org/resources/bio/152.html.

26. "Nag Hammadi," *Overlapping Magisteria* (blog), July 26, 2012 http:// magisteria.wordpress.com/tag/athanasius.

27. Paul Johnson, *The History of Christianity* (New York: Simon & Schuster, 1976), 55.

28. Dunin-Borkowski, "Hierarchy of the Early Church," in *The Catholic Encyclopedia*. (New York: Robert Appleton Company, 1910), accessed August 17, 2012, http://www.newadvent.org/cathen/07326a.htm.

29. Rodney Stark, *The Rise of Christianity: A Sociologist Reconsiders History*. (New Jersey, Princeton University Press, 1996), 6.

30. Paul Johnson, *The History of Christianity* (New York: Simon & Schuster, 1976), 78–79.

31. Richard L. Daft, *Organization Theory and Design* (Ohio, South-Western Cengage Learning, 2008), 341.

CHAPTER 3: THEY WERE CORRUPTED AND DIVIDED (1000–1499)

1. F. Heinrich Geffcken, *Church and State: Their Relations Historically Developed* (London: Longmans, Green, and Company, 1877), 193.

2. Herbert Edward John Cowdrey, *Pope Gregory VII, 1073–1085*, (New York: Oxford University Press, 1998), 546.

3. John of Salisbury, *Policraticus* (New York: Cambridge University Press, 1990).

4. "Nepotism" Dictionary.com, accessed August 24, 2012, http://dictionary .reference.com/browse/nepotism.

5. Nicholas Weber, "Pope Nicholas III," *The Catholic Encyclopedia* (New York: Robert Appleton Company, 1911), accessed July 26, 2012, http://www .newadvent.org/cathen/11056a.htm.

6. Michael Ott, "Pope Innocent VII," *The Catholic Encyclopedia* (New York: Robert Appleton Company, 1910), accessed July 26, 2012, http://www.newadvent.org /cathen/08019a.htm.

7. James Loughlin, "Pope Paul III," *The Catholic Encyclopedia,* (New York: Robert Appleton Company, 1911), accessed July 26, 2012, http://www .newadvent.org/cathen/11579a.htm.

8. Ibid.

9. Richard Butler, "Pope Sixtus IV," *The Catholic Encyclopedia* (New York: Robert Appleton Company, 1912), accessed July 26, 2012, http://www .newadvent.org/cathen/14032b.htm.

10. "Pope Sixtus IV," Mark Gstohl, Reformation Happens, accessed July 26, 2012, http://www.reformationhappens.com/people/sixtusiv.

11. Christopher Hibbert, *The Borgias and Their Enemies* (Florida, Houghton-Mifflin, 2008), 30.

12. "Cesare Borgia," *New World Encyclopedia*, accessed July 19, 2012, http://www.newworldencyclopedia.org/entry/Cesare_Borgia.

13. "Nepotism," *New Catholic Dictionary*, accessed July 26, 2012, http://saints .sqpn.com/ncd05726.htm.

14. Bertrand Russell, Bertrand, *History of Western Philosophy* (New York: Simon & Schuster, 1945), 384, emphasis added.

15. E. R.l Chamberlin, *The Bad Popes* (United States: Barnes and Noble, 1969), 70.

16. James Loughlin, "Pope Alexander VI," *The Catholic Encyclopedia* (New York: Robert Appleton Company, 1907), accessed July 26, 2012, http://www .newadvent.org/cathen/01289a.htm.

17. Nicholas Weber, "Pope Paul II," *The Catholic Encyclopedia* (New York: Robert Appleton Company, 1911), accessed July 26, 2012, http://www .newadvent.org/cathen/11578a.htm.

18. Robert Aldrich and Garry Wotherspoon, *Who's Who in Gay and Lesbian History* (New York: Routledge, 2001), 407.

19. "The Historical Origin of Indulgences," Enrico dal Covolo, Catholicculture .org, accessed July 26, 2012, http://www.catholicculture.org/culture/library/view. cfm?recnum=1054#4.

20. Johann Peter Kirsch, "The Reformation," *The Catholic Encyclopedia* (New York: Robert Appleton Company, 1911), accessed July 26, 2012, http://www .newadvent.org/cathen/12700b.htm.

21. "The Profession of the Pardoner," Dr. Nighan's British Literature and History of Western Philosophy Course, accessed July 26, 2012, http://www .stjohns-chs.org/english/Medieval/pdr.html.

22. "The Historical Origin of Indulgences," *Catholic Culture*, accessed July 26, 2012, http://www.catholicculture.org/culture/library/view.cfm?recnum=1054#4.

23. William Kent, "Indulgences," *The Catholic Encyclopedia* (New York: Robert Appleton Company, 1910), accessed July 26, 2012, http://www.newadvent.org /cathen/07783a.htm.

24. Jean Henri D'Aubigné, *History of the Great Reformation of the Sixteenth Century in Germany, Switzerland, & c.* (New York, Thomas Carter, 1843), 212.

25. "Piety," *Dictionary.com*, accessed July 19, 2012, http://dictionary.reference .com/browse/piety?s=t&ld=1086.

26. Aquinas on Torture," Jordan Bishop, Wiley Online Library, accessed July 21, 2012, http://onlinelibrary.wiley.com/doi/10.1111/j.0028-4289.2006.00142.x/ full.

27. "Growth of Episcopal Jurisdiction," Bulfinch's Mythology, accessed July 26, 2012, http://www.bibliotecapleyades.net/vatican/inquisition/Chapter07.htm.

28. William Turner, "Peter Abelard," *The Catholic Encyclopedia* (New York: Robert Appleton Company, 1907), accessed July 21, 2012, http://www.newadvent.org/ cathen/01036b.htm.

29. Henri Leclercq, "Fourth Lateran Council (1215)," *The Catholic Encyclopedia* (New York: Robert Appleton Company, 1910), accessed July 26, 2012, http:// www.newadvent.org/cathen/09018a.htm.

30. "The Cathars: Mass burning at Montsegur," Brenda Ralph Lewis, Medieval History, accessed uly 19, 2012, http://suite101.com/article/the-cathars-mass-burning-at-montsegur-1244-a346202.

31. "Franciscan Monks," Xtimeline, accessed July 19, 2012, http://www .xtimeline.com/evt/view.aspx?id=266395.

32. "William of Ockham," Stanford Encyclopedia of Philosophy, accessed July 19, 2012, http://plato.stanford.edu/entries/ockham.

33. Norman Cantor, *Civilization of the Middle Ages* (New York: HarperCollins, 1994), 203.

34. "John Wycliffe," Faithology, accessed July 19, 2012, http://www.faithology .com/bios/john-wycliffe.

35. Heiko Augustinus Oberman and Eileen Walliser-Schwarzbart, *Luther: Man between God and the Devil* (New York: Yale University Press, 2006), 54.

36. "Innocent VIII," *Encyclopedia Britannica Online*, accessed July 20, 2012, http://www.britannica.com/EBchecked/topic/288686/Innocent-VIII.

37. "Girolamo Savonarola," *Encyclopedia.com*, accessed July 19, 2012, http:// www.encyclopedia.com/topic/Girolamo_Savonarola.aspx.

38. Anotónio José Saraiva, "Introduction," *The Marrano Factory. The Portuguese Inquisition and Its New Christians*, H. P. Salomon and I. S. D. Sassoon, trans. (Boston: Brill, 2001).

39. Richard Urban Butler, "Pope Bl. Urban II," *The Catholic Encyclopedia* (New York: Robert Appleton Company, 1912), accessed July 27, 2012, http://www .newadvent.org/cathen/15210a.htm.

40. Louis Bréhier, "Crusades," *The Catholic Encyclopedia* (New York: Robert Appleton Company, 1908), accessed July 27, 2012, http://www.newadvent.org /cathen/04543c.htm.

41. Ibid.

42. "1054 The East-West Schism," George T. Dennis, *Christianity Today Library*, accessed July 20, 2012, http://www.ctlibrary.com/ch/1990/issue28/2820.html.

CHAPTER 4: THEY WERE REFORMED AND SCATTERED (1500 TO THE PRESENT)

1. David B. Barrett, *World Christian Encyclopedia* (New York: Oxford University Press, 2001), 3.

2. F. L. Glaser, *Pope Alexander VI and His Court: Extracts from the Latin Diary of Johannes Burchardus* (New York: Nicholas L. Brown, 1921), 154–55.

3. Ingrid D. Rowland, *Giordano Bruno: Philosopher/Heretic* (Chicago: University of Chicago Press, 2009), 3, 6, 112.

4. Dava Sobel, *Galileo's Daughter: A Historical Memoir of Science, Faith, and Love* (New York: Walker, 1999), 275–76.

5. Desiderius Erasmus, *The Praise of Folly* (London: Hamilton, Adams & Co. and Glasgow: Thomas D. Morison, 1887).

6. Henry Eyster Jacobs, *A History of the Evangelical Lutheran Church in the United States* (New York: Christian Literature Company, 1837), 41.

7. Richard, James William, *Philip Melanchthon: The Protestant Preceptor of Germany* (New York: Putnam, 1898), 379.

8. James J. Ellis, *William Tyndale* (New York: Thomas Whittaker, 1923), 19, 31.

9. Ibid, 32.

10. T. H. L. Parker, *Calvin: An Introduction to His Thought,* (London: Geoffrey Chapman, 1995), 128, 150.

11. John Calvin, "Separation of Church and State," *Theopedia,* accessed August 22, 2012, http://www.theopedia.com/john_calvin.

12. Mark Galli, "John Calvin," *131 Christians Everyone Should Know* (Nashville: Christianity Today, Inc., 2000).

13. Bruce Gourley "A Very Brief Introduction to Baptist History, Then and Now," Baptist History & Heritage Society, accessed July 27, 2012, http://yellowstone. net/baptist/overview.htm.

14. Jason K. Lee, *The Theology of John Smyth. Puritan, Separatist, Baptist, Mennonite* (Macon, GA: Mercer University Press, 2003), 91.

15. Mark A. Noll, *The Rise of Evangelicalism: The Age of Edwards, Whitefield and the Wesleys* (Downers Grove, IL, 2003), 107.

16. "The Moravians and John Wesley," Christianity Today Library, accessed August 22, 2012, http://www.ctlibrary.com/ch/1982/issue1/128.html.

17. "John Wesley, Conversion: Open-air Preaching," *tlogical,* accessed August 22, 2012, http://www.tlogical.net/biojwesley.htm#coap.

18. "Biography of John Wesley," *Christian Classics Ethereal Library,* accessed August 22, 2012, http://www.ccel.org/ccel/wesley.

19. M. M. Davis, *How the Disciples Began and Grew, A Short History of the Christian Church* (Cincinnati: The Standard Publishing Company, 1915).

20. C. Leonard Allen and Richard T. Hughes, *Discovering Our Roots: The Ancestry of the Churches of Christ* (Abilene, TX: Abilene Christian University Press, 1988).

21. Douglas Allen Foster and Anthony L. Dunnavant, "Walter Scott," *The Encyclopedia of the Stone-Campbell Movement: Christian Church (Disciples of Christ)* (Grand Rapids: Wm. B. Eerdmans Publishing, 2004).

22. Douglas Allen Foster and Anthony L. Dunnavant, "Alexander Campbell," *The Encyclopedia of the Stone-Campbell Movement: Christian Church (Disciples of Christ)* (Grand Rapids: Wm. B. Eerdmans Publishing, 2004).

23. "History of the Disciples of Christ," *About.com Christianity,* accessed September 28, 2012, http://christianity.about.com/od/Disciples-Of-Christ/a/ History-Of-The-Disciples-Of-Christ.htm.

24. Charles Taze Russell, "Series 4: The Battle of Armageddon," *Studies in the Scriptures, 1897,* accessed September 28, 2012, http://www.globallight.org.uk/ downloads/English%20Vol%204.pdf, 311.

25. George D. Chryssides, "Unrecognized Charisma? A Study of Four Charismatic Leaders," Center of Studies on New Religions, accessed August 22, 2012, http://www.cesnur.org/2001/london2001/chryssides.htm.

26. "The History of the Seventh-day Adventist Church," CARM, accessed September 28, 2012, http://carm.org/religious-movements/seventh-day-adventism/history-seventh-day-adventist-church.

27. Idígoras Tellechea and José Ignacio, *Ignatius of Loyola: The Pilgrim Saint* (Chicago: Loyola University Press, 1994), xxii.

28. Barry M. Horstman. "Billy Graham: A Man with a Mission." Barry M. Horstman, *The Cincinnati Post*, June 27, 2002. Accessed July 20, 2012, http://www.highbeam.com/doc/1G1-87912863.html.

29. "The Dead Sea Scrolls and Other Ancient Manuscripts" The United Methodist Women, accessed August 25, 2012, http://gbgm-umc.org/umw/bible/outside2.stm.

30. David B. Barrett, *World Christian Encyclopedia* (New York: Oxford University Press, 2001), 3.

31. "What Is an Evangelical? A Survey of How the Term Has Been Used and Abused," Phil Johnson, Grace to You, accessed July 21, 2012, http://www.gty.org/resources/articles/a363/what-is-an-evangelical-a-survey-of-how-the-term-has-been-used-and-abused.

32. Bruce Gourley "A Very Brief Introduction to Baptist History, Then and Now."

33. "Statistics," Baptist World Alliance, accessed July 19, 2012, http://www.bwanet.org/about-us2/statistics.

34. Alan Cooperman. "Southern Baptists Vote To Leave World Alliance," *Washington Post*, June 6, 2004, accessed July 20, 2012. http://www.washingtonpost.com/wp-dyn/articles/A44658-2004Jun15.html.

35. Cecil M. Robeck, Jr., *The Azusa Street Mission and Revival: The Birth of the Global Pentecostal Movement* (Nashville: Thomas Nelson, Inc., 2006), 4.

36. David B. Barrett, *World Christian Encyclopedia* (New York: Oxford University Press, 2001), 16.

37. David Hein and Gardiner H. Shattuck Jr., *The Episcopalians* (New York: Church Publishing, 2004), preface.

38. "Formation of the Assemblies of God," Assemblies of God, accessed July 21, 2012, http://ag.org/top/about/History/index.cfm#.

39. "History: Our Story," United Methodist Church, accessed July 21, 2012, http://www.umc.org/site/c.lwL4KnN1LtH/b.1720691/k.B5CB/History_Our_Story.htm.

40. "What is the United Church of Christ?" United Church of Christ, accessed July 19, 2012, http://www.ucc.org/about-us/what-is-the-united-church-of.html.

41. Evangelical and Reformed Historical Society, accessed July 20, 2012, http://www.erhs.info/Home.html.

42. "General Council of Congregational Christian Churches," *Encyclopedia Britannica Online*, accessed July 20, 2012, http://www.britannica.com/EBchecked/topic/228402/General-Council-of-Congregational-Christian-Churches.

43. "History," Seventh-day Adventist Church, accessed July 20, 2012, http://www.adventist.org//world-church/facts-and-figures/history/index.html.

44. Andrew Holden, Andrew (2002). *Jehovah's Witnesses: Portrait of a Contemporary Religious Movement* (New York: Routledge, 2002), 20.

45. David B. Barrett, *World Christian Encyclopedia* (New York: Oxford University Press, 2001), 11.

46. Ibid., 15.

47. Assemblies of God USA, "Why New Churches Fail," *Enrichment Journal*, accessed August 25, 2012, http://enrichmentjournal.ag.org/200004/022_why_new_chuches_fail.cfm.

48. Audrey Barrick, "Church Pastors' Pay Rises to More than $80,000," *The Christian Post*, August 19, 2008, accessed August 17, 2012, http://www.christianpost.com/news/church-pastors-pay-rises-to-more-than-80-000-33898.

SECTION 2: WHAT IS A CHRISTIAN? A DEFINITION

1. Alister E. McGrath, *Understanding the Trinity* (Grand Rapids: Zondervan, 1988), 97.

2. Leo Paul Giampietro, *The Wrath of Yeshu* (Bloomington, IN: AuthorHouse, 2008), 104.

3. Herbert Thurston, "Apostles' Creed," in *The Catholic Encyclopedia*, vol. 1 (New York: Robert Appleton Company, 1907), accessed July 27, 2012, http://www.newadvent.org/cathen/01629a.htm.

4. George Duce Wynne Ommanney, *The Athanasian Creed: an examination of recent theories respecting its date and origin* (London: Rivingtons, 1875), 120.

CHAPTER 5: IT'S CONFUSING ACCORDING TO THE WORLD

1. "Christian," *Merriam-Webster*, accessed July 20, 2012, http://www.merriam-webster.com/dictionary/christian.

2. "Christian," *Webster's Dictionary* (New York: Random House, 1996), 116.

3. "Christianity," *Encyclopedia Britannica Online*, accessed July 20, 2012, http://www.britannica.com/EBchecked/topic/115240/Christianity, retrieved 7/20/12.

4. "NCC at a Glance: Who Belongs, What We Do, How We Work Together," National Council of Churches USA, accessed July 22, 2012, http://www.ncccusa.org/about/about_ncc.html.

5. Ibid.

6. "Interfaith Relations and the Churches; A Policy Statement of the National Council of the Churches of Christ in the U.S.A. (November 10, 1999)," National Council of Churches, accessed July 22, 2012, http://www.ncccusa.org/interfaith/ifr.html.

7. "Edinburgh 2010," World Council of Churches, accessed August 25, 2012, http://www.oikoumene.org/programmes/unity-mission-evangelism-and-spirituality/mission-and-unity/towards-2010.html.

8. "What is the World Council of Churches?," World Council of Churches, accessed July 22, 2012, http://www.oikoumene.org/en/who-are-we.html.

9. "World Council of Churches 9th Assembly, February 14-23, 2006, Porto Alegre Brazil," World Council of Churches, accessed July 22, 2012, http://www.oikoumene.org/en/resources/documents/assembly/porto-alegre-2006/1-statements-documents-adopted/Christian-unity-and-message-to-the-churches/called-to-be-the-one-church-as-adopted.html.

10. "Who We Are," World Evangelical Alliance, accessed July 22, 2012, http://www.worldea.org/whoweare/introduction.

11. Ibid., mission.

12. Ibid., statement of faith.

13. "Constitution of the American Council of Christian Churches," American Council of Christian Churches, accessed July 22, 2012, http://www.amcouncilcc.org/constitution.asp.

14. Dr. John McKnight, President of the ACCC, email message to author, July 12, 2008.

15. "Doctrinal Statement of the American Council of Christian Churches," American Council of Christian Churches, accessed July 22, 2012, http://www.amcouncilcc.org/doctrine.asp.

16. "About us: Congregational Way," National Association of Congregational Christian Churches, accessed July 22, 2012, http://www.naccc.org/AboutUs/CongregationalWay.aspx.

17. Dr. Thomas M Richard, Executive Secretary, NACCC, email message to author, March 27, 2012

18. "Churches: membership in the NACCC," National Association of Congregational Christian Churches, accessed March 22, 2012, http://www.naccc.org/Churches/MembershipInNA.aspx.

19. Robert Welsh, President of the Council on Christian Unity, email message to author, June 15, 2008.

20. "Church Giving Drops $1.2 Billion Reports 2012 Yearbook of Churches," *National Council of Churches News*, accessed July 22, 2012, http://www.ncccusa.org/news/120209yearbook2012.html.

21. *Catechism of the Catholic Church*, 2nd ed, 1989, section 1229.

22. Ibid., section 776.

23. Anthony Bowen and Peter Garnsey, *Lactantius: Divine Institutes* (London: Liverpool University Press, 2003), 280.

24. *Catechism of the Catholic Church*, 2nd ed, 1989, section 224.

25. Ibid., 222.

26. "About Us—Meet Southern Baptists," *SBC.net*, accessed July 22, 2012, http://www.sbc.net/aboutus/default.asp.

27. Ibid., "The Baptist Faith and Message."

28. Ibid., "How to Become a Christian."

29. "Our Christian Roots," The United Methodist Church, accessed July 22, 2012, http://www.umc.org/site/c.lwL4KnN1LtH/b.2299859/k.13B7/Our_Christian_Roots.htm.

30. Ibid., "We Are Saved."

31. David B. Barrett, *World Christian Encyclopedia* (New York: Oxford University Press, 2001), 18.

32. "Statistical Report," The Church of Jesus Christ of Latter-day Saints, accessed July 22, 2012, http://www.lds.org/general-conference/2012/04/statistical-report-2011?lang=eng.

33. "Articles of Faith," *Mormon.org*, accessed July 22, 2012, http://mormon.org/articles-of-faith.

34. "Baptism," The Church of Jesus Christ of Latter-day Saints, accessed, July 22, 2012, http://www.lds.org/study/topics/baptism?lang=eng.

35. Ibid., "Sacrament."

36. M. Russell Ballard, "Faith, Family, Facts, and Fruits," *Liahona*, November 2007, 25–27.

37. "The Founder and Church History," The Church of God in Christ, Inc., accessed July 22, 2012, http://www.cogic.org/our-foundation/the-founder-church-history.

38. Ibid., "What We Believe."

39. "History of the National Baptist Convention, USA, Inc.," The National Baptist Convention, USA, Inc., accessed July 22, 2012, http://www.nationalbaptist.com/about-us/our-history/index.html

40. Ibid., "What We Believe."

41. Ibid.

42. "History of the ELCA," Evangelical Lutheran Church in America, accessed July 22, 2012, http://www.elca.org/Who-We-Are/History.aspx.

43. Ibid., "ELCA Confession of Faith."

44. Ibid., "Baptism" and "Holy Communion."

45. Miriam L. Woolbert, ELCA Communication Services, email message to author, January 10, 2008.

46. "What is Christianity?," Evangelical Lutheran Church in America, accessed July 22, 2012, http://www.elca.org/What-We-Believe/The-Basics/What-is-Christianity.aspx.

47. "History," National Baptist Convention of America, Inc., Int'l, accessed July 22, 2012, http://www.nbcainc.com/history.

48. "Brief History of the Assemblies of God," Assemblies of God USA, accessed July 22, 2012, http://ag.org/top/About/History/index.cfm.

49. Ibid., "Assemblies of God Fundamental Truth."

50. Zenas J. Bicket, Past-Chairman of the Doctrinal Purity Commission, email message to author, January 10, 2008.

51. "A Brief History of the Presbyterian Church in this Country," Presbyterian Historical Society, accessed July 22, 2012, http://history.pcusa.org/history/history.cfm.

52. "The Brief Statement of Faith," Presbyterian Mission Agency, accessed July 22, 2012, http://www.presbyterianmission.org/ministries/101/brief-statement-faith.

53. Ibid., "Word."

54. Ibid., "The Sacraments—Baptism."

55. Ibid., "The Sacraments."

56. Ibid., "The Sacraments—Lord's Supper."

57. Ibid., The Sacraments.

58. "The Authority of the Church in the World," National Council of Churches USA, accessed July 22, 2012, http://www.ncccusa.org/faithandorder/authority.small.htm.

59. "The Brief Statement of Faith," Presbyterian Mission Agency, accessed July 22, 2012, http://www.presbyterianmission.org/ministries/101/brief-statement-faith.

60. "Who is a Christian?" Religious Tolerance, accessed July 22, 2012, http://www.religioustolerance.org/chr_defn2.htm.

61. Ibid., "Which Definition Is Correct?"

62. "What is a Christian?," Christian Apologetics and Research Ministry, accessed July 22, 2012, http://carm.org/christianity/devotions/what-christian.

63. "What is a Christian,?" Got Questions.org, accessed July 22, 2012, http://www.gotquestions.org/what-is-a-Christian.html.

64. "What is a Christian?," Ray Pritchard, Christianity.com, accessed July 20, 2012, http://www.christianity.com/Christian%20Foundations/The%20Essentials/11541516/page2.

65. Mark M. Mattison, "What is a Christian?," (Auburn, AL: Auburn University), accessed July 3, 2012, http://www.auburn.edu/~allenkc/openhse/christian.html.

66. Mary Fairchild, "Christian," About.com, accessed July 23, 2012, http://christianity.about.com/od/glossary/g/christian.htm.

67. "What is the Orthodox Faith?" St. Andrews Greek Orthodox Church, accessed July 20, 2012, http://www.standrewslubbock.com/what_is_orthodoxy_.

68. Wilfred Cantwell Smith, The Meaning and End of Religion (Minneapolis: First Fortress, 1991), 5

69. Barry A. Kosmin and Ariela Keysar, "American Religious Identification Survey, Summary Report" (Connecticut: Trinity College, 2009)

70. "Religious Beliefs Vary Widely By Denomination," Barna Group, 2001, accessed July 22, 2012, http://www.barna.org/barna-update/article/5-barna-update/53-religious-beliefs-vary-widely-by-denomination.

CHAPTER 6: IT'S CLEAR ACCORDING TO THE BIBLE

1. "Deathly Word Study," Dr. Russell Norma Murray blog, April 16, 2011, quoting Strong's Exhaustive Concordance of the Bible, (Ontario: Welch Publishing Company, 1986), http://thekingpin68.blogspot.com/2011_04_01_archive.html.

2. "Messiah," *Online Etymology Dictionary*, accessed July 20, 2012, http://www .etymonline.com/index.php?term=messiah.

3. "God's Only Begotten Son," Institute for Creation Research, accessed August 26, 2012, http://www.icr.org/home/resources/resources_tracts_ godsonlybegottenson.

4. Louis Berkhof, *Systematic Theology* (Grand Rapids: William B. Eerdmans, 1949), 71.

5. "Fruit," *Vine's Dictionary of NT Words*, accessed July 22, 2012, http://www2 .mf.no/bibelprog/vines?word=%AFt0001150 – 3/30/12).

CHAPTER 7: IT'S REVEALING ACCORDING TO THE DATA

1. Christian Smith and Melinda Denton, *Soul Searching* (New York: Oxford University Press, 2005), 292.

2. Brian Steensland et al., *The Measure of American Religion: Toward Improving the State of the Art* (Chapel Hill: The University of North Carolina Press, 2000), 297.

3. The National Study of Youth and Religion, http://www.youthandreligion .org, whose data were used by permission here, was generously funded by Lilly Endowment Inc., under the direction of Christian Smith, of the Department of Sociology at the University of Notre Dame and Lisa Pearce, of the Department of Sociology at the University of North Carolina at Chapel Hill.

4. Christian Smith and Patricia Snell, *Souls in Transition* (New York: Oxford University Press, 2009), 309.

5. The National Study of Youth and Religion, http://www.youthandreligion .org, whose data were used by permission here, was generously funded by Lilly Endowment Inc., under the direction of Christian Smith, of the Department of Sociology at the University of Notre Dame and Lisa Pearce, of the Department of Sociology at the University of North Carolina at Chapel Hill.

6. "Religious Beliefs Vary Widely by Denomination" Barna Group, 2001, accessed July 22, 2012, http://www.barna.org/barna-update/article/5-barna-update/53-religious-beliefs-vary-widely-by-denomination.

7. Ibid

8. "Protestants, Catholics and Mormons Reflect Diverse Levels of Religious Activity," Barna Group, 2001, accessed July 22, 2012, http://www.barna.org/ barna-update/article/5-barna-update/54-protestants-catholics-and-mormons -reflect-diverse-levels-of-religious-activity.

9. Christian Smith and Melinda Denton, *Soul Searching* (New York: Oxford University Press, 2005), 308–9.

10. Recalculation of the Barna Group data from the 2001 study completed by Eric Shuster.

11. Paul Froese and Christopher Bader, *America's Four Gods: What We Say about God—and What That Says about Us* (New York: Oxford University Press, 2012), 1.

12. Data and sources previously cited with calculations by Eric Shuster.

13. "Sacrifice," The Church of Jesus Christ of Latter-day Saints, accessed July 22, 2012, http://www.lds.org/scriptures/gs/sacrifice?lang=eng.

14. Kenda Dean, *Almost Christian: What the Faith of Our Teenagers Is Telling the American Church* (New York: Oxford University Press, 2012), 45.

CHAPTER 8: IT'S COMPLICATED ACCORDING TO THE CRITICS

1. "Pharisee," *Online Etymology Dictionary*, accessed July 23, 2012, http://www.etymonline.com/index.php?allowed_in_frame=0&search=Pharisee&searchmode=none.

2. Mitchell G. Bard, "The Pharisees," *Jewish Virtual Library*, accessed July 22, 2012, http://www.jewishvirtuallibrary.org/jsource/History/sadducees_pharisees_essenes.html.

3. "Woman Riding in Swaggart Car Says She's a Prostitute," Associated Press, *Los Angeles Times*, October 12, 1991, accessed July 22, 2012, http://articles.latimes.com/1991-10-12/news/mn-202_1_jimmy-swaggart.

4. "Jim Bakker," Infoplease, accessed July 22, 2012, http://www.infoplease.com/biography/var/jimbakker.html.

5. "Ted Haggard Mocks Cathjolicism, Islam, Mormonism and the Jews," Evangelical Right, accessed July 24, 2012, http://www.evangelicalright.com/2006/10/ted_haggard_mocks_catholicism_islam_mormons_and_jews.html.

6. Katherine T. Phan, "Ted Haggard Shares Shocking Details in Interview," January 7, 2011, accessed February 2013, http://www.christianpost.com/news/ted-haggard-shares-shocking-details-in-new-interview-48697.

7. Brian Kaylor, "Reports Conflict About Fred Thompson's Church Membership, Attendance," *Ethics Daily*, accessed July 23, 2012, http://www.ethicsdaily.com/news.php?viewStory=9407.

8. Dan Gilgoff, "Dobson Offers Insight on 2008 Republican Hopefuls." *US News and World Report*, March 28, 2007. Accessed July 23, 2012, http://usnews.com/usnews/news/articles/070328/28dobson.htm.

9. Sally Quinn, "Southern Baptist Convention leader talks Christianity, cults and 2012," *The Washington Post*, October 11, 2011, accessed July 23, 2012, http://www.washingtonpost.com/blogs/on-faith/post/southern-baptist-convention-leader-talks-christianity-cults-and-2012/2011/10/10/gIQAvm0PcL_blog.html.

10. source: http://www.foxnews.com/opinion/2012/11/03/cnn-religion-blogger-attacks-christian-conservatives-for-supporting-romney/).

11. Richard B. Morris, *Seven Who Shaped Our Destiny: The Founding Fathers as Revolutionaries* (New York: Harper & Row, 1973).

12. David L. Holmes, *The Faiths of the Founding Fathers* (New York: Oxford University Press, 2006), 61.

13. Ibid., 59–60.

14. Ibid., 62

15. Jared Sparks, *Writings of George Washington* (Boston: American Stationers, 1847), in David L. Holmes, *The Faiths of the Founding Fathers* (New York: Oxford University Press, 2006), 62.

16. Ellen Judy Wilson and Peter Hanns Reill, *Encyclopedia of the Enlightenment* (New York: Book Builders, 2004), 146–47.

17. Holmes, *The Faiths of the Founding Fathers*, 66.

18. James Madison, *A Nation Mourns: Bishop James Madison's Memorial Eulogy on the Death of George Washington* (Mount Vernon, VA: Mount Vernon Ladies' Association, 1999), in Holmes, *The Faiths of the Founding Fathers*, 68.

19. Herbert Baxter Adams, *The Life and Writings of Jared Sparks: Comprising Selections from His Journals and Correspondence (1893)* (Boston: Houghton Mifflin, 1893), in Holmes, *The Faiths of the Founding Fathers*, 71.

20. Owen Aldridge, "The Alleged Puritanism of Benjamin Franklin," in Leo Lemay, *Reappraising Benjamin Franklin: A Bicentennial Perspective* (Newark: University of Delaware Press, 1993), in Holmes, *The Faiths of the Founding Fathers*, 53–54.

21. Holmes, *The Faiths of the Founding Fathers*, 54.

22. Ibid., 55–56.

23. Franklin Dexter, *The Literary Diary of Ezra Stiles* (New York: C. Scribner's Sons, 1901), 387.

24. "Letter from Benjamin Franklin to Ezra Stiles," Beliefnet, accessed July 22, 2012, http://www.beliefnet.com/resourcelib/docs/44/Letter_from_Benjamin_Franklin_to_Ezra_Stiles_1.html.

25. Holmes, *The Faiths of the Founding Fathers*, 56.

26. Ibid., 76.

27. N. Weber, "Unitarians." *The Catholic Encyclopedia*. vol. 15 (New York: Robert Appleton Company, 1912), accessed July 28, 2012, http://www.newadvent.org/cathen/15154b.htm.

28. Holmes, *The Faiths of the Founding Fathers*, 77.

29. "Letter from John Adams to Benjamin Rush," Beliefnet, accessed July 22, 2012, http://www.beliefnet.com/resourcelib/docs/75/Letter_from_John_Adams_to_Benjamin_Rush_1.html.

30. John Adams to Thomas Jefferson, April 19, 1817, in *Microfilms of the Adams Papers*, reel 123, in Holmes, *The Faiths of the Founding Fathers*, 78.

31. Holmes, *The Faiths of the Founding Fathers*, 79–80.

32. Edwin S. Gaustad, *Sworn on the Altar of God: A Religious Biography of Thomas Jefferson* (Grand Rapids: Wm. B. Eerdmans, 1996), xiii–xiv.

33. Holmes, *The Faiths of the Founding Fathers*, 80–81.

34. "The Letters of Thomas Jefferson: 1743–1826: The Morals of Jesus," "To Dr. Benjamin Rush, with a Syllabus Washington, Apr. 21, 1803," accessed July 29, 2012, http://www.let.rug.nl/usa/P/tj3/writings/brf/jefl153.htm.

35. Holmes, *The Faiths of the Founding Fathers*, 82.

36. Ibid., 83.

37. Edwin S. Gaustad, *The Religious History of America: The Heart of the American Story from Colonial Times to Today* (San Francisco: HarperCollins, 2004), 136.

38. Holmes, *The Faiths of the Founding Fathers*, 85.

39. Ibid., 92.

40. Ibid., 93.

41. George S. *Hillard, Life, Letters, and Journals of George Ticknor* (New York: Houghton Mifflin, 1909), 30.

42. Gillard Hunt, *The Writings of James Madison* (New York: G.P. Putnams's sons, 1910), 230.

43. "Religious Affiliation of the Founding Fathers of the United States of America," Adherents, accessed July 23, 2012, http://www.adherents.com/gov/Founding_Fathers_Religion.html.

44. "Adolf Hitler—Early Years (1889–1919)," Global Security, accessed July 23, 2012, http://www.globalsecurity.org/military/world/europe/de-hitler-1.htm.

45. Richard Steigmann-Gall, *The Holy Reich: Nazi Conceptions of Christianity 1919–1945* (New York: Cambridge University Press, 2003), 252.

46. "Hitler and Religion: Ratzinger is wrong," The Richard Dawkins Foundation, accessed July 23, 2012, http://richarddawkins.net/discussions/518979-hitler-and-religion-ratzinger-is-wrong.

47. Tim Reiterman, *Raven: the Untold Story of The Revelation Jim Jones and His People* (New York: Penguin, 1982).

48. "Cult Crimes Jim Jones," Oppapers.com, accessed July 23, 2012, http://www.oppapers.com/essays/Cult-Crimes-Jim-Jones/191595.

49. "Peoples Temple," Encyclopedia.com, accessed July 23, 2102, http://www.encyclopedia.com/topic/Jim_Jones.aspx.

50. "Who is Paul Hill," Army of God, accessed July 23, 2012, http://www.armyofgod.com/PaulHillWhoIs.html.

51. Kathy Sawyer. "Turning From 'Weapon of the Spirit" to the Shotgun." Washington Post, August 7, 1994. Accessed July 23, 2012, http://www.washingtonpost.com/wp-srv/national/longterm/aborviolence/stories/hill/htm.

52. Sheryll Shariat, Sue Mallonee, and Shelli Stephens-Stidham, *Summary of Reportable Injuries in Oklahoma* (Oklahoma City: Oklahoma State Department of Health, 1998), 1.

53. "An Accurate Look at Timothy McVeigh's Beliefs," Bruce Prescott, *Ethics Daily*, accessed July 23, 2012, http://www.ethicsdaily.com/news.php?viewStory=15532.

54. Robert McFadden, "Terror in Oklahoma: The Suspect; One Man's Complex Path to Extremism," *New York Times*, April 23, 2995, accessed July 22, 2012, http://www.nytimes.com/1995/04/23/us/terror-in-oklahoma-the-suspect-one-man-s-complex-path-to-extremism.html?pagewanted=all&src=pm.

55. "McVeigh Took Last Rites before Execution," CNN: Justice, June 11, 2001, accessed July 23, 2012, http://articles.cnn.com/2001-06-11/justice/mcveigh.03_1_timothy-mcveigh-first-federal-execution-mcveigh-attorney?_s=PM:LAW.

56. "The Transformation of Fred Phelps," Joe Taschler and Steve Fry, *The Topeka Capital-Journal*, accessed July 29, 2012, http://www.rickross.com/reference/westboro/westboro4.html.

57. "Repentance in Pasadena," *Time*, June 11, 1951, accessed July 29, 2012, http://www.time.com/time/magazine/article/0,9171,814897,00.html.

58. Nedra Pickler, "Bush Says U.S. Must Honor War Dead." *The Washington Post*, May 30, 2006, accessed July 29, 2012, http://www.washingtonpost.com/wp-dyn/content/article/2006/05/30/AR2006053000134.html.

59. Mark Potok, "Hate Groups Increase Numbers, Unite Against Immigrants," *Southern Poverty Law Center Intelligence Report* (Spring 2006):121, accessed July 29, 2012 http://www.splcenter.org/get-informed/intelligence-report/browse-all-issues/2006/spring/the-year-in-hate-2005.

INTRODUCTION TO SECTION 3: WHERE ARE THE CHRISTIANS?

1. David B. Barrett, *World Christian Encyclopedia* (New York: Oxford University Press, 2001), 3.

2. "Global Christianity: A Report on the Size and Distribution of the World's Christian Population, December 2011," 43, Pew Research Center, accessed February 2013, http://www.pewforum.org/uploadedFiles/Topics/Religious_ Affiliation/Christian/Christianity-fullreport-web.pdf.

3. "World Getting More Corrupt Poll Reveals," *Modern Ghana*, accessed July 29, 2012, http://www.modernghana.com/news/307900/1/world-getting-more-corrupt-poll-reveals.html.

4. Dave Graham, "U.S. Slips to Historic Low in Global Corruption Index," Reuters, accessed July 29, 2012, http://www.reuters.com/article/2010/10/26/us -corruption-transparency-idUSTRE69P0X620101026.

5. "Entire World—Prison Population Rates per 100,000 of the National Population," International Centre for Prison Studies, accessed July 29, 2012, http:// www.prisonstudies.org/info/worldbrief/wpb_stats.php?area=all&category=wb_ poprate.

6. Lara Jakes Jordan, "FBI Chief: Are Americans Becoming More Crooked?," Free Republic, accessed July 29, 2012, http://www.freerepublic.com/focus/f-news/2003680/posts.

7. "Prison Incarceration and Religious Preference, Adherents," accessed July 29, 2012, http://www.adherents.com/misc/adh_prison.html.

CHAPTER 9: THEY'RE DEPARTING—BELIEVERS LOSING THEIR BELIEF AS DEPARTING CHRISTIANS

1. Lauren Green, "State of the Bible," Fox News, April 18, 2012, accessed July 29, 2012, http://www.foxnews.com/us/2012/04/18/state-bible-2012 /#ixzz1tdmF4PCo.

2. Ibid.

3. Lamar Vest, "Does the Bible Still Matter in 2012?" Fox News, April 29, 2012, accessed July 29, 2012, http://www.foxnews.com/opinion/2012/04/29/does-bible-still-matter-in-2012/#ixzz1tdmLUbWF.

4. "Bart D. Ehrman," The University of North Carolina at Chapel Hill Faculty Bios, accessed July 29, 2012 http://religion.unc.edu/people/current-faculty/ faculty-bios/bart-d.-ehrman.

5. M. Alex Johnson, "Bible Edits leave some feeling cross," Fox News.com. Accessed July 29, 2012, http://www.msnbc.msn.com/id/42215497/ns/us_news -life/t/bible-edits-leave-some-feeling-cross/#.T6WfQMWePvM).

6. "Church Giving Drops $1.2 Billion Reports 2012 Yearbooks of Churches," National Council of Churches, accessed July 29, 2012, http://www.ncccusa.org /news/120209yearbook2012.html.

7. "America Becoming Less Christian, survey finds," *CNN: Living*, March 9, 2009. Accessed July 29, 2012, http://articles.cnn.com/2009-03-09/living/ us.religion.less.christian_1_american-religious-identification-survey-christian-nation-evangelical?_s=PM:LIVING).

8. Jason Pitzl-Waters, "Accessing ARIS," Patheos. Accessed July 29, 2012, http:// www.patheos.com/blogs/wildhunt/2009/03/assessing-aris.html.

9. Dan Harris, "America Is Becoming Less Christian, Less Religious," ABC News, March 9, 2009, accessed July 29, 2012, http://abcnews.go.com/US /story?id=7041036&page=1#.T6G7I8WePvM.

10. Daniel Stone, "One Nation Under God?," The Daily Beast, accessed July 29, 2012, http://www.thedailybeast.com/newsweek/2009/04/06/one-nation-under-god.html.

11. Frank Newport, "This Christmas, 78% of Americans Identify as Christian," December 24, 2009, Gallup, accessed July 29, 2012, http://www.gallup.com/ poll/124793/this-christmas-78-americans-identify-christian.aspx.

12. Sven Erlandson, "The Shrinking of Evangelical Christianity," Yahoo Voices, accessed July 29, 2012, http://voices.yahoo.com/the-shrinking-evangelical -christianity-458744.html.

13. Ibid.

14. David B. Barrett, *World Christian Encyclopedia* (New York: Oxford University Press, 2001), 3.

15. Ibid., 5.

16. Ibid.

17. "The End of Christian America," *The Daily Beast*, April 3, 2009, accessed August 24, 2012, http://www.thedailybeast.com/newsweek/2009/04/03/the-end-of-christian-america.html.

18. Ibid.

19. Ibid.

20. "Americans Draw Theological Beliefs From Diverse Points of View," October 8, 2002, Barna Group, accessed August 20, 2012, http://www.barna.org/barna-update/article/5-barna-update/82-americans-draw-theological-beliefs-from-diverse-points-of-view.

21. Ibid.

22. Cathy Lynn Grossman, "Mixing Their Religion," December 10, 2009, *USA Today*, December 12, 2009, accessed July 29, 2012, http://www.usatoday.com/ NEWS/usaedition/2009-12-10-1Amixingbeliefs10_CV_U.htm.

23. Ibid.

24. Matt Canham, "Mormon Portion of Utah Population Steadily Shrinking," *Salt Lake Tribune*, July 24, 2005, accessed July 29, 2012, http://www.sltrib.com /ci_2886596.

25. Christian Smith, *Lost in Transition* (New York: Oxford University Press, 2011).

26. "Five Myths About Young Adult Church Dropouts," November 16, 2011, Barna Group, accessed July 29, 2012, http://www.barna.org/teens-next-gen-articles/534-five-myths-about-young-adult-church-dropouts.

27. Ibid.

CHAPTER 10: THEY'RE HIDING—NOT PRACTICING THEIR FAITH AS ADEQUATE CHRISTIANS

1. "US Religious Knowledge Survey," September 28, 2012, Pew Research Center, accessed July 29, 2012, http://www.pewforum.org/uploadedFiles/Topics/Belief_ and_Practices/religious-knowledge-full-report.pdf.

2. "Most Americans Christians Do Not Believe that Satan or the Holy Spirit Exists," April 10, 2009, Barna Group, sccessed July 29, 2012, http://www.barna. org/barna-update/article/12-faithspirituality/260-most-american-christians-do-not-believe-that-satan-or-the-holy-spirit-exis.

3. Associated Press, "Bishops Strategize on Wayward Catholics," MSNBC, November 13, 2006, accessed July 29, 2012, http://www.msnbc.msn.com/ id/15697161/ns/us_news-life/t/bishops-strategize-wayward-catholics.

4. Michelle A. Vu, "U.S. Evangelicals Pessimistic about Christianity in America," *Christian Post*, June 3, 2009, accessed July 29, 2012, http://www.christianpost. com/news/u-s-evangelicals-pessimistic-about-christianity-in-america-38959.

5. Craig Groeschel, *The Christian Atheist* (Grand Rapids: Zondervan, 2010).

6. Ibid.

7. "Christian Witness to Nominal Christians Among Roman Catholics," The Lausanne Movement, accessed July 29, 2012, http://www.lausanne.org/en/ documents/lops/55-lop-10.html.

8. "Casual Christians and the Future of America," May 22, 2009, Barna Group, accessed July 29, 2012, http://www.barna.org/barna-update/article/13-culture/268-casual-christians-and-the-future-of-america.

9. Ibid.

10. Alan Cooperman. "Evangelicals at a Crossroads As Falwell's Generation Fades." *Washington Post*, May 22, 2007, accessed July 29, 2012, http://www .washingtonpost.com/wp-dyn/content/article/2007/05/21/AR2007052101581 .html.

11. Richard Stearns and Lamar, "Christians losing their way." *Washington Post*, December 14, 2009, accessed July 29, 2012, http://newsweek.washington post.com/onfaith/guestvoices/2009/12/call_for_christians_to_help_poor.html.

CHAPTER 11: THEY'RE VACILLATING–LIVING UNDER THEIR POTENTIAL AS HESITANT CHRISTIANS

1. "Gian Carlo Menotti Quotes," Brainy Quotes, accessed July 29, 2012, http:// www.brainyquote.com/quotes/authors/g/gian_carlo_menotti.html.

2. "Geoffrey Gaberino Quotes, " I Love Quotes, accessed July 29, 2012, http:// www.1-love-quotes.com/quotes/author/Geoffrey/Gaberino.

3. "Yoke" The Free Dictionary, accessed August 28, 2012, http://www. thefreedictionary.com/yoke.

4. "Hesitation," *The Free Dictionary*, accessed July 29, 2012, http://www. thefreedictionary.com/hesitation.

5. Richard Stearns and Lamar, "Christians Losing Their Way," *Washington Post*, December 14, 2009, accessed July 29, 2012, http://newsweek.washingtonpost .com/onfaith/guestvoices/2009/12/call_for_christians_to_help_poor.html.

6. "He Who Hesitates is Lost," Dictionary.com, accessed July 29, 2012, http:// dictionary.reference.com/browse/he+who+hesitates+is+lost.

CHAPTER 12: THEY'RE ENDEAVORING–LIVING DISCIPLESHIP IN THE GOSPEL OF CHRIST AS LABORING CHRISTIANS

1. "Mother Teresa of Calcutta (1910–1997)," Vatican News Services, accessed July 29, 2012, http://www.vatican.va/news_services/liturgy/saints/ns_lit_doc_ 20031019_madre-teresa_en.html.

2. "Mother Teresa Did Not Feel Christ's Presence for Last Half of Her Life, Letters Reveal," August 24, 2007, Fox News, accessed February 2013, http:// www.foxnews.com/story/0,2933,294395,00.html.

3. Mark Galli, *131 Christians Everyone Should Know* (Nashville: Christianity Today, Inc., 2000).

4. Ibid.

5. Ibid.

6. Ibid.

7. Ibid.

8. Ibid.

9. "History of the Catholic Charities Network," Catholic Charities USA, accessed July 29, 2012, http://www.catholiccharitiesusa.org/history.

10. William P. Barrett. "The 200 Largest US Charities." *Forbes*, November 30, 2011, accessed July 29, 2012, http://www.forbes.com/lists/2011/14/200-largest-us-charities-11.html.

CHAPTER 13: WHAT KIND OF CHRISTIAN ARE YOU?

1. "Endure," Dictionary.com, accessed July 29, 2012, http://dictionary.reference.com/browse/endure.

2. "William Law Quotes," Goodreads.com, accessed August 4, 2012, http://www.goodreads.com/author/quotes/66863.William_Law.

3. Damien Cave, "What Would Jesus Do—about Copyright?," Salon, accessed July 29, 2012, http://www.salon.com/2000/10/25/wwjd.

INTRODUCTION TO SECTION 4: HOW IS CHRISTIANITY TO UNITE?

1. Henry Chadwick, *Origen: Contra Celsum* (New York: Cambridge University Press, 1953), 313.

2. Nikolai Berdyaev, "Unifying Christians of the East and the West," Chebucto, accessed July 29, 2012, http://www.chebucto.ns.ca/Philosophy/Sui-Generis/Berdyaev/essays/unifying.htm.

3. "Grid Computing," *PC Magazine Encyclopedia*, accessed July 29, 2012, http://www.pcmag.com/encyclopedia_term/0,1237,t=grid+computing&i=43962,00.asp.

CHAPTER 14: STRENGTHEN THE INDIVIDUAL

1. David Kerr, "Pope Says Uniting Christianity Requires Conversion." Catholic News Agency, January 18, 2012, accessed July 29, 2012, http://www.catholicnewsagency.com/news/pope-says-uniting-christianity-requires-conversion.

2. Ibid.

3. Ibid.

CHAPTER 15: STRENGTHEN THE FAMILY

1. "The Family, a Proclamation to the World," The Church of Jesus Christ of Latter-day Saints, accessed July 29, 2012, http://www.lds.org/family/proclamation.

2. "About Focus on the Family," Focus on the Family, accessed July 29, 2012, http://www.focusonthefamily.com/about_us.aspx.

3. James Dobson, "The State of the Family: James Dobson's July 2001 Newsletter," accessed July 29, 2012, http://www.ldolphin.org/family.html.

4. "Apostolic Exhortation, Familiaris Consortio," Vatican, accessed July 29, 2012, http://www.vatican.va/holy_father/john_paul_ii/apost_exhortations/documents /hf_jp-ii_exh_19811122_familiaris-consortio_en.html.

5. Philip Pullella, "Stop Disintegration of the Family in Europe: Pope," June 5, 2011, accessed July 29, 2012, http://www.reuters.com/article/2011/06/05/us-pope-croatia-idUSTRE7540QI20110605.

6. Patrick Fagan, "The Real Root Causes of Violent Crime: The Breakdown of Marriage, Family, and Community," The Heritage Foundation, March 17, 1995, accessed July 29, 2012, http://www.heritage.org/research/reports/1995/03 /bg1026nbsp-the-real-root-causes-of-violent-crime.

7. Patrick Fagan, "The Child Abuse Crisis: The Disintegration of Marriage, Family and the American Community," The Heritage Foundation, May 15, 1997, Accessed July 29, 2012, http://www.heritage.org/research/reports/1997/05/ bg1115-the-child-abuse-crisis).

8. "Homily of John Paul II, Perth (Australia), 30 November 1986," Vatican, accessed July 29, 2012, http://www.vatican.va/holy_father/john_paul_ii/homilies /1986/documents/hf_jp-ii_hom_19861130_perth-australia_en.html.

9. "Jerry Falwell Quotes," Brainy Quote, accessed July 29, 2012, brainyquote. com/quotes/authors/j/jerry_falwell.html.

10. "Mother Teresa Quotes," Goodreads.com, accessed August 4, 2012, http:// www.goodreads.com/quotes/show/62266.

11. "Daily Media Use Among Children and Teens Up Dramatically From Five Years Ago," Kaiser Family Foundation, January 20, 2010. Accessed July 29, 2012, AGOhttp://www.kff.org/entmedia/entmedia012010nr.cfm.

12. "Winston Churchill Quotes," Thinkexist.com, accessed July 29, 2012, http://thinkexist.com/quotation/there_is_no_doubt_that_it_is_around_the _family/161333.html.

13. Michael D. Tanner, "The American Welfare State: How We Spend Nearly $1 Trillion a Year Fighting Poverty—And Fail," CATO Institute, accessed July 29, 2012, http://www.cato.org/publications/policy-analysis/american-welfare-state-how-we-spend-nearly-$1-trillion-year-fighting-poverty-fail.

14. Patrick Fagan, "The Real Root Cause of Violent Crime: The Breakdown of the Family," Hillsdale College, accessed July 29, 2012, http://www.hillsdale.edu/news/imprimis/archive/issue.asp?year=1995&month=10.

15. "The Family, a Proclamation to the World," The Church of Jesus Christ of Latter-day Saints, accessed July 29, 2012, http://www.lds.org/family/proclamation.

16. Steven R. Covey, *The Seven Habits of Highly Effective Families* (New York: Golden Books, 1997).

17. Ibid., 2.

18. "Remarks of Mrs. Bush at Wellesley College Commencement," Wellesley College, 1990, accessed July 29, 2012, http://www.wellesley.edu/PublicAffairs/Commencement/1990/bush.html.

19. "15 Secrets of Happy Families," Denise Mann, WebMD, accessed July 30, 2012, http://www.webmd.com/parenting/features/15-secrets-to-have-a-happy-family.

20. "Raising a Happy Family," Aha Parenting, accessed July 29, 2012, http://www.ahaparenting.com/parenting-tools/Family.

CHAPTER 16: STRENGTHEN THE CHURCH

1. Drew Zahn, "Why Can't Christians Unite to Change America's Ways?," World Net Daily, September 27, 2009. Accessed July 29, 2012, http://www.wnd.com/2009/09/111154.

2. Ibid.

3. Ibid.

4. Ibid.

5. "Not Every Sin is Pride," St. Augustine: Anti-Pelagian Writings," Christian Classics Ethereal Library, accessed July 29, 2012, http://www.ccel.org/ccel/schaff/npnf105.xii.xxxvii.html.

6. "What Does the Bible Say about Racism, Prejudice, and Discrimination?" Gotquestions.org, accessed July 29, 2012, http://www.gotquestions.org/racism-Bible.html.

7. "Aristotle," Quote DB, accessed July 29, 2012, http://www.quotedb.com/quotes/924.

8. "Women Clergy," United Methodist Church, accessed August 28, 2012, http://archives.umc.org/interior.asp?mid=1021.

9. Sam Hodges, "One in Four Presbyterian Pastors Is Female, and Nearly Half the Membership Is 65 or Older," *Dallas Morning News*, accessed August 29, 2012, http://religionblog.dallasnews.com/2010/02/one-in-four-presbyterian-pasto.html.

10. Bonnidell Clouse et al., *Women in Ministry: Four Views* (Downers Grove, IL: InterVarsity Press, 1989).

11. Anthony McFarland, "What Does the Bible Say About Ending Personality Conflict?" Abundant Harvest Christian Center, accessed July 29, 2012, http://www.abundantharvest.info/endingpersonalityconflict.php.

12. Lucy Buckland, "The Battle of Bethlehem: 100 Rival Priests Clash at Church Built to Mark the Birth of Jesus," December 29, 2011, accessed July 29, 2012, http://www.dailymail.co.uk/news/article-2079328/Priests-brawl-Bethlehems-Church-Nativity-clergy-fight-Christmas-cleaning.html.

13. Saul McLeod, "Maslow's Hierarchy of Needs," Simply Psychology, updated 2012. Accessed July 29, 2012, http://www.simplypsychology.org/maslow.html.

14. "Fellowship New Members, Remain Faithful and True, Prophet Counsels," *Church News*, April 12, 1997. Accessed July 29, 2012, http://www.ldschurchnews.com/articles/29106/Fellowship-new-members-remain-faithful-and-true-prophet-counsels.html.

CHAPTER 17: STRENGTHEN THE COMMUNITY

1. Patrick Geddes, "A Man of All Reason," National Library of Scotland, accessed July 29, 2012, www.nls.uk/about-us/publications/discover-nls/2009/patrick-geddes.

2. Michelle Bauman. "National Day of Prayer opportunity for Americans to seek God," *Catholic News Agency*, April 18, 2012, accessed July 29, 2012, http://www.catholicnewsagency.com/news/national-day-of-prayer-opportunity-for-americans-to-seek-god.

3. Travis Reed, "Group Limits Mormon Participation in National Day of Prayer." May 4, 2004, accessed July 29, 2012, http://www.rickross.com/reference/mormon/mormon161.html.

4. Jimmy Akin, "The History of Anti-Catholicism," Catholic Answers, accessed July 29, 2012, http://archive.catholic.com/thisrock/2001/0103bt.asp.

5. Michael Gordon, *The Orange Riots: Irish Political Violence in New York City* (New York: Cornell University, 1993).

6. "Marcus Tullius Cicero Quotes," Thinkexist.com, accessed July 29, 2012, http://thinkexist.com/quotation/the_enemy_is_within_the_gates-it_is_with_our_own/191672.html.

7. "Ecumenism," *The Free Dictionary*, accessed July 29, 2012, http://www.the freedictionary.com/ecumenism.

8. "Evangelicals & Catholics Together: The Christian Mission in the Third Millennium," Leadership U, accessed July 29, 2012, http://www.leaderu.com /ftissues/ft9405/articles/mission.html.

9. Ankerberg, Kennedy, MacArthur, and Sproul, "Irreconcilable Differences: Catholics, Evangelicals, and the New Quest for Unity," 1995, lecture and discussion (Ft. Lauderdale, FL), Grace to You, accessed July 29, 2012, http:// www.gty.org/resources/sermons/GTY54/irreconcilable-differences-catholics -evangelicals-and-the-new-quest-for-unity-parts-13.

10. "Joint Declaration on the Doctrine of Justification," Vatican, accessed September 5, 2012, http://www.vatican.va/roman_curia/pontifical_councils /chrstuni/documents/rc_pc_chrstuni_doc_31101999_cath-luth-joint-declaration_en.html.

11. "Proposition 8," California Voter Guide 2008, accessed July 29, 2012, http:// voterguide.sos.ca.gov/past/2008/general/text-proposed-laws/text-of-proposed -laws.pdf#prop8.

12. "About Us," Christian Churches Working Together, accessed August 30, 2012, http://christianchurchestogether.org/?page_id=6.

13. "Christian Churches Together Focuses on Poverty, Evangelism during Annual Meeting," Episcopal News Service, January 2008, accessed September 6, 2012, http://sojo.net/press/christian-churches-together-focuses-poverty-evangelism -during-annual-meeting.

14. "About Us," Love INC, accessed August 30, 2012, http://www.loveincdouglas .org/about-us/who-we-are.html.

15. *Love INC June-July 2011 Newsletter*, accessed August 30, 2012, http://www .loveincdouglas.org/images/pdf/loveinc_july-august2011_newsletter.pdf.

16. "History and Mission," Nortwest Assistance Ministries Online, accessed July 29, 2012, http://www.namonline.org/site/c.ktJYJ7MNIuE/b.5062845/k.91E7 /Facts_and_Figures.htm.

17. "Covenant and Supporting Congregations," Nortwest Assistance Ministries Online, accessed July 29, 2012, http://www.namonline.org/site/c.ktJYJ7MNIuE/ b.2035485/k.3B76/Covenant__Supporting_Congregations.htm.

18. Phone interview conducted by Eric Shuster with Anais Watsky, former Director of NAM on Thursday, June 7, 2012.

19. "What We Do," Neighborhood Interfaith Movement, accessed July 30, 2012, http://www.nimphilly.org/what-we-do.

20. "History," Neighborhood Interfaith Movement, accessed July 30, 2012, http://www.nimphilly.org/who-we-are/history.

21. Phone interview conducted by Eric Shuster with Dick Fernandez, former director of Neighborhood Interfaith Movement, June 12, 2012.

22. "History of IFM," Inter-Faith Ministries of Wichita, accessed July 30, 2012, http://www.interfaithfaithwichita.org/index.php/about.

23. Ibid.

24. D. L. Eck, *A New Religious America* (New York: HarperCollins, 2001), 31.

FINAL THOUGHTS ON THE WHO, WHAT, WHERE, AND HOW

1. Will L. Thompson, "Have I Done Any Good?" *Hymns of The Church of Jesus Christ of Latter-day Saints*, accessed July 30, 2012, http://library.lds.org/nxt/gateway.dll/Curriculum/music.htm/hymns.htm/special%20topics.htm/223%20have%20i%20done%20any%20good.htm#JD_Hymns.223 – Have I done any good?"

ABOUT THE AUTHOR

ERIC SHUSTER HAS DEDICATED HIS WRITING CAREER TO BUILDING bridges of understanding between Christians. His first book, *Catholic Roots, Mormon Harvest*, chronicles the faith journey of he and his wife, including the respectful comparison of dozens of doctrines between Catholicism and Mormonism. His second book, *The Biblical Roots of Mormonism* (coauthored with Charles Sale), provides a common scriptural platform for Christians to better understand Mormon doctrine using over 1,000 scriptural references from the Bible. With his professional research background, directorship at the Foundation for Christian Studies, and his unique life experiences, Mr. Shuster is able to delve into complex spiritual subject matter and make it understandable and enjoyable to the everyday reader.

Mr. Shuster is a veteran of the information technology industry and has held several executive positions in a variety of business disciplines, including CEO of IntelliClear, a global market research and business strategy firm. Mr. Shuster holds an industrial engineering management degree from San Jose State University and an MBA from the University of Phoenix. Mr. Shuster and his wife, Marilyn, have been married for twenty-five years and have several biological and adopted children.